# DOING BUSINESS IN KOREA

Much of the existing research looks at the outflow of companies and people from Korea to foreign countries, whilst less is known about foreign firms and workers in Korea. Considering the immense interest of both academics and practitioners in the business opportunities in Korea, this book provides a comprehensive overview of doing business in Korea and recommendations on how foreign companies and individuals can succeed in this market.

This book covers a wide range of relevant topics, including the Korean business environment, market entry into Korea, management issues and entrepreneurship in Korea. This is a must-read for anyone interested in or already doing business in Korea.

**Fabian Jintae Froese** is Chair Professor of Human Resource Management and Asian Business at the University of Göttingen, Germany, and Editor-in-Chief of *Asian Business & Management*. Previously, he was Professor of International Business at Korea University. He obtained a doctorate in International Management from the University of St. Gallen, Switzerland, and another doctorate in Sociology from Waseda University, Japan. His research interests lie in international human resource management and cross-cultural management. His work has been published in journals such as the *British Journal of Management*, *Human Resource Management*, the *Journal of Organizational Behavior* and the *Journal of World Business*.

"Fabian J. Froese's *Doing Business in Korea* is one of the most comprehensive books describing dynamic Korean business and management today. The updated contents and cases about Korean business will be ideal learning materials for graduate students. The book could also serve as an excellent reference for foreign managers and executives interested in learning about Korean market environment and Korean companies. I find this book interesting, updated, and insightful."

> — *Mannsoo Shin, Professor of International Business,*
> *Korea University Business School, Korea*

"This new book is a very welcome addition to a sparse literature for a trio of reasons. First, it is edited by a leading and well-respected academic grounded in practice in the area. Second, its three-part structure comprehensively locates the key issues of management and market entry in the crucial operating environment. Third, interesting cases are provided."

> — *Professor Chris Rowley, Kellogg College, University of Oxford &*
> *Cass Business School, City, University of London, Editor,*
> Asia Pacific Business Review

"The book includes what all foreign executives need to know and can be considered as a deep source of information. That is why the book is a must for all newly arrived executives in order to get quickly on-boarded to run a business successfully in Korea. *Doing Business in Korea* is also valuable for people being here on the ground for some years, as it makes your picture complete."

> — *Christoph Heider, President of the European*
> *Chamber of Commerce in Korea*

"Korea has been considered one of the most challenging markets for foreign companies and individuals to achieve a good outcome. This book offers a very useful guidance for them to better understand not only the contexts but also the strategies and the practices that will bring success in conducting business in Korea."

> — *Yongsun Paik, Director of the Center for Asian Business,*
> *Professor of International Business & Management,*
> *Loyola Marymount University, USA*

# DOING BUSINESS IN KOREA

*Edited by Fabian Jintae Froese*

LONDON AND NEW YORK

First published 2020
by Routledge
2 Park Square, Milton Park, Abingdon, Oxon OX14 4RN

and by Routledge
52 Vanderbilt Avenue, New York, NY 10017

*Routledge is an imprint of the Taylor & Francis Group, an informa business*

*British Library Cataloguing-in-Publication Data*
A catalogue record for this book is available from the British Library

*Library of Congress Cataloging-in-Publication Data*
A catalog record for this book has been requested

ISBN: 978-1-138-54943-2 (hbk)
ISBN: 978-1-138-54944-9 (pbk)
ISBN: 978-1-351-00047-5 (ebk)

Typeset in Bembo
by Apex CoVantage, LLC

MIX
Paper from
responsible sources
FSC
www.fsc.org  FSC™ C013985

Printed in the United Kingdom
by Henry Ling Limited

# CONTENTS

# FIGURES

# TABLES

# ABBREVIATIONS

| | |
|---|---|
| 4Ps | product, promotion, price, place |
| CSA | country-specific advantage |
| DJ | (Kim) Dae-jung |
| EOI | export-oriented industrialization |
| KDB | Korea Development Bank |
| FBA | fair transactions in franchise business act |
| FDI | foreign direct investment |
| FETL | foreign exchange transaction law |
| FIPL | foreign investment promotion law |
| FSA | firm-specific advantage |
| FTA | free trade agreement |
| GDP | gross domestic product |
| GNI | gross national income |
| GNP | gross national product |
| GSC | global start-up center |
| HR | human resources |
| HRM | human resource management |
| HQ | headquarters |
| IB | international business |
| ICT | information communication technology |
| ISI | import substitution industrialization |
| KIC | Korea Innovation Center |
| KOSDAQ | Korean Securities Dealers Automated Quotations |
| KOTRA | Korea Trade-Investment Promotion Agency |
| KRW | Korean Won |
| M&A | mergers and acquisitions |
| MNE | multinational enterprise |

| | |
|---|---|
| MOCIE (Korea) | Ministry of Commerce, Industry, and Energy |
| MOTIE (Korea) | Ministry of Trade, Industry, and Energy |
| NGO | non-government organization |
| NIPA | National IT Promotion Agency |
| PCT | Patent Cooperation Treaty |
| PE&SE | political, economic, and social environment |
| PSPD | People's Solidarity for Participatory Democracy |
| R&D | research and development |
| SIE | self-initiated expatriate |
| SME | small and medium-sized enterprise |
| TMT | technology, media, and telecom |
| USD | US dollars |

# CONTRIBUTORS

**Samuel Davies** is a research associate and doctoral candidate at the Chair of Human Resource Management and Asian Business at the University of Göttingen, Germany. His research interests lie in the interface of (international) human resource management and organizational behavior and characteristics of and issues vital to internationally mobile employees, as well as domestic employees, drawing on social psychology and other surrounding social sciences. His work has been published in international academic journals including the *International Journal of Human Resource Management*.

**Fabian Jintae Froese** is Chair Professor of Human Resource Management and Asian Business at the University of Göttingen, Germany, and Editor-in-Chief of *Asian Business & Management*. Previously, he was a Professor of International Business at Korea University. He obtained a doctorate in International Management from the University of St. Gallen, Switzerland, and another doctorate in Sociology from Waseda University, Japan. His research interests lie in international human resource management and cross-cultural management. His work has been published in journals such as the *British Journal of Management*, *Human Resource Management*, the *Journal of Organizational Behavior* and the *Journal of World Business*.

**Stephan Gerschewski** is Lecturer in International Business and Strategy at Henley Business School, University of Reading, UK. He is also Programme Director for the degree programme BA International Management and Business Administration with French/German/Italian/Spanish (IMBA) at University of Reading. Prior to moving to Henley Business School, he worked as Assistant Professor of International Business at two major universities in South Korea: Hankuk University of Foreign Studies (HUFS) in Seoul and Hannam University in Daejeon. His research interests mainly relate to international entrepreneurship, small and medium-sized enterprises SMEs and export strategies of firms. His work has been published in various academic journals, including the *Journal of World Business, International Business Review, International Small Business Journal, Multinational Business Review* and *Thunderbird International Business Review.*

**Martin Hemmert** is Professor of International Business at Korea University. His research interests include international comparative studies of management systems, innovation systems and entrepreneurial ecosystems, organizational boundaries of firms and interorganizational research collaborations. He has published several books, including most recently *The Evolution of Tiger Management: Korean Companies in Global Competition* (Routledge, 2018) and numerous articles in journals such as the *Journal of Product Innovation Management*, the *Journal of World Business, Research Policy* and *Technovation.*

**Sven Horak** is Associate Professor at The Peter J. Tobin College of Business of St. John's University in New York City, where he researches and teaches in the area of international management and organization. Most of his research focuses on the role informality plays in human interactions at the dyadic, group and network level, predominantly in an international context. By drawing on insights from the neighboring social sciences, in particular economic and organizational sociology, social psychology and ethics, his work advances knowledge on the anatomy of informal institutions and how they moderate managerial behavior.

**Hyunji Lee** is a graduate student at the University of Göttingen. She has worked as a research assistant at the Chair of Human Resource Management and Asian Business.

**In Hyeock (Ian) Lee** is Associate Professor of International Business and Strategy in the Quinlan School of Business, Loyola University Chicago. He has published in leading journals such as *Regional Studies*, the *Journal of Business Research, IEEE Transactions on Engineering Management*, the *Journal of International Management* and *Small Business Economics*, among others. He currently serves as an editorial board member of *Entrepreneurship Theory & Practice*, the *Journal of International Management* and *Asian Business & Management*. Prior to joining academia, he was Deputy Director at the Ministry of Trade, Industry & Energy in Korea for eight years.

**Richard Lee** is Associate Professor of Marketing at the University of South Australia (UniSA). Prior to joining UniSA in 2007, Richard spent 15 years managing sales and marketing functions with Asian IT/telecommunication companies. His research expertise and publications are mainly in international and ethnic marketing, with particular focus on Asian markets. Richard has also won several industry grants that focus on how Australian SMEs can capitalize on FTAs and on enhancing the export competitiveness of Australian food and wine companies. His teaching experience includes consumer behavior, marketing planning, customer relationship management and market research.

**You-il Lee** is Associate Professor of International Business at the University of South Australia (UniSA). He has published widely in leading journals in the areas of Asian Studies, Asian business management and Asian political economy. He has had considerable experience in advising companies and government departments on a range of Asian business environment and various policy issues. He has met with more than 200 CEOs of multinational corporations over the years and currently teaches on Asian political economy, Asian community and cross-cultural management as part of the UniSA Business School's 5-star MBA and International MBA programs.

**Jinxi Michelle Li** is Associate Professor in the College of Business at Gyeongsang National University, South Korea. She received her PhD in management from Ewha Womans University, South Korea, and her master's in Speech Communication from Southern Illinois University Edwardsville, US. She was a consultant in POMIC (POSCO Management & Innovation Consulting) and a researcher in Hyundai Research Institute. Her research interests include cultural adjustment, cross-cultural training programs and organizational culture, among others. Her papers have appeared in the *Journal of Organizational Change Management, International Area Studies Review* and *Tourism Management Perspectives*.

**Yong Suhk Pak** is Professor of International Business at Yonsei University. He is also Director of Institute of East and West Studies, one of the oldest research centers at Yonsei University. He was Associate Dean of the MBA programs at Yonsei School of Business and was the editor of the *International Business Journal*, which is published by the Korean Academy of International Business. His research interest began with the conventional IB topic of foreign market expansion strategies, expanded into the knowledge management of international joint ventures and post-merger integration of cross-border M&As and now focuses on global mindset and global talent management. He has published more than a dozen articles in the leading IB journals such as *Management International Review, Journal of World Business* and *International Business Review*.

**Justin Paul** is Professor at the University of Puerto Rico, San Juan, US. He previously served as Associate Professor with the University of Washington, US, and Nagoya University of Commerce & Business, Japan. He has published four textbooks, including *Export-Import Management* (2nd edition). He has published more than 25 articles in refereed journals such as *International Business Review, Harvard Business Review, The International Trade Journal, International Journal of Consumer Studies,* the *Journal of Retailing & Consumer Services, Marketing Intelligence & Planning* and the *Journal of Consumer Marketing*.

**Sarah Reckelkamm** is a graduate student at the University of Göttingen. She has worked as a research assistant at the Chair of Human Resource Management and Asian Business.

**Jitendra Uttam** is Assistant Professor at India's Jawaharlal Nehru University and teaches East Asian affairs at the School of International Studies. His research focuses on political economy/capitalism of East Asia. Holding a PhD from Seoul National University, Korea, he has wide-ranging publications, including two recent books, *The Political Economy of Korea: Transition, Transformation and Turnaround* and *Varieties of Capitalism in Asia: Beyond the Developmental State*, co-authored with David Hundt. His other publications include "Economic Growth in India and China: A Comparative Study" for the journal *International Studies* and "Korea's New Techno-Scientific State: Mapping a Strategic Change in the Developmental State" in *China Report*.

**Yi Yang** is Assistant Professor of International Business at Gachon University and a researcher at Yonsei Business Research Institute. Her research topics and publications have focused on the post-merger management of cross-border M&As, competence and growth of MNEs from emerging markets, localization strategies of MNEs and international human resource management. She teaches international strategy and international management and has practical business experience participating and advising Chinese firms about cross-border M&As of Korean biotech and cosmetics firms.

# 1

# INTRODUCTION

## Korea – land of great opportunities

*Fabian Jintae Froese*

In the 1960s, South Korea (henceforth Korea) was a poor and relatively unknown country, with a GDP per capita of US$158, which was similar to most African countries at the time (World Bank, 2015). However, Korea has achieved tremendous and rapid economic growth within the last few decades, the so-called miracle of the Han River. Nowadays, Korea is an established member of the OECD and boasts the 11th-largest economy in the world, with a GDP per capita of US$38,260, similar to Italy or Spain (World Bank, 2017). Unlike most Western European countries, Korea's economy continues to grow substantially with an average of 3.1% during the last ten years (World Bank, 2018). The Korean economy is well connected internationally, having developed 15 free-trade agreements with 52 countries, including ASEAN (Association of Southeast Asian Countries), European Union (28 countries), India, and New Zealand. Korea is currently ranked fifth worldwide for exports worth US$573 billion and imports worth US$478 billion (World Trade Organization, 2017). All this makes Korea an attractive destination for foreign companies.

Korea is particularly strong in manufacturing and high technology. Huge investments in R&D and infrastructure have provided the basis for this development. In 2016, Korea spent about 4.3% of its GDP on research, well ahead of the US (2.5%), China (2.0%), and the EU (1.9%) (van Nooden, 2016). Furthermore, Korea has the highest average internet connection speed in the world (Statista, 2018), and 99.2% of all households have access to broadband internet (Ramirez, 2017). E-commerce plays an important role in Korea. Large Korean conglomerates, so-called chaebols, such as Samsung and Hyundai have emerged in this environment and have become world leaders. Samsung, the largest chaebol, accounts for more than 20% of the entire market value of the Korean Stock Exchange and accounts for around 15% of Korea's entire economy (Ullah, 2017).

Beyond business, Korea has gained worldwide attention through its media and entertainment. Korean music and TV dramas have started a 'Korean wave', an increase in the global popularity of Korean culture, particularly within Asia. For instance, the music video 'Gangnam Style' has been watched over 3 billion times on YouTube. The boy band EXO claimed the number one spot on Billboard's World Music chart, and the band Super Junior remained on top of the music charts in Taiwan for more than two years (Culture trip, 2018). This remarkable success in recent years has attracted a huge influx of foreign companies, workers, students, and tourists, into Korea. In response, universities around the globe have initiated and/ or expanded programs on Korean studies. For instance, the University of Tuebingen, Germany, launched a Korean Studies program in 2010 and currently employs 14 teaching staff, including three professors, teaching 399 students (University of Tuebingen, 2019).

In short, there is a huge interest in doing business in Korea, yet the academic and non-academic literature is still somewhat lagging behind. Numerous books and articles have analyzed the economic development of Korea (e.g., Uttam, 2014; Lee, 2016). If international business is concerned, the majority of research has focused on the international activities of Korean companies (e.g., Hemmert, 2018). However, much less research has looked at foreign business in Korea (for exceptions, see, e.g., Bader et al., 2018; Froese, 2010). To conduct business in a foreign country successfully, it is imperative to understand the underlying business environment; otherwise, companies may fail. For instance, Walmart failed to adapt to local preferences and eventually had to retreat from Korea. Korea has a unique business environment and the political, legal, and cultural environments differ substantially from those in the rest of the world. The political and legal environments were influenced by the US, Germany, and Japan, but they developed their own characteristics along the way. The culture is influenced by Confucianism and emphasizes seniority and personal relations while also embracing Western features in recent years (Froese et al., 2008). These topics are covered in this book.

The purpose of this book is to provide insights into and recommendations for how foreign companies and individuals can succeed in Korea. Thus, this book covers a wide range of relevant topics, including the Korean business environment, market entry into Korea, and management issues in Korea. The book will be useful for investors, organizations, managers, and students interested in doing business or already doing business in/with Korea. Researchers interested in doing research on foreign companies and workers in Korea might also find this book a useful resource in obtaining a broad understanding. The contributors to this book are well-known scholars based in America, Asia, Australia, and Europe, further demonstrating the global reach and interest in doing business in Korea.

## Outline of volume

The book is divided into three parts. Part I provides an overview of the economic, political, and cultural environments that shape the way of doing business in Korea.

This is an important foundation to better understand why and how to do business in Korea. Part II covers market access into Korea and specifically focuses on exporting and M&A, two common entry modes, and how foreign companies can learn from Korea. Part III discusses typical management issues that foreign companies and managers face in Korea, including marketing, human resource management, and expatriate management. Furthermore, since a substantial proportion of foreign students and adults in Korea find employment through starting their own business, we also have a chapter on how to found a company.

## Part I: business environment

The following chapter, Chapter 2, provides a historical overview of the recent economic development in Korea. You-il Lee and Richard Lee, both from the University of South Australia, Australia, structure their overview into the three phases from 1960 until today. The first phase focuses on state-led international trade development through export-oriented industrialization between the 1960s and 1990s. The second phase sees a neo-liberal, market-oriented development enabling FDI inflows and international trade through free-trade agreements starting from the late 1990s. The third phase describes the present period of Korea as an industrialized nation. This chapter is very important for understanding the Korean economic structure.

Chapter 3, written by Jitendra Uttam from Jawaharlal Nehru University, India, introduces the Korean political environment. This chapter focuses on two events that shaped the political and social landscape in Korea: the Asian financial crisis in 1997 and the political crisis in 2016, which resulted in the impeachment of the Korean president. While the triggers were different, both events reduced the influence of the government in business. This chapter provides important insights into the role of formal and informal institutions in Korean business.

Chapter 4 explains the unique features of the Korean culture relevant to doing business in Korea. The cultural environment of South Korea is typically regarded as being shaped by Confucian ideals, a low level of trust, and a high degree of collectivism. Sven Horak, St. John's University, US, introduces a more focused view by redefining trust viewed through the lens of informal networks, which characterize Korean society. Social ideals in Korea can be described as simultaneously individualistic and collectivistic. This chapter provides practical implications that are important for the management of expatriates in connection to ethical behavior.

## Part II: market access

Chapter 5 analyzes FDI inflows into Korea. In Hyeock (Ian) Lee, Loyola University, US, analyzes a large data set to demonstrate the pattern of FDI inflow and explain such patterns. Findings show that inbound FDI into Korea has consistently increased over the studied period, mainly coming in from Asia-Pacific countries and often within the service industries and in the greater Seoul area. Based on the analysis, this chapter provides important managerial and policy implications.

Chapter 6 is dedicated to exporting, as the majority of foreign firms do business in Korea via exports. Justin Paul, University of Puerto Rico, USA, and Hyunji Lee, University of Goettingen, Germany, discuss the advantages and disadvantages of direct versus indirect exporting. Furthermore, the chapter provides an analysis of the typical challenges foreign firms encounter in Korea. Based on their analysis, the authors give suggestions for how foreign firms can prepare themselves and implement direct and indirect exporting to Korea.

Chapter 7, written by Yong Suhk Pak and Yi Yang, Yonsei University, Korea, introduces both inbound and outbound cross-border M&As of Korean firms, including deal cases, value, location, and industry distributions. Moreover, the chapter discusses the main regulations and foreign investment guidance and the procedures for foreign companies acquiring Korean firms. Given that the success and failure of cross-border M&As will be decided during the integration phase, this chapter provides a contextual analysis, paying particular attention to language and cultural challenges. The authors provide important managerial implications for foreign companies integrating Korean target companies.

Chapter 8 discusses how foreign companies can learn from Korea. First, Martin Hemmert, Korea University, Korea, describes the strengths of Korean companies. Technical knowledge in knowledge-intensive industries, such as semiconductors and mobile communications, as well as certain managerial practices, might be particularly interesting for foreign companies. Close relationships and rich communication channels are also important for absorbing knowledge. Technological and managerial learning is often first conducted most effectively via foreign companies' local subsidiaries in Korea, which may subsequently transfer the knowledge they have absorbed to other locations.

## Part III: marketing and managing in Korea

Chapter 9 focuses on marketing in Korea. Fabian Jintae Froese and Sarah Reckelkamm, both from the University of Goettingen, Germany, introduce international marketing strategies and current consumer trends in Korea. Guided by the '4Ps', this chapter critically analyzes whether and how alterations in terms of product/services, price, promotion, and place are important to success in the Korean market. The chapter provides important managerial implications for how foreign companies could modify their products and services to better reach Korean consumers.

Chapter 10, written by Jinxi Michelle Li, Gyeongsang National University, Korea, and Fabian Jintae Froese, University of Goettingen, Germany, deals with HRM in Korea. First, the chapter overviews typical human resource management practices prevalent in Korea. Then, the chapter discusses typical human resource management challenges and possible solutions, also providing important recommendations for how foreign companies can attract, recruit, and manage Korean talent.

Chapter 11, written by Samuel Davies and Fabian Jintae Froese, both from the University of Goettingen, Germany, is devoted to expatriate management. This chapter focuses on highly skilled employed foreigners who do not intend to live in Korea permanently, so-called expatriates. This chapter discusses the major challenges and opportunities for expatriates in Korea. Dealing with a different culture, language, understandings of work–life balance, and social exclusion can complicate expatriates' cross-cultural adjustment. Preparation, high motivation, cultural intelligence, and a supportive family can help alleviate these challenges. This chapter provides practical implications for potential and current expatriates as well as organizations wishing to employ expatriates in Korea.

Chapter 12 provides an overview of how foreign entrepreneurs can start a business in Korea, including the rules and regulations and general advice on doing business in Korea. Stephan Gerschewski, University of Reading, UK, begins by outlining the general SME sector in Korea and then examines key industries that are attractive for foreigners to start up their businesses. In addition, the chapter analyzes how foreign entrepreneurs can do business in Korea, including the legal types of businesses, visa types for foreigners, start-up incubators for foreigners, and key tax information for foreign start-ups.

## References

Bader, K., Froese, F. J., & Kraeh, A. 2018. Clash of cultures? German expatriates' work-life boundary adjustment in South Korea. *European Management Review*, 15: 357–374.

Culture trip. 2018. *The 10 most popular K-Pop artists and bands.* https://theculturetrip.com/asia/south-korea/articles/the-10-most-popular-kpop-artists-and-groups/. Accessed 15 March 2019.

Froese, F. J. 2010. Success and failure in managing foreign acquisitions in South Korea and Japan: Lessons from Renault, General Motors and DaimlerChrysler. *Global Business and Organizational Excellence*, 30(1): 50–59.

Froese, F. J., Pak, Y. S., & Chong, L. C. 2008. Managing the human side of cross-border acquisitions in South Korea. *Journal of World Business*, 43(1): 97–108.

Hemmert, M. 2018. *The evolution of tiger management: Korean companies in global competition.* New York: Routledge.

Lee, J. W. 2016. *The republic of Korea's economic growth and catch-up: Implications for the people's republic of china.* Asian Development Bank Institute (ADBI) Working Paper Series No.571. Tokyo: ADBI.

Ramirez, E. 2017. *Nearly 100% of households in South Korea now have internet access, thanks to seniors.* www.forbes.com/sites/elaineramirez/2017/01/31/nearly-100-of-households-in-south-korea-now-have-internet-access-thanks-to-seniors/#4603b9cb5572. Accessed 15 March 2018.

Statista. 2018. *Internet usage in South Korea.* www.statista.com/topics/2230/internet-usage-in-south-korea/. Accessed 15 March 2019.

Ullah, Z. 2017. *How Samsung dominates South Korea's economy.* https://money.cnn.com/2017/02/17/technology/samsung-south-korea-daily-life/index.html. Accessed 15 March 2019.

University of Tuebingen. 2019. *Geschichte der Koreanistik in Tuebingen* (History of Korean Studies in Tuebingen). https://uni-tuebingen.de/fakultaeten/philosophische-fakultaet/fachbereiche/aoi/koreanistik/abteilung/geschichte/. Accessed 15 March 2019.

Uttam, J. 2014. *The political economy of Korea: Transition, transformation and turn-around,* Basingstoke, Hampshire, New York: Palgrave Macmillan.

Van Nooden, R. 2016. *South Korea stretches lead in research investment*. www.nature.com/news/south-korea-stretches-lead-in-research-investment-1.19333. Accessed 15 March 2019.

World Bank. 2015. *GDP per capita*. https://data.worldbank.org/indicator/NY.GDP.PCAP.CD?end=2015&start=1960. Accessed 15 March 2019.

World Bank. 2017. *World development indicators*. http://databank.worldbank.org/data/source/world-development-indicators. Accessed 15 March 2019.

World Bank. 2018. GDP growth https://data.worldbank.org/indicator/NY.GDP.MKTP.KD.ZG?locations=KR. Accessed 15 March 2019.

World Trade Organization. 2017. *International trade and market access data*. www.wto.org/english/res_e/statis_e/statis_bis_e.htm?solution=WTO&path. Accessed 15 March 2019.

# PART I
# Business environment

# 2

# ECONOMIC ENVIRONMENT

*You-il Lee and Richard Lee*

## Introduction

Within approximately a single generation, Korea, the *Miracle on the River Han*, has transformed itself from an aid-dependent developing country following the Korean War (1950–53) to being one of the richest countries in the world. Where it was once a basket-case economy that relied on foreign aid for survival, it is now a donor country that is pulling its weight as a global citizen. Even as the 1997 Asian financial crisis threatened to cast a dark and lengthy shadow on the country, by 2016 Korea had emerged to become the 11th-largest economy in the world and fourth in Asia after China, Japan and India (World Bank, 2017).

Fuelled by the government's strategy of "income-led growth", the OECD forecasts that Korea's economy will grow at an average of three percent until the end of this decade (OECD, 2017). The strategy aims to drive growth through increasing public employment, raising the minimum wage and increasing social spending. Although the current high level of household debt (at 160% of household disposable income) and persistent unemployment rate (at 3.7%) may continue to remain a headwind to private consumption (OECD, 2017), Korean consumers still possess relatively high disposable income. These factors bode well for Korea's domestic consumption. Indeed, recent data by the World Bank reveals that Korea's per capita GNI is about US$36,000, putting the country as the 30th richest in the world (by GNI). In summary, in a relatively short time span, Korea has experienced *the* most rapid rate of economic development and has now undoubtedly become wealthy and competitive with a rapid ascent in the world of high-technology products (i.e., Samsung, SK, LG, POSCO, Hyundai). This remarkable development of post-war industrialization has transformed the national brand image of Korea from a backwater developing country to a 21st-century economic and high-technology powerhouse.

Against this backdrop, this chapter provides an overview of Korea's recent economic development in a historical context and offers an analysis of the social relations (political and institutional) that have successfully driven Korea's rapid economic growth in a relatively short period of industrialization. The chapter provides a discourse into the evolution of Korea's economic success through three phases. The first phase, from the 1960s to 1997, recounts how the state enacted policies to propel trade development through EOI. The neo-liberal, market-oriented focus of the second phase saw the government facilitating inflows of foreign direct investment and regional integration through FTAs. This phase started in the late 1990s and further expanded Korea's trade with their international counterparts, despite the setbacks of the Asian financial crisis of 1997. Finally, the third phase chronicles Korea's journey to becoming a modern-day high-tech powerhouse. This analysis also serves as an important prelude to later chapters of this volume by offering a historical overview of Korea's recent economic development.

## First phase of industrialization – 1960s–1997

### EOI-led international trade development

Korea's industrialization, late particularly by Western timelines, kick-started in the early 1960s, joined by the formation of the chaebol (i.e., mostly family-owned and - managed Korean conglomerates such as Samsung, LG, SK, Hyundai), to spearhead large-scale export-oriented industrialization. According to a recent report by Deloitte (GMCI, 2016), Korea's manufacturing industry accounted for about 86% of total merchandise exports. Korea's economic past of the period between the 1960s and 1980s has been hailed by the global community as a 'miracle'. The country has come a long way since the post-Korean Wars (1950–1953) period when manufacturing accounted for a mere 12% of GDP and grew from US$1.9 billion during 1960 to more than US$400 billion by 1996. Average GDP growth rates in the 1960s exceeded 7%, 8.6% in the 1970s and 9% in the 1980s, respectively (Lee, 2016: 4). However, the industrialization objectives and characteristics, articulated in successive five-year plans under different administrations, differed vastly during the early post-war days in comparison to recent times.

Korea was predominantly an agricultural economy up until the Korean War. In the beginning (early 1960s), the government's import substitution industrialization (ISI) policies were aimed to make Koreans self-reliant while increasing their wealth (Chung, 1974), although some have argued that the approach was a mistake (e.g., see Harvie & Lee, 2003). Korea chose this policy (EOI) due to various unfavorable national conditions for economic development such as limited natural resources, negligible domestic savings and the lack of development experience. The change of economic policy from ISI to EOI involved a revaluation of the currency (about 12%) in 1964 and an establishment of a Free Export Zone for industries such as electronics and motor vehicles.

Economic conditions in Korea in the 1960s were similar to those of most resource-poor, low-income developing countries. The population was growing at an annual rate of 2.9%, and there was widespread unemployment. The 1962 per capita GNP in current prices was only US$120, and the level of domestic savings was negligible. The nation had no significant exports, which amounted to only US$54 million, and had run a chronic balance of payments deficits ever since the establishment of the independent government in 1948. Through successive five-year plans, the Korean government systemically enacted import substitution policies through tariffs and subsidies as well as through regulations and restrictions on foreign investments and technology transfers in order to develop strong local companies that could compete internationally. The omnipresence of the state in guiding or even regulating private industries has benefited major family-owned chaebol as major financial resources and coveted public infrastructure projects are channelled to them. In turn, the chaebol invested heavily in R&D that would eventually bring about world-class brands including the likes of Samsung and Hyundai (Shin, 2005). The characteristics of the country's industrialization process are long considered as one underpinned by political nationalism.

Through succeeding five-year economic plans since the early 1960s, the Korean government systemically enacted import substitution policies through tariffs and subsidies, as well as through regulations and restrictions on foreign investments and technology transfers in order to develop strong local companies that are capable of competing internationally. Some credit for the rapid success of Korea's industrialization should also be attributed to the government's development of special economic zones (SEZs) starting from the 1970s. These zones serve to attract foreign investments through policy (e.g., one-stop-shop processing of import/export customs procedure) and financial incentives (e.g., cheaper access to land for rental) in order to enhance the competitiveness of Korean exports (Jeong & Pek, 2016). Among them, the Masan Export Processing Zone (later renamed as the Masan Free Trade Zone) was the first designated bonded processing zone. Consequently, many prominent multinational corporations, such as Nokia, Sony, Sanyo, and Matsushita, set up businesses within the zone. This not only formed a concentrated cluster that synergized the development of support businesses by Korean companies; it also facilitated the transfer of advanced technologies and business know-how that would later feed the competitiveness and growth of Korean businesses.

The major determinants of Korea's phenomenal economic success and the 1997 financial crisis have been the subject of debate among economists, political scientists and political economists, and institutionalists. Literature advances a range of explanations, from market mechanisms to the strong role of the state and the role of state policy in facilitating private- and public-sector coordination.

Liberal market economists or neo-classical theorists have found Korea's high-speed economic growth in its pursuit of EOI along with policies that favor a market orientation and minimal government intervention (Westphal, 1978, 1990; Krueger, 1982, 1990; Riedel, 1988; Little, 1990). They also see that the success of Korea's industrialization was mainly because Korea adopted a 'neutral policy' regime in which free trade and private markets played a major role. To them, government intervention in economic markets creates distortion and breeds inefficiency. Instead, the free play of market forces should be promoted. For example, Krueger argues against the restrictive 'direct control' of ISI regimes, which she maintains, 'fight the market' and lead to a highly complex and erratic incentive structure which eventually results in a decline in output and productivity. Instead, she links Korea's rapid growth to their reliance on EOI.

While the neo-classical approach attempts to explain the rise of the Korean economy in terms of the shifting patterns of comparative advantage and its management, a new breed of scholars, known as statists, began to investigate domestic political processes and structures in Korea in relation to its rapid economic growth. Despite the considerable debate about the character of successive post-war Korean governments, the consensus of the literature is perhaps most evident in its view on the state dominance over the economy, market and labor. What really matters in the context of Korea's economic success from the statist perspective is the domestic political structures that shape policy choices and implementation and ultimately determine economic outcomes (Jones & Sakong, 1980; Moon, 1988; Wade, 1988; Woo, 1991). What they suggest is that rather than emphasizing policy itself, the nature of economic policy-making should first be analyzed in examining the nature of Korean economic development. Accordingly, the adoption of an EOI strategy was not a result of market forces but the result of a conscious state choice to realize economic and political objectives. The state's consistent and coherent implementation has been facilitated by state strength unique to Korea. In particular, Amsden's work on Korean industrialization challenges the free-market orthodoxy (Amsden, 1987a, 1987b, 1992, 1994). The crux of her argument is that although low wages and the exclusion of the popular sector are the foundation of Korea's successful late industrialization, low wages themselves are not adequate stimuli for success, nor does the pursuit of comparative advantage ensures success. Instead, pervasive state intervention, combined with large-scale guaranteed external sources including technological and foreign capital (i.e., aid and loan), which eventually enabled the Park Chung-Hee regime (1963–1979) to dominate the economic and financial sectors (Choi, 1993: 22), is effective and necessary to produce a nation's dynamic comparative advantage. In short, the state interventionist nature of the Korean political economy is probably the most critical aspect of Korea's first phase of EOI industrialization.

## Second phase of industrialization: globalization

### 1997 financial crisis

Korea's remarkable economic achievement during the first phase of industrialization is not free of problems. Korea faced many uncertainties triggered by the so-called economic miracle in the 1980s. For example, since the mid-1980s, the country has been confronted by a variety of issues. They included the emergence of new protectionism from the advanced industrial countries, particularly from the United States, the European Union and looming competition from the newly emerging economic superstars of Southeast Asia such as Indonesia, Thailand and Malaysia. At home, Korea also had to contend with other challenges. These included increasing social and political tensions such as labor and management conflicts and the growing discrepancy between the 'haves' and 'have-nots'. Moreover, there were worsening infrastructural imbalances of the economy, particularly in the high-tech industries, where there was an underdevelopment of small and medium-sized firms.

With rising labor costs since 1987, Korean industries and the economy had to some extent shed their competitive luster in the global market as a manufacturing base. While during the 1970s and 1980s, Korea achieved the most spectacular economic growth among the developing countries, yet, in the latter part of the 1990s, Korea became the first country among the "East-Asian Tigers" to receive what was a record-breaking US$58 billion rescue package from the International Monetary Fund (IMF) to remedy its ailing economy as a result of the so-called 1997 Asian Financial Crisis. This marked the end of the country's long-hailed reputation as a newly industrialized country and even as an advanced industrial country. Korea's financial crisis has brought various but serious economic problems for Korea. The GDP growth rate in the first quarter (January-March) of 1998 was 3.8% year on year, which was the lowest since the 7.8% growth rate in 1980. Changes in the unemployment and inflation rates since November 1997 were also remarkable. From 2.6% at the end of November 1997, the unemployment rate rose drastically to 6.8% by the end of 1998, and the number of unemployed already exceeded 1.5 million (Moon et al., 1999: 14). The consumer price index rose from 4.3% in November 1997 to 7.5% in 1998, largely because of the exchange rate devaluation (Moon et al., 1999: 33). The United Nations Conference on Trade and Development (UNCTAD, 1998) in its annual report on trade and development estimated that Korea's unemployment rate would reach around 10% by the end of 1998. The most significant drop in terms of employees since the currency crisis was in manufacturing, particularly in key sectors of the Korean economy related to infrastructure and automobile.

As briefly discussed earlier, two distinct schools (neo-classical and statist) on Korea's rapid growth have their own unique explanations. While the neo-classical school treats Korea's success as a classic economic model that shows the virtues of the Western capitalist system, the state or institutionalists see the case as a different paradigm from this Western perspective and argue the difference is the key to its economic triumph (Frankel, 1998). However, how do scholars explain the crisis of the time given that Korea's economic success was rooted either in the nation's adherence to market principles and minimal state intervention, so-called Western capitalism, or in the strong capacity of the state? Why did the Korean economy under such circumstances collapse?

Economists tend to contribute various macroeconomic (capital inflows, real exchange rate application) and microeconomic (credit expansion, financial regulation and supervision) factors to the Asian financial crisis (Radelet & Sachs, 1998). Corsetti et al. (1998) suggest that the cause of the crisis is rooted in the inconsistency of policies aimed at simultaneously sustaining growth, investment and risk-taking, as well as maintaining stable exchange rates and providing guarantees to underregulated financial institutions. In the absence of fully developed and sophisticated securities markets, these policies caused large account imbalances. Similarly, Paul Krugman (1998) suggests that the Asian financial crisis might have been only incidentally about currencies, but it was mainly about bad banking and its consequences. Krugman places the problem of a moral hazard asset bubble, which created severe inflation – not of goods but of asset prices such as land and stock – as a major contender for a leading role in the crisis (Krugman, 1998). On the contrary, unlike the neo-classical economists, state-centered theorists see the problems and causes in relation to the capacity of the developmental state. Weiss and Hobson (1998), for example, argue that the Asian financial crisis was fundamentally rooted in the vulnerability of government capacity to the strong winds of global finance.

One of the most painful IMF conditions for Korea was the opening of its industry to foreign competition, including foreign investment reforms in financial services and trade reform and liberalization. Korea has had a long history of economic nationalism stimulated initially by a negative response to earlier interactions with foreign regimes and then by the desperate need for economic survival. This nationalistic economic doctrine was the binding force that gave direction to Korea's industrialization policies over the last half-century (Lopez-Aymes, 2010). Furthermore, a strong belief in self-sufficiency has inevitably resulted in a tough business climate that is seemingly hostile to foreign companies. This is because as indicated earlier, Korea's economic policies used to be state-chaebol-driven and had a strong protectionist nature regarding foreign competition in the local market. To turn the distorted Korean economy into a healthy economy, the new government under Kim Dae-jung (DJ; 1998–2002) had shown a strong commitment to the priorities and steps prescribed by the IMF to be taken by restructuring the financial sectors, mostly banks and the chaebol. Ironically, however, the financial crisis coupled with externally driven pressures imposed by the IMF rescue package provided opportunities to implement major reforms, including hostile mergers and acquisitions (M&As), full opening of the domestic market to foreign products, massive restructuring of financial institutions and, more important, curbing the power of the large corporate groups or the chaebol.

## FDI and FTA-led international trade model

The outbreak of the currency crisis and its seriousness to the Korean economy resulted in a striking transition in Korea's attitude towards foreign companies and products. First, to turn the distorted Korean economy into a healthy economy, the DJ administration had shown strong commitment by making decisive reform efforts in sectors, mostly involving finance and corporate (chaebol) restructuring. The aim was to eliminate Korea's chronic disease, which is its tight government–business collusion, to enhance transparency and supervision, and to restore market confidence. It is now generally accepted by the DJ administration and the Korean people since the eruption of the currency meltdown that foreign capital is critical to remedy its ailing economy. Not only did foreign direct investment in Korea stabilize the foreign exchange market, but also it eventually helped in restructuring the economy and increasing economic efficiency. The November 1998 Foreign Investment Promotion Act abolished restrictions on the foreign ownership of land and hostile cross-border M&As and allowed foreign participation in large public enterprises and key industries (EAAU, 1999). This draconian change in the government's policy toward inbound investments had the effects of shifting the Korean economy toward a more of market-oriented neo-classical economic growth paradigm based on inward FDI and replaced the old model of the state-led development strategy.

Under the guidance of the IMF since early 1998, the Korean economy rebounded from its late 1997 meltdown faster than expected. After falling by nearly 7% in 1998, real GDP was almost 11 % in 1999 and near 9% in 2000. Since the opening of its market to the outside, international capital flows into Korea rose from a meagre US$27.4 million in 1987 to more than US$32 billion in 1996 (Economist Intelligence Unit, 2002: 8). Beginning in the early 1990s, the affiliates of more than 16,000 MNEs had established operations in fields ranging from consumer products to high-tech industries operating in Korea. In addition to IMF-mandated structural reforms, a lower value of the local currency (won), the declining status of the chaebol, and the government's strong push for investment liberalization measures meant there was an upsurge of FDI inflows into Korea (Chang, 1998; Weiss & Hobson, 1998; Kim & Rowley, 2001; Noland, 2005; Shin, 2005). While the amount of total inward FDI during the period from 1962 to 1997 was minimal, total FDI during the eight-year period from 1998 to 2005 alone tallied about US$91 billion on a notification basis, which is nearly quadruple the US$25 billion posted during the previous 35 years, or about 79% of the US$115 billion aggregate FDI figure recorded from 1962 to 2005 (Ministry of Commerce, Industry and Energy, 2007).

Korea has also been very determined since the 1997 Asian financial crisis to become a regional FTA hub nation in order to overcome its relatively small domestic market and participate actively in a rapidly regionalized world. In fact, until its first FTA with Chile in 2004, Korea had established no bilateral trade agreements, nor did it have any plans for FTA with foreign countries. The 1997 Asian financial crisis that hit Korea hard was a key triggering factor behind Korea's aggressive pursuit for FTA as a matter of survival. As discussed earlier, the major structural reforms mandated by the IMF consisted of restructuring troubled financial institutions, improving corporate governance and enhancing labor market flexibility. The IMF also demanded equally important external reforms. One of the top economic policy priorities of the DJ administration centered on engaging with foreign companies to attract FDI into Korea. In terms of trade liberalization, the DJ administration started kicking off a series of FTA negotiations in 1998 with the aim of overcoming the currency crisis, strengthening the competitiveness of Korean industry and boosting exports (Ye, 2017: 151). As of June 2017, 659 notifications of regional trade agreements (RTAs) had been received by the General Agreement on Tariffs and Trade (GATT) and then the World Trade Organization (WTO). These WTO figures correspond to 445 physical RTAs, of which 279 are currently in force. Over 20% of 279 were FTAs wherein one of the signatories was an East Asian country (World Trade Organization, 2017).

Dramatically, the late 1990s saw the sudden emergence of Korea as a major recipient of foreign capital for both strategic and non-strategic industrial areas, ranging from consumer products (e.g., alcohol, tobacco, cosmetics, textiles, etc.) to telecommunications. Consequently, the 1990s witnessed the flood of foreign products as well as an increasing number of foreign MNEs operating in Korea. Since the outbreak of Korea's financial crisis, more than 1,500 MNEs have established operations in Korea in fields ranging from consumer products to high-tech industries. This implies that the Korean market is rapidly changing and open to outsiders offering opportunities to maximize market benefits. This is one of the most revolutionary features of the Korean economy in the 20th century, contrasting with the previous four decades of the Korean political economy. Many neo-liberal supporters such as international financial institutions described Korea's "economic recovery and financial stabilization" as remarkable (Crotty & Lee, 2001: 183). Consequently, Korea's IMF loans were paid off by mid-2001. Regarding its regional integration strategy, as of January 2017, Korea had concluded 15 FTAs with 52 countries, namely those with ASEAN (Association of Southeast Asian Countries, 10 countries), Australia, Canada, Chile, China, Colombia, EFTA (European Free Trade Association, 4 countries), EU (European Union, 28 countries), India, New Zealand, Peru, Turkey and the United States of America.

However, the role of FDI and FTA throughout Korea's legacy of economic development has been insignificant. to say the least. In fact, the level of FDI/FTA relative to the size of the economy had been quite negligible when compared to that of other countries in East Asia. This fact can be verified by several indicators. According to the United Nations Conference on Trade and Development's (UNCTAD, 2006) World Investment Report 2006, the inward FDI stock in Korea as a percentage of current GDP in 2005 was 8%, above Japan (2.2%) but below the levels of Taiwan (12.1%), China (14.3%) and Singapore (15.8%). What then has accounted for the relatively minor role played by FDI/FTA in Korea's economic development in comparison with its Asian neighbors? In the initial period of Korea's modern economic growth during the 1960s, the inflow of foreign capital was encouraged to make up for the shortage of domestic savings and foreign reserves. However, the Korean government preferred foreign borrowing, which then allowed them to control foreign resources, over FDI. The general fear of Korean industries being dominated by foreign entities, which was deeply rooted in Korea's then recent history of Japanese colonization from 1910 to 1945, was too widespread inside Korea for the government to accommodate foreign management. Even today there is a lingering suspicion that FDI/FTA is just a conduit through which foreigners/foreign countries attempt to control Korean industries. While the Korean leaders today show preferences towards FTAs, they yet face strong domestic interest groups and oppositions (Ye, 2017: 152). But undoubtedly, Korea has emerged in recent decades as one of the most active states in attracting FDI and pursuing FTAs with partners across the globe. Ravenhill (2003) points to three factors to explain the prevalent trend toward bilateral FTAs: (a) an increasing awareness of the weakness of existing regional institutions and initiatives, (b) perceptions of positive demonstration effects from regional agreements in other parts of the world and (c) changing domestic economic interests after the economic crisis.

## Korea today – a high-technology nation

As the 1970s saw Korea relying on heavy industries as the growth engine of its economy, the 1980s initiated seismic shifts towards high-technology products. The shift may in part be because Korea is finding itself sandwiched between its two neighboring countries, China and Japan. The emergence of China has changed the landscape for trade in Asia, if not the whole world. As China grows on the back of its government's strategy to boost key heavy and chemical industries (HCI), especially in the steel, petrochemical and construction industries, China is fast closing the gap with, if not having already overtaken, Korea as the Asian heavy industrial powerhouse. Concurrently, Korea continues to lag Japan in high technology innovation and manufacturing.

However, Korean technology products in those early days were still stigmatized by the nation's heavy-industry image. At the start of the high-technology evolution, Korean companies mostly functioned as low-cost assembly lines for foreign consumer electronic firms. But by the 1990s, Korea's continued emphasis on high-technology had led to the country moving up the value chain to include sectors such as aerospace and micro engineering. According to a recent report by Deloitte, Korea is the global leader in market share for LCD (Liquid Crystal Display) TVs and memory chips and second to China in the manufacture of smartphones (GMCI, 2016). By 2014, high technology exports had occupied 58% of total manufactured exports.

Korea's rapid ascent in the world of high-technology products is no less due to the government's emphasis on research and development. In 2016, Korea had spent about 4.3% of its GDP on research, well ahead of the United States (2.5%), China (2.0%) and the EU (averaging 1.9%; van Nooden, 2016) and nearly twice the global average of 2.23%, according to the World Bank (2015). The success of Korea's transformation to a high-technology economy and the weight it puts on research and development are exemplified by the dominance of Korean smartphone products. In 2017, Samsung and LG combined held more than a 70% share of the smartphones market in Korea, with Apple a distant third at 24%. *Similarly, on a worldwide basis, Samsung still dominates with a share of 31%, followed by Apple at about 20%* (Statcounter, 2018).

According to the ranking by Brandirectory (2018), in a short span of two decades and even as Korea was embroiled in the Asian financial crisis, Samsung has gone on to surpass the Japanese electronics giant Sony in brand value. Indeed, the company is ranked higher than quintessential U.S. brands like Microsoft, American Express, McDonald's, Coca-Cola and even Facebook. Samsung Group, which comprises the combined consumer Electronics, information technology and mobile communications businesses, is also five times more valuable than the next Korean brand (ranked 79th), Hyundai Motors (Brandirectory, 2018).

Interestingly, Samsung, who is currently undoubtedly the biggest of the chaebol groups, was already a successful domestic company at the start of Korea's industrialization process. The firm's main activities were insurance, property and low-technology product manufacturing with a sprawling network of more than 80 subsidiaries that account for more than 20% of the entire market value of the Korean Stock Exchange and account for about 15% of Korea's entire economy (Ullah, 2017). The year 1969 was Samsung's first foray into foreign markets by teaming up with the Japanese consumer electronics company, Sanyo, to assemble low-cost transistor radios and black-and-white TVs. This joint venture gave Samsung the opportunity to send its employees to be trained by Sanyo (and others). Samsung subsequently not only mastered the manufacturing process but also became innovative with manufacturing and product improvements. By 2007, it had registered 2,725 patents in the United States alone and operated 17 research centers around the globe with an annual R&D spent of about US$5.6 billion.

In their *Harvard Business Review* article, Khanna et al. (2011) asserted that Samsung's success is due in part to the company's ability to tap into its traditional low-cost manufacturing base and augment it with innovations to quickly bring to market high-quality, high-margin products. In doing so, it has melded a traditional Confucian top-down management philosophy with meritocratic Western business practices, where pay and promotion are tied to performance rather than by seniority by length of stay in the company. This hybrid approach to strategic management has guided Samsung to multiple years of record profit in the wake of the Asian financial crisis in the late 1990s; Khanna et al. (2011) reported that Samsung's profit was higher than the five largest Japanese competitors (Sony, Panasonic, Toshiba, Hitachi, Sharp) combined. Such public and international prominence leaves little doubt that advanced technology (just like the case of Germany or Japan) is a representative factor of foreigners' perception of Korea's national brand image of a high technology country (Kinsey & Chung, 2013). The country also possesses the world's highest penetration of broadband in households. A recent Forbes report indicated that 99.2% of the 19 million households in Korea have broadband internet access (Ramirez, 2017). Moreover, 99% of the household users went online at least once a week and spent an average of 14.3 hours per week on the internet. Given the world dominance of the smartphone market by Samsung and LG, it is also not surprising that mobile phones and smart devices are the most popular means to access the internet. The icing on the cake is the recent announcement that Korea has won the race by being the first country to launch commercial fifth-generation (5G) mobile services at the 2018 Winter Olympics at PyeongChang (SCMP, 2018).

Similarly, a study by Pew Research Centre (2016) found that Korea has the highest penetration (about 88%) of smartphone users in the world against a global median of 43%. The population's openness to new technology has resulted in Korea's tech-savvy population being early adopters of technology. For example, according to a report by global market analytics firm eMarketer, nearly one-third of its smartphone users will make mobile payments for goods or services at a point of sale in 2018. Mobile payment adoption took off following the launch of mobile payment services such as Samsung Pay and LG Pay in 2015.

Despite the emphasis on the high technology industry, Korea's heavy industry past has persisted to the present day. Just look at the makeup of Fortune 500 companies. A total of 15 Korean companies made the Fortune Global 500 list in 2017, which was the same as the previous year and only three more than in 2000. While Samsung Electronics, at 15th position in the list, is the highest-ranking Korean company, the next few remaining Korean companies in the list are in the heavy, chemical and construction industry, including Hyundai Motor (78th), SK Holdings (95th), Korea Electric Power Corporation (177th) and with LG Electronics (201st) rounding up the top five. It thus seems that Korea has not totally shed its heavy industry image, nor is it in the country's best interest to do so. Indeed, it is not uncommon for nations to excel in different industry sectors and hence possess multiple brand images, although one image may stand out more than the others. For example, as much as France is known as the fashion capital of the world with its line of luxury brands, France is also known for its heavy industry manufacturing (think Renault and Airbus).

It thus seems that Korea's nation brand image, at least in present times, is rooted in its industrialized past. It harbors the pedigree of a competitive heavy-industry nation, coupled with the image of a global high-technology powerhouse.

## Conclusion

This chapter has reviewed perhaps the most striking feature of the Korean economy in the late 20th century (i.e., the rise to and fall from economic eminence). During the 1970s and 1980s, Korea achieved the most spectacular economic growth among the developing countries. Yet, in the latter part of the 1990s, Korea became the first country among the 'East-Asian Tigers' to receive what was then a record-breaking rescue package from the IMF to remedy its ailing economy. It was obvious that Korea's state-led growth model, embedded in a mercantilist leadership, had to face the severe challenges brought about by the unavoidable market-driven globalization force (i.e., IMF). These have led the Korean government to the dramatic shift towards a neo-liberal FDI and FTA oriented international trade model (i.e., FTA and international business hub). However, this impressive and positive portrayal of Korea's openness to trade and FDI in the aftermath of the financial crisis should not mislead readers into thinking that Korea's reform measures have proceeded smoothly. To the contrary, painful and difficult decisions must be made and were made, along the road toward conforming to global standards.

As Korea looks to the next decade and beyond, the country will continue to grapple with the challenges of assuring buoyant economic growth, consumer welfare gains and job creation through expanded trade and investment between the two and even maintaining or even improving its nation brand image in the face of increasing competition globally. And then there are rising threats from a resurgent Japan, its inability to compete with China on scale, and a menacing northern neighbor. Korea wants its international standing to be commensurate with the economic success it has built since the 1960s. Hence, what dominant shape Korea's competitiveness and its high-tech nation brand image shall take in the future would depend on the industries (i.e., fourth industrial revolution) that the country is able to develop and sustain competitively.

## Acknowledgments

This research was supported by the Seed Program for Korean Studies through the Ministry of Education of the Republic of Korea and the Korean Studies Promotion Service of the Academy of Korean Studies (AKS-2017-INC-2230006).

## Bibliography

### Key references

Amsden, A. 1987. *Asia's next Giant: South Korea and late industrialization*. New York: Oxford University Press.
Khanna, T., Song, J., & Lee, K. 2011. The paradox of Samsung's rise. *Harvard Business Review*, 89 July–August: 142–147.
Lee, J. W. 2016. *The republic of Korea's economic growth and catch-up: Implications for the people's republic of China*. Asian Development Bank Institute (ADBI) Working Paper Series No.571. Tokyo: ADBI.
Shin, J. 2005. Globalization and challenges to the developmental state: A comparison between South Korea and Singapore. *Global Economic Review*, 34(4): 379–395.

### Online sources

Organization for Economic Cooperation and Development. 2017. *Korea – Economic forecast summary*. www.oecd.org/korea/korea-economic-forecast-summary.htm. Accessed 10 May 2018.
Pew Research Centre. 2016. *Smartphone ownership and internet usage continues to climb in emerging economies*. www.pewglobal.org/2016/02/22/smartphone-ownership-and-internet-usage-continues-to-climb-in-emerging-economies/. Accessed 11 March 2018.
World Bank. 2015. *Research and development expenditure* (% of GDP). https://data.worldbank.org/indicator/GB.XPD.RSDV.GD.ZS. Accessed 10 March 2018.
World Bank. 2017. *World development indicators*. http://databank.worldbank.org/data/source/world-development-indicators. Accessed 10 May 2018.

World Trade Organization. 2017. *Regional trade agreements: Facts and figures*. www.wto.org/english/tratop_e/region_e/regfac_e.htm. Accessed 22 August 2017.

# References

Amsden, A. 1987a. *Asia's next Giant: South Korea and late industrialization*. New York: Oxford University Press.

Amsden, A. 1987b. *Republic of Korea – Country study*. Helsinki: World Institute for Development Economics Research of the United Nations University.

Amsden, A. 1992. A Theory of government intervention in late industrialization. In L. Putterman & D. Rueschemeyer (Eds.), *State and market in development: Synergy or rivalry?*: 53–84. Boulder and London: Lynne Rienner Publishers.

Amsden, A. 1994. Why isn't the whole world experimenting with the East Asian model to develop? Review of the East Asian miracle. *World Development*, 22(4): 627–633.

Brandirectory. 2018. *The world's most valuable brands in 2018*. http://brandirectory.com/league_tables/table/global-500-2018. Accessed 1 March 2018.

Chang, H. 1998. South Korea: The misunderstood crisis. In K. S. Jomo (Ed.), *Tigers in Trouble*: 223–231. London: Zed Books.

Choi, J. 1993. Political cleavages in South Korea. In H. Koo (Ed.), *State and society in contemporary Korea*: 13–50. Ithaca, London: Cornell University Press.

Chung, K. H. 1974. Industrial progress in South Korea. *Asian Survey*, 14(5): 439–455.

Corsetti, G., Pesenti, P., & Roubini, N. 1998. Paper tigers? A preliminary assessment of the Asian Crisis. *Paper Presented at the Conference on NBER-Bank of Portugal International Seminar on Macroeconomics*. Lisbon, 14–15 June.

Crotty, J., & Lee, K. 2001. Economic performance in post-crisis Korea: A critical perspective on neoliberal restructuring. *Seoul Journal of Economics*, 14(2):183–242.

EAAU. 1999. *Korea rebuilds: From crisis to opportunity*. Canberra: Department of Foreign Affairs and Trade.

Economist Intelligence Unit (EIU). 2002. *Magnet or Morass? South Korea's prospects for foreign investment*. Hong Kong: Economist Intelligence Unit.

Frankel, J. 1998. The Asian model, the miracle, the crisis and the fund. *Paper Delivered at the US International Trade Commission*. Accessed 16 April.

GMCI. 2016. *Global manufacturing competitiveness index*. https://www2.deloitte.com/content/dam/Deloitte/us/Documents/manufacturing/us-gmci-skorea.pdf. Accessed 5 April 2018.

Harvie, C., & Lee, H. H. 2003. Export-led industrialisation and growth: Korea's economic miracle, 1962–1989. *Australian Economic History Review*, 43(3): 256–286.

Jeong, H. G., & Pek, J. H. 2016. *Special economic zones: What can developing countries learn from the Korean experience?* www.ksp.go.kr/common/attdown.jsp?fidx=692&pag=0000700003&pid=209. Accessed 1 March 2018

Jones, L., & Sakong, I. 1980. *Government, business, and entrepreneurship in economic development: The Korean case*. Cambridge: Harvard University Council on East Asian Studies.

Khanna, T., Song, J., & Lee, K. 2011. The paradox of Samsung's rise. *Harvard Business Review*, 89 (July-August): 142–147.

Kim, J., & Rowley, C. 2001. Managerial problems in Korea – Evidence from the nationalized industries. *The International Journal of Public Sector Management*, 14(2): 129–148.

Kinsey, D. F., & Chung, M. 2013. National image of South Korea: Implications for public diplomacy. *Exchange: The Journal of Public Diplomacy*, 4(1): Article 2.

Krueger, A. 1982. Newly industrializing economies. *Economic Impact*, 40(4): 26–32.

Krueger, A. 1990. Government failures in development. *Journal of Economic Perspectives*, 4(3): 9–23.

Krugman, P. 1998. Saving Asia: It's time to get radical. *Fortune*, 7 September: 75–80.

Lee, J. W. 2016. *The republic of Korea's economic growth and catch-up: Implications for the people's republic of China*. Asian Development Bank Institute (ADBI) Working Paper Series No.571. Tokyo: ADBI.

Little, I. 1990. *Economic development theory, policy and international policy*. New York: Praeger.

Lopez-Aymes, J. F. 2010. Automobile, information and communication technology and space industries as icons of South Korean economic nationalism. *Pacific Focus*, 25(2): 289–312.

Ministry of Commerce, Industry and Energy (MOCIE). 2007. *Press Release* (in Korean), 4 January.

Moon, C. 1988. The demise of a developmentalist state?: Neoconservative reforms and political consequences in South Korea. *Journal of Developing Societies*, 4: 67–84.

Moon, H., Lee, H., & Yoo, G. 1999. *Economic crisis and its social consequences*. Seoul: Korea Development Institute.

Noland, M. 2005. *South Korea's experience with international capital flows*. Working Paper Series, No. 05–4, Washington, DC: Institute for International Economics.

OECD. 2017. *Korea – Economic forecast summary*. www.oecd.org/korea/korea-economic-forecast-summary.htm. Accessed 10 May 2018.

Pew Research Centre. 2016. *Smartphone ownership and internet usage continues to climb in emerging economies*. www.pewglobal.org/2016/02/22/smartphone-ownership-and-internet-usage-continues-to-climb-in-emerging-economies/. Accessed 11 March 2018.

Radelet, S., & Sachs, J. 1998. *The East Asian financial crisis: Diagnosis, remedies, prospects*: 26–27 March. Washington, DC: Brookings Panel.

Ramirez, E. 2017. *Nearly 100% of households in South Korea now have internet access, thanks to seniors*. www.forbes.com/sites/elaineramirez/2017/01/31/nearly-100-of-households-in-south-korea-now-have-internet-access-thanks-to-seniors/#4603b9cb5572. Accessed 1 March 2018.

Ravenhill, J. 2003. The new bilateralism in the Asia Pacific. *Third World Quarterly*, 24(2): 299–371.

Riedel, J. 1988. Economic development in East Asia: Doing what comes naturally? In H. Hughes (Ed.), *Achieving industrialization in East Asia*: 1–38. Cambridge: Cambridge University Press.

SCMP. 2018. *KT wins race in launching world's first 5G service at PyeongChang 2018 Olympics*. www.scmp.com/country-reports/business/topics/south-korea-business-report/article/2116061/kt-wins-race-launching. Accessed 20 May 2018.

Shin, J. 2005. Globalization and challenges to the developmental state: A comparison between South Korea and Singapore. *Global Economic Review*, 34(4): 379–395.

Statcounter. 2018. *Mobile vendor market share republic of Korea* http://gs.statcounter.com/vendor-market-share/mobile/south-korea. Accessed 5 March 2018.

Ullah, Z. 2017. *How Samsung dominates South Korea's economy*. https://money.cnn.com/2017/02/17/technology/samsung-south-korea-daily-life/index.html. Accessed 19 November 2018.

UNCTAD (United Nations Conference on Trade and Development). 1998. *Trade and development report 1998*. New York, Geneva: United Nations.

UNCTAD (United Nations Conference on Trade and Development). 2006. *World investment report 2006*. New York, Geneva: United Nations.

Van Nooden, R. 2016. *South Korea stretches lead in research investment.* www.nature.com/news/south-korea-stretches-lead-in-research-investment-1.19333. Accessed 15 April 2018.

Wade, R. 1988. The role of government in overcoming market failure: Taiwan, republic of Korea and Japan. In H. Hughes (Ed.), *Achieving industrialization in East Asia*: 129–163. Cambridge: Cambridge University Press.

Weiss, L., & Hobson, J. 1998. *State power and economic strength: Revisited: What's so special about the Asian crisis?* Paper presented at the Conference on From Miracle to Meltdown: The End of Asian Capitalism. Asia Research Centre, Murdoch University, Perth, Australia.

Westphal, L. 1978. The republic of Korea's experience with export-led industrial development. *World Development*, 6(3): 347–382.

Westphal, L. 1990. Industrial policy in an export-propelled economy: Lessons from South Korea's experience. *Journal of Economic Perspectives*, 4(3): 41–59.

Woo, J. 1991. *Race to the swift: State and finance in Korean industrialization.* New York: Columbia University Press.

The World Bank. 2015. *Research and development expenditure* (% of GDP). https://data.worldbank.org/indicator/GB.XPD.RSDV.GD.ZS. Accessed 10 March 2018.

World Bank. 2017. *World development indicators.* http://databank.worldbank.org/data/source/world-development-indicators. Accessed 10 May 2018.

World Trade Organization. 2017. *Regional trade agreements: Facts and figures.* www.wto.org/english/tratop_e/region_e/regfac_e.htm. Accessed 22 August 2017.

Ye, M. 2017. South Korea's free trade strategy and East Asian Regionalism: A multistage approach. *Asian Perspective*, 41(1): 147–174.

# 3

# POLITICAL ENVIRONMENT

## Between systemic informality and attempted formality

*Jitendra Uttam*

## Introduction

In recent times, South Korea's (hereafter Korea) twin disjunctions – the '1997 financial crisis', which pushed the country to seek International Monetary Fund (IMF) emergency funds and the '2016 political turbulence' culminating in the president's impeachment – have caused profound changes in the changes in the country's political economic & social environment (PE&SE). The first disjunction, in the form of the 1997 financial crisis, invited widespread social ire and prompted a number of serious reform measures that concentrated on changing financial, industrial and corporate structures while leaving crucial political and social reforms behind. The old political system, shaped by the needs of authoritarian polity, operated in tandem with the demands of a distinct 'developmental alliance', which facilitated the convergence of interests between state, big business and conservative political class to achieve very high economic growth. This famed alliance functioned more on the basis of push and pull applied by 'informal sociopolitical networks', which were based on regional, family or alumni relationships, than on the basis of a rule-based formal institutional system. The system's informality under authoritarian polity, suffering from a democratic deficit, grew leaps and bounds and finally culminated in 'crony capitalism', which played a key role in enabling the financial crisis of 1997.

Interestingly, unlike the 1997 crisis when the demand to reform business came from international institutions led by IMF, Korea's second disjunction in the form of the 2016 political crisis has invoked an increasingly empowered civil society demanding wide-ranging political reforms. Social restlessness channeled through organized civil society institutions has brought progressive polity once again at the fore. The forces triggered by system-shaking crises called for a total overhaul of the country's PE&SE and argued for fairness in the economy by consolidating democracy, liberalizing the economy and humanizing society.

Moreover, the fast-changing focus of economic regime in Korea from labor-intensive to capital-intensive and now to knowledge-intensive has also been dictating fundamental changes in the nation's PE&SE. In fact, labor- and capital-intensive phases in Korea benefited from the authoritarian polity deriving logic from its traditional Confucian collective social consciousness. The ongoing transition to a knowledge-intensive phase, however, does not require authoritarian polity and collective social consciousness; rather, it needs democratic polity and individual consciousness to push for innovation and invention to develop new technologies. Nonetheless, economic changes are easier to accomplish than altering political structures deeply rooted in a country's social norms, cultural traditions and identity patterns.

It is too early to assess how the return of progressive politics in Korea under the leadership of Moon Jae-in, who became president in 2017, has strengthened institutional infrastructure to create transparent and reasonably efficient mediation between state and business. Nonetheless, it can be a very difficult task to carefully eliminate informal content in state–business interaction by inserting a degree of formal institutional mediation but without burdening the business process with too many regulations. Any mismanagement in reforming PE&SE has the potential to adversely impact Korea's business environment, which has been largely business-friendly.

## Rise in systemic informality: Korean PE&SE under 'statist developmentalism'

In order to fully grasp the contours of increased systemic informality in Korea, a clear understanding of the PE&SE during the decades of 'statist developmentalism' is crucial. A distinctly informal political, economic and social culture spread throughout Korea after military general Park Chung-Hee established his dictatorial rule in 1961. Quickly reverting the failed developmental legacy of Korea's first president Syngman Rhee, the authoritarian administration under Park Chung-Hee wasted no time revising the nation's industrialization strategy away from import substitution to fully concentrate on export promotion (Moon, 2016). At this point in time, Park's experience studying at the Tokyo Military Academy provided him with valuable first-hand experience of an outward-oriented mass-producing economic system (Kim & Vogel, 2011). Korea largely emulated the Japanese-style export-led industrialization strategy, with one crucial difference. Unlike Japan, where the banking sector was under private control, the Korean state nationalized its banking industry to build a domestic industrial class. In order to assert state control, in October 1961, the Korean government repossessed the commercial bank shares held by large stockholders on the basis that these were illegally hoarded properties. Under the Temporary Act of Bank Administration, the voting interest of any single stockholder was restricted, which made government the dominant stockholder with comprehensive control over the banks. The government believed that privately owned banks would contribute to the concentration of economic power along the lines Japan experienced.

This desire to follow the Japanese style of economic development clearly had a strategic imperative as well. With the sudden departure of the Japanese colonial state and en masse flight of the Japanese capitalist class from Korea created a vacuum in its commercial-industrial sphere. More so, confronting aggression from the North, this economic vacuum has acquired greater strategic significance.[1] In order to fill this strategic void, the Park administration embarked on an ambitious project to promote national capital in the form of a powerful domestic industrial class capable of being the state's ally in a time of national crisis. The Park administration not only initiated an export-promotion industrialization strategy, but later in the early 1970s it tilted towards heavy and chemical industries with the explicit aim of potentially augmenting the nation's capacity to develop a military industrial complex. As a late entrant in the development foray, the Korean state was in a hurry to produce high economic growth even at the risk of accumulating high debt. This 'high-debt, high-growth' strategy was successful due to exceptional determination by a powerful 'developmental alliance', where state, business and conservative polity worked together to produce double-digit economic growth. Due to a clear focus on labour-intensive mass-manufacturing industries, as well as export orientation, Korea was able to achieve full-employment conditions, which created the basis for a mass-participatory economy with reasonable systemic efficiency. Korea's developmental success was acknowledged by works such as *Asia's Next Giant* (Amsden, 1989), *Han Unbound* (Lie, 1998) and *Race to the Swift* (Woo, 1992).

In this race for economic development, rigorous and detailed scrutiny was compromised in the process of economic development to achieve pre-targeted results. In a bid to leapfrog industrial hierarchy, Korea heavily relied on an unwritten, informal system that was based on relationships developed through personal ties, such as attending the same high school or university, having similar regional roots or sharing family ties. This informality proved to be much more resilient than many initially thought as it effectively penetrated in the formal rules and procedures spelled out by the country's laid-out legislative process, government decrees and orders and their institutional interpretations. The informal network created a shadow world with non-transparent, and often corrupt, business deals taking center stage. 'This system helped develop some of the largest and most innovative companies in the world, but not without a cost as their cosy relationship with government make[s] the *Chaebols* particularly vulnerable to corruption' (Brannon, 2017).

The undue reliance on informal connections to achieve consensus in conducting business effectively bypassed the rule-based formal system. Complexity embedded in the informality worked as an instrument to promote domestic business interests and discouraged foreign firms from conducting business in Korea. This arrangement worked well in favour of Korea's national capital, which witnessed rapid expansion mostly at the cost of international capital interests. This systemic informality gave rise to an internalized system of finance, administration and corporate governance. Korea successfully lowered transaction costs below the market-determined price through the avoidance of often-cumbersome detailed market processes. By avoiding numerous procedures, Korea was able to create an 'economy of speed'. Such a change revolutionized Korea's productivity, with the economy growing at a phenomenal pace. Still, the rampant corruption, collusion and collaboration distorted the internal system.

## Cost of systematic informality: crony capitalism and the crisis of 1997

The systemic informality that Korea used to propel decades of double-digit growth had another side to it (Rachman, 2013). In a bid to expedite economic development, the Korean state acted paternalistically to become the 'senior partner', and the big businesses readily accepted the position of 'junior partner' (Kim, 1997). This exceptionally close partnership gave rise to informal and non-transparent links in the state's dealings with businesses. The informal system's success led to the rise of an 'internal capital market' as the authoritarian administration was pressed to produce economic growth to gain political legitimacy and credibility. Political determination, commitment and general will to mediate transactions virtually replaced market-determined transactions.

In the initial phase of Korean economic development, political mediation in the form of 'monthly meetings' was quick and cost-effective. President Park Chung-Hee, various economic ministers, heads of banks, export firms and various trade promotion bodies attended these meetings to make important decisions. Personal and singular attention accorded by the highest office in the country helped the informal system produce better results than any formal system would have achieved. Korea's hyper economic growth during the early 1970s to the mid-1990s has been a testimony of Korea's political commitment to a 'growth-first strategy' (Yoon, 2001; Lim, 1994). However, with the rapid growth in economic size and the associated rise in managerial complexities, the cost of politically mediated transactions started to outweigh the market-mediated transactions.

The informal system made it easier for businesses to bypass formal rules but ignoring informal commitments and obligations given to political leaders devoted to 'GNP nationalism' became much more difficult.[2] With the nation's strategic and economic interest at the stake, the authoritarian polity was fully committed to producing economic development as a potent instrument to safeguarding the nation's strategic interests. This situation augmented the developmental determination that made the Korean state push the corporate sector to maximize exports. Indeed, this informal push produced high economic growth, but at the same time those verbal commitments and unofficial obligations gave rise to non-transparent links between the state and business (Kang, 2002). Firms following government directives were rewarded with lucrative business contracts and subsidized credits, which meant that formal business rules were undermined. Korea witnessed the emergence of informal, unwritten power circles involved in facilitating business processes ranging from securing the supply of subsidized credit to arranging numerous tax benefits, including administrative support to procure inter-mediated goods and materials.

Finally, non-transparency embedded in the informality grew into a full-blown crisis of the system. A nexus of these inter-linkages created a *de facto* system that has been labelled 'crony capitalism' (Kang, 2002; Woo et al., 2000). As a result, the top 10 per cent of the population possessed 46 per cent of the country's total wealth, while the bottom 50 per cent of the population possessed 9.5 per cent wealth in 2012 (Rodrik, 1994).

Cronyism quickly engulfed many industrial areas, leading to negative consequences and finally culminating in the financial crisis of 1997. The crisis that began with the financial sector eventually became economic and social as well (Robb, 1998). Rapid depreciation of currency led to a stock price plunge, causing a 'negative wealth effect' that precipitated sharp price correction in the other asset classes, including real estate. Consequently, a downward spiral hit the Korean economy hard resulting in a chain of corporate bankruptcies pushing dramatically high unemployment rate. For instance, in January 1997, Korea's second-largest steelmaker, Hanbo Iron and Steel, was unable to honour its promissory notes and went bankrupt, followed by other midsize Chaebols, such as Kia Motor, Jinro and Haitai, among others. Korea had no option left but to ask the IMF for emergency bailout funds.

The question that arises is, if the Korean economy operated primarily by a system of informal networks based on socially trusted relationships, then what caused the system's reasonable efficiency, sustainability and credibility? The answer takes us to Korea's partial market conformity due to its heavy reliance on exports. It can be argued that operating under informal rules meant Korea's productive system was disciplined by the pressures of the market forces that were able to penetrate in the domestic market by the country's uncompromising focus on exports. Korea's singular focus on promoting exports compelled the state to link its subsidized credit exclusively to firms' performance in the global marketplace. With the government's unambiguous backing to supply cheap credit for export-oriented industries, corporate Korea, led by big business, transformed itself into a formidable export machine. This indirect market discipline supported Korea's continuous maintenance of reasonable efficiency in the midst of systemic informality.

## Causes of the 1997 crisis and the direction of reforms

Debates on the causes of the 1997 financial crisis identified two sets of factors: those that are structural in nature and those related to sequencing of financial sector reforms under foreign pressure. The direction of structural reforms post-1997 crisis has been closely related to the widespread belief in Korea that international pressure largely contributed to pushing them to choose the wrong sequencing in financial sector reforms (Chang et al., 1998). This perception helped the Korean state to entirely shift the blame of the financial crisis to big business. In result, both the state and society found consensus to initiate far-reaching reforms exclusively in the economic and business sphere, leaving state and polity outside the purview of reforms. Despite evidence that the causes of the crisis were systemic and political in nature, by shifting the blame of the crisis to business, the state was able to carry out partial reforms focused exclusively on the corporate sector.

A long-term effective cure of the crisis should have included reforms in the political sphere as well, but reforming politics is a daunting task as political logics are deeply embedded in the country's sociocultural norms and values, which are not easy to change. The problems impacting Korean politics are manifold. One problem is that 'the ruling party typically dominates all positions within government; the president names the heads of most agencies or has a strong say in their appointment. "Despite such vast powers, presidents often become lame ducks early on, because they are limited to a single five-year term – a safeguard from 1987 intended to prevent a return to authoritarianism" (Economist, 2017). Others see that

> [p]arties . . . are constantly mutating to stay in power. Since the republic was founded in 1948, the main liberal party has changed its name 14 times and splintered 11 times; its conservative counterpart has fared little better, with ten name-swaps and ten fractures. The endless manoeuvring makes it impossible to pursue a concerted legislative agenda – and hard for voters to keep track.
>
> *(Economist, 2017)*

The fluid nature of political parties did not allow Korea's inherent systemic informality to subside. During the two progressive administrations, pre-existing informal networks seemingly became redundant or simply replaced by other types of networks. Mindful of eradicating its informal business practices, Korea worked to establish credible institutions; however, at this juncture, the focus of the reform program was limited to restructuring finance, corporate governance, industrial policy and economic bureaucracy, leaving a vast area of polity and its close relations with business aside. The reform and restructuring worked well for the Korean economy as it rebounded sharply post-1997 crisis. However, the quickest reform in the Korean economy came largely due to the export boom owing to massively devalued local currency. In fact, the rebound was less due to structural changes and more due to the nation's time-tested export orientation. During the three years of the IMF structural adjustment programme, beginning in December 1997, approximately 95 per cent of the net inflow of foreign currency reserves came from exports, while capital inflow in the form of portfolio and direct investment was insignificant and even negative in the case of credits (Kalinowski, 2008). Moreover, Kim Dae-Jung's administration was quick to arrange a large financial package amounting to US$150 billion to recapitalize big business.

However, the return of conservative polity under the administrations of Lee Myung-Bak from 2008 to 2013 and Park Geun-Hye from 2013 to 2017 allowed informal sociopolitical networks to make a comeback. These well-entrenched networks mediated state – business relations mostly in a non-transparent manner of secrecy and anonymity. The causes of this secrecy are rooted in the lack of diversity in the country's mass media, which had earned a bad reputation in articulating public demands. "The World Press Freedom Index placed South Korea in 70th position last year, below Haiti and Malawi" (Economist, 2017). Moreover, kinship networks, by default, maintained secrecy by revolving critical information within the extended family network.

This return of conservative polity after two progressive administrations clearly signaled to Korean chaebol firms that the informality of Park Chung-Hee's era in 'doing business' was back. Powerful developmental alliance partners, including state, businesses, bureaucrats and the conservative political class brought the process of political economic reforms to a grinding halt during the two successive conservative administrations. This was even more apparent during the Park Geun-Hye administration, which provided a symbolic affiliation with her father's two-decade-long 'developmental informalism'. It is important to note that though conservative polity in Korea was back in power, progressive politics was still very much alive and kicking. Park Geun-Hye won her presidential bid only by a margin of 3 per cent. Working through grass-roots civil society organizations, the progressive polity was busy monitoring the revival of the state – business closeness. Civil society networks often controlled by progressive polity kept an eye on apparent misdeeds by the state. When a hint of non-transparent dealing came to light, the progressives invoked civil society to revolt against Park Geun-Hye, which resulted in her conviction and sentencing to prison in 2017.

## Fallout of the crisis: systemic informality under social scrutiny

### Lingering legacy of informality

Korea's authoritarian polity that operated through informal, invisible social networks was not easy to be restructured. Even a long-drawn reform and restructuring following the financial crisis could not fully neutralize socially rooted power relationships. In fact, habits of operating under the strong tradition of 'statist developmentalism', progressive polity,[3] in Korea came under the pressure of a formidable lobby representing the interest of big business, which eventually forced Korea to adopt an ambivalent approach towards chaebol reforms. Kim Dae-Jung's administration's (president from 1998 to 2003) resolve to save the export-oriented industrial complex by creating a scheme called 'the public fund', under which 156.7 trillion won was redirected to recapitalize the banking sector that had been reeling under the burden of bad loans (Uttam, 2014).

In a time-tested one-step-forward, two-steps-backward model, progress being made during two progressive administrations led by Kim Dae-Jung (1998–2003) and Roh Moo-Hyun (2003–2008) leveled off due to the return of conservative rule under the Lee Myung-Bak and Park Geun-Hye administrations.[4] Sensing that renewed conservatism had brought informality back, chaebol groups quickly moved to gain state support to socialize their losses. To narrow its self-interest, big business looked back on the nation's developmentalist past, but society, worried about unprecedented wealth concentration, demanded a more equitable and harmonious Korea. This contradiction where business aimed to gain concessions from the state's intervention in the market place while society wanted the state to remain at 'arm's-length distance' from the marketplace started to create tension. This tension became out of control in 2016, bringing a crisis to the country's presidential office.

The return of conservative polity as a governing outfit was unwilling to take instructions from an organized civil society focused on correcting systemic malfunctioning; rather, polity developed an affinity to some distinct civil society groups that were trying to siphon off state resources. Conservative polity could not understand the country's fundamentally changed social aspirations and thus was caught off-guard when a massive candlelight vigil gathered momentum. The rise of civil society as a new variable in shaping the Korean political economy is a historically important development. Under this constant social pressure, the Korean polity has begun to formalize and institutionalize state–business ties and is working hard to persistently eliminate informal constraints.

## Emerging trend of social monitoring

Korea's financial crisis of 1997 has been remembered for its disastrous economic upheaval, but its social consequences were far greater than the economic consequences. The crisis shook the very foundation of Korean society that had grown by adhering to Confucius social values and norms marked by overreaching societal conformity, collective solidarity and unquestionable hierarchy. Korea's 'developmental alliance' carefully utilized these social values to motivate and discipline the workforce for the benefit of its expanding export-oriented mass-manufacturing industries. Indeed, Korea's statist developmental strategy went along well with this social tradition and thus successfully produced what many prefer to call the 'miracle on the Han River'.

Surprisingly, in 1997 Korea witnessed an unprecedented financial shake-up that disrupted Korea's social convictions that preferred conformity with authority and despised individual self-interest over societal well-being. The financial crisis worked as a catalyst to change conformity into curiosity and made society ready to raise many questions, particularly against the massive wealth concentration under few chaebol hands. Korea's giant chaebols were also perceived as guilty for causing the crippling financial crisis. Korea's bending to the IMF did hurt the country's nationalist sentiments. Humiliating IMF conditions pushed society to invoke 'second state' where collective social desire could effectively constrain the state's policy choices.[5] By invoking social control over economics, the collective social desire greatly mobilized by the citizen's movement worked as a mutually embedded symbiotic relationship between state and society. This mutual embeddedness was promoted during the two progressive-era administrations when the state was willing to accept certain societal constraints affecting its policy choices (Kim, 1988).

Restlessness in the Korean society post-1997 crisis and subsequent civil society consolidation led by the NGO revolution (Shin, 2006) at the grassroots level created institutional structures that were able to monitor state–business relations, specifically during the second conservative rule. A business lobby that benefited during developmentalism started to again become dangerously close to political power. Having the history of a close nexus with the chaebol groups, conservative rule quickly earned social ire. Civil society institutions started to keep a close eye on illicit chaebol activities, particularly actions related to corner state favours. The inauguration of the Park Geun-Hye administration harkened back to Park Chung-Hee's administration, an event which alerted society about shadow activities occurring during previous administrations. In 2016, society's desire to monitor non-transparent links between state and business manifested in the 'candlelight vigils'[6] that largely contributed to bringing down the presidency of Park Geun-Hye.

Conservative polity and associated social forces failed to understand post-1997 societal restlessness desiring systemic overhaul. Korea's power of *minjung ideas*[7] that have a long-documented history of mobilizing people for collective action was at its best during the months-long candlelight vigils in the streets of the capital city. The political crisis of 2016 was a grim reminder that the continuation of informality in managing Korea's political, economic and business affairs would not be successful. It also highlighted that democratic consolidation itself is not the cure of non-transparency and corruption between state and business. Without having active institutional mediation, informality may return to the state and businesses promoting their cronies.

The fallout of Korea's political revolution in 2016 has galvanized progressive political forces seeking economic justice based on democracy, equity and fairness. Represented by the competent leadership of progressive polity, the people's collective will was successful in ousting the conservatives from the ruling system. Sensing the mood of the society, the progressive polity actively tried to contain and control systemic informality in the country. Sandwiched between the twin crises, consensus in Korea favored the empowerment of formal workable institutions capable of reducing informal constraints hindering the system. It is evident that Korea's highly mobilized and organized civil society wants to see the effectiveness of institutional mediation between state and business. Social pressure to have systemic change seems to be justified as Korea paid an enormous price for systemic informality in the form of the financial meltdown in 1997. However, many fear that a formal system may drastically increase the cost of doing business in Korea.

## Towards new PE&SE: rebalancing between 'social' and 'economic' forces

Korea's recent social restlessness has emerged out of a widening gap between changed economic regulations and a stagnated political reform process. This has caused pessimism in society, which is at the core of undeterred collective action to correct the mistakes of the political process. An unprecedented number of people took to the streets to protest the growing non-transparent dealings between state and business through sustained 'candlelight vigils'. The enormous power of grass-roots mobilization based on Korea's age-old tradition of protest in the form of *Minjung* has been successful in mounting a collective social demand to reform the nation's political culture. *Minjung* has been at the core of Korean society's historical struggle against the injustice done by the ruling political classes. Social protests erupting during the Jeju Uprising in 1948 against the national police employed by the US military government in Korea, the student protest against the corrupt autocratic rule of the Rhee administration (April 1960) and the Gwangju uprising against the authoritarian rule of Chun Doo-Hwan (May 1980) demonstrate Korea's collective resolve to correct the ills of the political process.

In 2016, a culture that permitted informality and ad hoc–ism in the decision-making process by top government officials and heads of the giant business conglomerates has become the target of broad societal concern:

> massive protests were about much more than bringing Ms. Park to book. A sense of injustice had been simmering for years. The number of graduates out of a job, or who have given up looking for one, recently exceeded 3.5 million out of a total of roughly 14 million. An educational rat-race and intense competition for socially respected jobs, concentrated in the biggest conglomerates, makes life for teens and 20-somethings stressful.
>
> *(Economist, 2017)*

According to Pew's surveys, only 20% of teens and people in their twenties are satisfied with the direction of their country, compared with 40% of those aged 50 and over – despite the fact that among the elderly the rates of both poverty and suicide are the highest among wealthy nations (Economist, 2017). Korea has become a unique OECD country where, given the choice, large numbers of people are willing to leave for foreign lands. 'Their disillusion is compounded by the knowledge that those with money and connections can evade the rat-race' (Economist, 2017). Families are often anxious for their children's entrance to best universities because, in a Confucian society, the best social networking is done in the learning institutions such as schools or universities.

It is important to note that the forces pushing for the economic reforms post-1997 and social constituencies clamoring for political reforms after 2016 are different in their origin, orientation and outlook. International pressure in the form of neo-liberal policy prescriptions and advisory by foreign investors were the prime movers of the structural economic and financial reforms that Korea underwent in the late 1990s; whereas recent political reforms are backed by increasingly restless social forces that have been empowered by *Minjung* ideas, memories of the post–land reform egalitarian economics and wider information circulation regarding the ills of the system's malfunctioning. This differentiation in the origin of forces clamoring for fundamental change has the potential to impact the pace, reach and sustainability of systemic reform process.

In fact, Korea has been able to reverse international pressures imposed by the IMF conditions, but indigenous societal forces seeking sociopolitical reforms have shown a determination not to allow Korea to derail the process. This time, Korea would not be able to avoid the reform-minded society. As Korea's economic development was imposed by a 'developmental alliance', the change in the economic system was demanded by a nexus of international institutions such as IMF–OECD–Wall Street, but this time the demand to reform the political culture has come from the wider civil society and thus the momentum to alter the political order would last longer.

Moon Jae-in's administration symbolizes the hopes and aspirations of the common people who rose *en masse* to end Park Geun-Hye's presidency. Leading the second wave of progressive polity, President Moon is trying to bring systemic transparency by formalizing informal channels of mediation between and among state, society and market interrelationships. Transforming informal networking practices into formal rules and enforceable regulations monitored by credible institutions is a long and cumbersome process. Korea needs to match post-1997 economic reforms with the post-2016 political change. A new socio-economic and political consensus in Korea has emerged to debate, legislate and implement verifiable and transparent institutional mediation aimed at reducing the informal or gray areas.

## Reforms in the midst of old systemic inertia

The inertia of the old system has been so powerful that Korea needed crisis situations – such as the 1997 financial crisis and the 2016 political revolution – to initiate worthwhile systemic changes. The beneficiaries of the systemic informality are still around and, given the opportunity, they could once again regroup to hinder the progress in making system formal and transparent. Korea's twin crises came as reminders that informal networks giving legitimacy to an internalized capital market and non-transparent state – business relations may have a few merits in the initial phase of development, but it cannot be effective in managing the needs of a large diversified economy.

The two progressive administrations were successful in eliminating many old business practices, but sociopolitical reforms were left untouched. In order to fill the gaps left by government reform initiatives, an NGO revolution rescued the reform process (Joo, 2000). Greatly empowered NGOs embarked on scrutinizing issues related to corporate governance, workers' salary, rights of minority shareholders and so on. Many civil society institutions worked to remove the ills of economic injustice emanating from unprecedented wealth concentration, non-transparent business deals leading to corporate governance issues and replacing family management with professional management, among other aspects. For instance, a powerful NGO, the PSPD led a campaign to introduce systemic reforms aimed at improving corporate governance and monitored progress in corporate and financial-sector restructuring. A societal push to make polity accountable, transparent and formal created a generation that was much more vocal than their predecessors. It has been noted that 'South Koreans . . . are growing more comfortable with speaking out. In the 1980s many parents discouraged their children from joining anti-government demonstrations. . . [but] this time they went together, sometimes with grandparents' (Economist, 2017).

The civil society institutions emerging post-1997 crisis were not antagonistic to the state, as both the state and society shared progressive ideals. Thus, a number of NGOs started to work in tandem with state objectives to help develop institutional mechanisms to ensure a degree of transparency, accountability and verifiability in the system. Big business was not used to having social scrutiny and, as a result, felt uneasy with rising civil society meddling in time-tested informal business practices. With the return of conservative polity, big business started to, again, work very closely with the government and objected to society's enhanced role in scrutinizing business activities. Facing an increasingly restless society that acquired the habit of fighting for economic injustice and social inequalities, Korea's big business devised technocratic solutions to hide from the rule-based systemic accountability. Among others, the chaebols parked their stakes in philanthropic non-profit foundations, which facilitated them keeping control without paying heavy taxes. Furthermore, chaebols created new firms that strike lucrative and friendly business deals with other firms they control (Mullany, 2017). The tension between political and economic elite eager to operate in the old system with fuzzy and invisible rules collided with the society increasingly demanding transparency and accountability. This uneasy tension burst out of control in 2016 when a society united by collective demands forced the president out of office.

Many still suspect that, heeding to social demands, Moon Jae-in's administration has begun a path of accountability and regulatory rationality through instituting political reforms. Given the deep-seated state – business proximity, 'only naïve observers regard the image of a former president and heir to Korea's largest corporation in prison garb as proof that the country will finally see meaningful political reform' (Brannon, 2017). Brannon (2017) clarifies:

> In Korea's legal system, judges' rise through the ranks of a system that has the appearance of a meritocracy, but is overshadowed by politics. However bright and earnest judges may seem in rendering judgments, they are far more than technicians applying specific statutory provisions to discrete pieces of evidence . . . judicial process that must be reformed before any substantive economic reforms can be accomplished.

The successful rebalancing of society's demands and the needs of Korea's businesses is a daunting task ahead of Moon Jae-in administration.

## Changing the Korean business environment

Korea's social society is trying to change its economics by controlling the political sphere. This empowered social movement, which has been successful in removing conservatives from power, now looks towards a new administration to establish a 'fair economy' based on institution-led, rule-based mediation between state and business. Pragmatism, however, demands that an economy facing enormous challenges from the unfolding fourth industrial revolution must resist the temptation of 'regulatory overreach'. In the name of transparency, overregulation can potentially add further complexities to Korea's business environment. The government in Korea has to strike a delicate balance between social aspirations seeking equity and fairness in the economy and business looking towards maximizing profit without much of social responsibility.

An analysis of factors impacting business encourages economies to compete towards more efficient regulations, offer measurable benchmarks for reforms and serves as a resource for academics, journalists, policy makers and others interested in knowing the business climate. According to a World Bank Report (2019), Korea is ranked fifth in the ease of doing business. Findings of this report suggest that Korea's score on the different verticals of doing business has witnessed remarkable progress except in terms of paying taxes. The report says that in 2016, Korea made paying taxes more complicated and costly for companies by requiring separate filing and payment of the local income tax and by increasing the rates for unemployment insurance and national health insurance paid by employers.

This same World Bank Report (2019) confirms that due to reducing costs, allowing online payment of registration taxes, setting time limits for value added tax registration and eliminating the minimum capital requirement and notarization requirements in 2010, starting a business in Korea has become easier. Furthermore, the introduction of a new online one-stop shop, Start-Biz, in 2012 and the elimination of the post-registration procedure in 2017 have also contributed to faster business setup (see Chapter 12 for further details). Similarly, registering property in Korea has been made easier by reducing the time needed to buy housing bonds and to register the property transfer in 2015. Getting credit was made simpler as well when Korea revised its secured transactions framework by creating new types of security rights that can be publicized through registration. Moreover, in terms of labour-market regulation, Korea has increased the maximum duration of fixed-term contracts.

The World Bank Report (2019) also indicates that Korea has accelerated its corporate income tax reduction program, shortening it from five to three years in 2010. It adds that in 2012, Korea further eased the administrative burden of paying taxes for firms by merging several taxes, allowing labour taxes and contributions to be paid jointly and continuing to increase the use of the online tax payment system. Korea strengthened investor protections by making it easier to sue directors in cases of prejudicial-related party transactions. In terms of enforcing contracts, World Bank Report (2019) stresses that Korea has made filing a commercial case easier by introducing an electronic case-filing system. In order to simplify trading across borders, Korea upgraded the electronic data interchange system. Then, in 2013, Korea reduced the cost of electricity by introducing a new connection fee schedule and an instalment payment system. Dealing with corporate insolvencies was also updated by introducing post-filing financing, granting super priority to the repayment of loans given to companies undergoing reorganization in 2011. Furthermore, in 2013, Korea expedited the insolvency process by implementing a fast track for company rehabilitation.

On top of changes brought by conservative administrations, ongoing regulatory rationalization based on the progressive political vision of 'an economy pursuing co-prosperity' with 'fair business practices' may possibly bring a few added complications for businesses. Recently, Korean fair trade-related laws, including the Monopoly Regulation and Fair Trade Act (FTA) and the Fair Transactions in Franchise Business Act (FBA), have been revised. The FTA has introduced criminal punishment for refusal and obstruction of investigations. Similarly, in failing to meet reporting obligations, businesses now have to pay financial penalties. The revised FBA also includes punitive damage provisions (Park, 2017).

The preceding changes to the Korean business environment hint that the Moon administration is ratcheting up its efforts to impose stronger regulations and enforcement to realize the social aspirations of equity and justice. In this new emerging business environment, companies failing to adjust their business practices may risk exposing themselves to serious losses. To successfully adjust with the changing regulatory environment, companies need to understand the revised regulations, closely track policy developments and be careful to avoid activities in their business operations that will run afoul of the FTA's new rules and requirements. Certainly, ongoing formalization of the business process may entail extra cost to businesses.

## Conclusion

Korea's PE&SE has witnessed a paradigmatic shift during two distinct phases of economic development – 'statist developmentalism' prior to 1997 and 'liberal developmentalism' in the post-1997 phase. In the era of 'statist developmentalism', the rule-based formal system in Korea witnessed insurmountable informal constraints dominated by powerful social networks. This widespread informality produced high economic growth, but at the same time, it negatively impacted the system's transparency, accountability and possibly efficiency as well. In the post-1997 period, Korea witnessed attempts to remove informal constraints and witnessed a degree of success during the two progressive-leaning administrations. Nonetheless, with the return of conservative political forces under the leadership of Lee Myung-Bak and Park Geun-Hye, informal constraints in the form of family and kinship networks tied with school–university affiliations returned and clouded transparency gains in country's state–business relations.

Korean states' understanding and interpretation of the causes of the 1997 financial crisis led to the blame being shifted to big business. This careful political maneuvering made the state to place itself beyond any scrutiny and led the charge to reform the chaebol system. As a result, IMF-mandated economic reforms that had a narrow business-centred vision were readily accepted by the

Korean 'developmental state'. In a bid to safeguard the credibility of the state system, partners in the developmental alliance did not see non-transparency, unaccountability and systemic inefficiency as having their origin in the political system. As a result, Korea's elusive sociopolitical reforms were left unattended. This mismatch between a reformed economy and stagnated polity gave rise to a major disjunction that surfaced in the form of the Park Geun-Hye's impeachment. This time, pressure did not come from the international institutions, but instead, it was Korean society that took to the streets demanding political reforms. The impeachment came as a grim reminder that economic reforms alone cannot bring accountability and transparency in the system. In order to succeed in augmenting systemic efficiency and transparency, economic reforms must be matched by equally important political reforms.

Korea, pressed between economic change and political continuity, had no other way out but to create a visible, transparent and accountable institutional mediation. There have been various attempts to institutionalize relations between state and business, however informal constraints embedded in the nation's sociopolitical reality hindered effective functioning of these institutions. The new administration is working to fulfil aspirations and trust that sociopolitical forces have endowed with the progressive Moon administration. Thus, it can be concluded that on the face of relentless domestic social pressure, Korea is on track to evolve the institutional framework that can bring the needed transparency to its state–business relations. This can certainly contribute to making the Korean business environment much more predictable, transparent and friendly. A well-balanced PE&SE would lead to a better balance between big and small businesses as well as between national and international firms doing business in Korea.

## Notes

This work was supported by the Core University Program for Korean Studies through the Ministry of Education of the Republic of the Korea and Korean Studies Promotion Service of the Academy of Korean Studies (AKS-2016-OLU-2250008).

1 Specifically, after Nixon's visit to China in 1971, Korea was griped under the 'fear of abandonment' by the United States. Responding to this fear, Korea swiftly moved to 'self-help mode' with HCI as an instrument to achieve strategic flexibility.
2 The monthly export meetings basically brought the country's political leadership face-to-face with major economic agents in the country. For details, see Ahn (1986).
3 'Progressive politics' favours larger social spending and redistribution of wealth and despised the giant Chaebols and argues for their division into smaller firms.
4 'Conservative politics' in Korea defends laissez-faire economics with private firms or chaebol, as in case of Korea, as engines of growth.
5 'Second State' refers to mutual embeddedness of state and society. For details, see Uttam (2014) Also, it addresses how society in state can constrain its choices (Migdal, 1988).
6 'Candlelight vigils' or series of protests against President Park Geun-Hye occurred throughout South Korea from November 2016 to March 2017.
7 *Minjung* refers to the impoverished majority in Korea that has been oppressed but capable of rising up against oppression. It derives its logical core from Korea's past when society was organized horizontally. For details, see Namhee Lee (2007).

# Bibliography

## Key references

Chang, K. S. 2019. *Developmental liberalism in South Korea: Formation, degeneration, and trans-nationalization.* London: Palgrave Macmillan.

De Mente, B. L. 2014. *Korean way in business: Understanding and dealing with the South Koreans in business.* Tokyo: Tuttle Publishing.

Kim, Y. 2018. *Korea's quest for economic democratization: Globalization, polarization and contention.* London: Palgrave Macmillan.

Lee, S., & Rhyu, S. Y. 2019. *The political economy of change and continuity in Korea: Twenty years after the crisis.* Switzerland, AG: Springer.

## Online sources

Alshamsi, A. K. M. 2011. *The global developmental state: The triple non-alliance of state bureaucrats, domestic capital and foreign capital in Korean economic development,* Doctoral thesis, Northumbria University. http://nrl.northumbria.ac.uk/2212/ Accessed 13 June 2018.

World Bank Report. 2019. *Doing business 2019: Economic profile of the republic of Korea,* Washington, DC: The world Bank Group. www.doingbusiness.org/en/data/exploreecono mies/korea. Accessed 13 June 2018.

# References

Ahn, C. Y. 1986. Economic development of South Korea, 1945–1985: Strategies and performance. *Korea and World Affairs,* 10(1): 91–117.

Amsden, A.H. 1992. Asia's Next Giant: South Korea and Late Industrialization. New York: Oxford University Press.

Brannon, I. "A System on Trial: South Korean Political Reform Requires Evidence, Not Stagecraft", Forbes, Sep 27, 2017. Available at: https://www.forbes.com/sites/ikebrannon/2017/09/27/a-system-on-trial-south-korean-political-reform-requires-evidence-not-stagecraft/#2becadda357b. Accessed 6 June 2018.

Chang, H. J., Park, H. J., & Yoo, C. G. 1998. Interpreting the Korean crisis: Financial liberalisation, industrial policy, and corporate governance. *Cambridge Journal of Economics,* 22(6): 735–746.

Economist. 2017. Post-Park life: The revolution that ousted South Korea's president is unfinished. *Economist.* www.economist.com/asia/2017/05/04/the-revolution-that-ousted-south-koreas-president-is-unfinished. Accessed 6 June 2018.

Eun, M. K. 1988. From dominance to symbiosis: State and Chaebol in Korea. *Pacific Focus,* 3(2): 105–121.

Jo, H. Y. 2000. *Hanguk simin sahoe-ui yeoksa: hyeonhwang-gwa jeonmang* (The History of Korean NGOs: Fact and Prospect). In Kim Dong-chun et al (Eds.), *NGO-ran mu-eosinga? (What is NGOs?),* Seoul: Arche.

Joo, S. S. 2000. Understanding the NGO revolution in Korea. *Global Economic Review,* 29(4): 3–19.

Kang, D. C. 2002. *Crony capitalism: Corruption and development in South Korea and the Philippines* (Cambridge Studies in Comparative Politics). New York: Cambridge University Press.

Kalinowski, T. 2008. Korea's recovery since the 1997/98 financial crisis: The last stage of the developmental state. *New Political Economy,* 13(4): 447–462.

Kim, E.M. 1988. From Dominance to Symbiosis: State and Chaebol in Korea. *Pacific Focus*, 3(2): 105-121.

Kim, E. M. 1997. *Big business, strong state: Collusion and conflict in South Korean development, 1960–1990.* Albany: State University of New York Press.

Kim, B. K., & Ezra, F.V. 2011. *The Park Chung Hee Era: The transformation of South Korea.* Cambridge, MA: Harvard University Press.

Lee, B. C. 2006. Political economy of Korean development after liberation: A critical reflection. *Korea Journal*, 46(3): 49–79.

Lie, J. 1998. *Han Unbound: The Political Economy of South Korea.* Stanford: Stanford University Press.

Lim, D. 1994. Explaining the growth performances of Asian developing economies. *Economic Development and Cultural Change*, 42(4): 829–844.

Migdal, J. S. 1988. *Strong societies and weak states: State-society relations and state capabilities in the third world.* Princeton, NJ: Princeton University Press.

Moon, H. C. 2016. *The strategy for Korea's economic success.* New York: Oxford University Press.

Mullany, G. 2017. South Korea's presidential election: A look at the pivotal issues, *New York Times.* www.nytimes.com/2017/05/08/world/asia/south-korea-election-president.html. Accessed 13 June 2018.

Namhee, L. 2007. *The making of Minjung: Democracy and the politics of representation in South Korea.* Ithaca: Cornell University Press.

Park, K. C. 2017. *South Korea: Amendment of Korean fair trade-related laws, lee international.* www.inhousecommunity.com/article/south-korea-amendment-korean-fair-trade-related-laws/. Accessed 31 January 2019.

Rachman, G. 2013. The dark side to the South Korean miracle, *Financial Times.* www.ft.com/content/277e4c5c-8063-3d7b-9839-cbb565054894. Accessed 13 June 2018.

Robb, C. M. 1998. Social impact of the East Asian Crisis: Perceptions from poor communities. *Paper prepared for the East Asian Crisis Workshop, IDS*, University of Sussex, UK.

Rodrik, D. 1994. *King Kong meets Godzilla: The world bank and the East Asian miracle, in mirage or design: Lessons from the east Asian experience.* OCD Policy Essay No.11.

Shin, K.Y. 2006. The Citizens' movement in Korea. *Korea Journal*, 46(2): 5–34.

Uttam, J. 2014. *The political economy of Korea: Transition, transformation and turn-around.* Basingstoke, New York: Palgrave Macmillan.

Woo. J.E. 1991. Race to the Swift: State and Finance in Korean Industrialization. New York: Columbia University Press.

Woo, W.T., Sachs, J. D., & Schwab, K. (Eds.). 2000. *The Asian financial crisis: Lessons for a resilient Asia.* Cambridge, MA: MIT Press.

World Bank Report. 2019. *Doing business 2019: Economic profile of the republic of Korea,* Washington, DC: World Bank Group.

Yoon, H. 2001. Development strategy in Korea re-examined: An interventionist perspective. *The Social Science Journal*, 38: 217–231.

# 4

# CULTURAL ENVIRONMENT

## Cultural context, informal networks, and *Yongo*

*Sven Horak*

## Introduction

Conventionally, the cultural context for international management activities in Korea is described as generally low in trust ascriptions towards others and high in ingroup collectivism, group orientation, and group harmony. While this description is certainly not wrong, it still is quite broad, which could be misleading and increase the risk of false ad hoc interpretations. This chapter presents some alternative insights into the cultural environment in Korea. It proposes some novel views and reinterprets traditional ones by first putting the pervasive informal networks that span Korean society – as yet underresearched in management studies – at the forefront of the debate. Second, it suggests that, instead of regarding Korea as a collectivist society, a change towards the view of Korea as a network society would be more insightful. Consequently, the view of trust needs to be adjusted to better suit the nature of network societies (Horak & Yang, 2017a). Third, in the context of new insights provided, practical implications and challenges are discussed for local networking and managing people, respectively, which will be of interest to international managers. First and foremost, this chapter aims to make informal networks central in explaining the Korean cultural context as the most relevant feature for successful local management activities (Horak, 2014a; Horak, 2016; Horak & Yang, 2017a). Similar to *Guanxi* in China (Li, 2007), understanding informal networks in Korea is pivotal for any sustainably successful business activity in Korea.

Informal networks in Korea differ in characteristics and can be distinguished into three different categories, named in Korean as follows: *Inmaek, Yongo* and *Yonjul* (Horak, 2014a). Whereas *Inmaek* is simply translated into the English term "network," *Yongo* and *Yonjul* have a wider meanings. Characteristic of Korea are *Yongo* networks that can be distinguished further at the dyadic as well as at the network level into sentimental ties based on former university or high school affiliation;

second, ties based on the place of birth or hometown; and, third, ties based on family (i.e., blood ties). Though by trend transforming and adjusting to modern times, *Yongo* is a powerful force in social interactions in business, politics, and society at large. *Yongo* characterizes the Korean society. Remarkably, *Yongo* is described as immutable and irreversible; it is, to a great extent, predefined. Consequentially, and especially important for international managers engaging in business in Korea, it is difficult to acquire and maintain, as it is hard for foreigners to establish *Yongo*. *Inmaek*, on the contrary, can be established, but whether it is as powerful as *Yongo* in business remains a subject for further research. Both *Yongo* and *Inmaek* can serve as a potential base on which to establish *Yonjul*, which has a rather negative connotation and is often referred to when unethical aims are pursued (Horak, 2014a, 2016). These concepts can overlap and can hardly be separated clearly from each other. Nevertheless, on an aggregate level, it can be stated that informal networks characterize Korean society; that is, they shape and define social relationships in Korea and influence decision-making behavior in business and politics. Surprisingly, they have not yet been analyzed in detail in the management literature.

Informal ties and networks are not only extraordinarily pronounced in the business sphere; since they are societal phenomena, they naturally penetrate all spheres of interpersonal affairs. This is, in principle, a similar case to *Guanxi* in China. In the past, often assessed from a Western perspective, East Asian societies have been classified as societies in which collectivism is pronounced. However, collectivism is a rather broad term and can easily be misunderstood in the East Asian context. As we will see later in the case of Korea, Koreans do not act collectivistically per se; it basically depends on the context, more specifically the *relational context*, which determines whether behavior becomes collectivistic or individualistic. The term *collectivism* does not capture this sufficiently; thus, among others, this chapter proposes an alternative term to collectivism that is more precise, that is, *network society*.

Finally, since many expatriation preparation trainings for Korea and East Asia at large center on the collectivism and in-group harmony paradigm, it is important to elaborate what living in a network society and in particular what being exposed to informal networks in business mean for the effectiveness of international staff on a comparatively short-term (i.e., 3–5 years) business mission in Korea. Since *Yongo* ties are pronounced and influential but cannot be acquired since they are to a certain extent predefined, that is, partly given by birth, it is important to understand how typical expatriates of a different ethnicity and without any family roots in Korea can establish informal ties that are helpful in business (Horak & Yang, 2016). In a network society, informal ties are a valuable asset that defines the status and power of an individual. Can expatriates compete in that regard? Can they fulfill their mission in Korea without informal ties? These are important questions that need to be considered not only by firms sending managers to Korea but also by the manager and his or her family since the more expatriates integrate into social networks, the more satisfied with their life and the more successful in business they are. Foreign managers in Korea will first recognize the prevalence of pronounced hierarchies in business and social relationships as a result of Confucian ideals.

# The cultural environment

## *Confucian ideals and hierarchy*

Korea has been described as possessing vertical collective rather than horizontal work relationships, pronounced power distance, and top-down decision making (Hofstede, 1991; Shim et al., 2008; Yang, 2014). It has often been described as "the most Confucian country in Asia" (Holcombe, 2017: 6). Although Korea is a secular state today, with most people not belonging to any religion, Buddhist and Christian beliefs are widespread. Surprisingly, however, only a fraction of people would identify as Confucianists. The latter group makes up only 2 percent of the population (H. Shim, 2004). Approximately 15 percent identify as Buddhists, 28 percent as Christians and the large majority of about 57 percent as either atheists or as belonging to an unregistered religious or spiritual group (census data, KOSTAT, 2015). Despite Confucianism not being organized and not requiring members to officially register, classic Confucian virtues and moral norms are vital today (Jun & Rowley, 2014; Warner & Rowley, 2014). Among registered Christians, about 90 percent of Catholics and 76 percent of Protestants can be identified as Confucianists and among Buddhists, all (i.e. 100 percent) believe in Confucian virtues and moral norms and practice Confucian rituals (comp. Koh, 1996; Shim, 2004). Table 4.1 shows the classic Confucian virtues and moral norms that are assumed to explain the continuously strong pronounced social hierarchies in Korea today. Four out of five of them describe hierarchical relationships as the order principle between people and only 'trust among friends' puts forward a notion of equality between people.

In a business context, hierarchies derived from Confucian ideals represent the underlying philosophy of managing people in Korea (Horak & Yang, 2017a). For company employees, not only monetary incentives play a role in career progression. Whereas both monetary reward and promotion are typically determined by seniority (Horak & Yang, 2017b), the higher status that accompanies advancement through organizational ranks was seen in the past as the highest-valued reward. Besides, organizational promotion adds to family prestige and increases a person's social standing (Milliman et al., 1993). However, while some scholars have assumed the role of seniority would recede, current research has found that seniority is still

**TABLE 4.1** Classic Confucian virtues and moral norms

| *Virtues* | *Moral norms* |
| --- | --- |
| Benevolence | Justice between ruler and subject |
| Justice | Love between father and son |
| Morality | Differentiation between man and woman |
| Wisdom | Order between younger and older people |
| Loyalty | Trust among friends |

*Source*: Horak & Yang (2017a).

a dominant component to decide on promotion, among other factors (Horak & Yang, 2017b). Furthermore, seniority is closely connected to and reflected in job titles. If firms prefer seniority to play a marginal role in exchange for individual performance orientation, they need to implement modifications to the end of hierarchical job titles and their meaning accordingly; otherwise, the performance orientation will be jeopardized. The firms that have been interviewed tried to implement changes in this direction, with mixed success, as a president of a large MNC explains:

> We once had the policy to abolish hierarchical job titles but that failed. Employees just ignored it. So, we reintroduced the traditional job titles. Job titles indicate seniority, hierarchy, and privileges that seniors just have over juniors. That is something very cultural. It was not possible to change that with a new corporate policy. Even staff at Starbucks in Korea address each other with hierarchical job titles followed by the name. That fact taught us that it is something very important.
>
> *(interview ID42expat)*

In sum, it can be claimed that Confucian ideals are still strong and influence management techniques as reflected by the several studies conducted over the last decades. Lesser knowledge has been so far accumulated along a second strand of Confucianism, helping to manifest hierarchies, which can be seen in affection, empathy or benevolence between the one at the top and the inferior. Social hierarchies in Confucianism are not a one-way street.

It has been suggested that affective ties embedded in a Confucian value system developed into large informal networks, giving the hierarchical system efficiency and stability. How can affective ties and networks in Korea be characterized in detail?

### Affective ties and informal networks in Korea

In Western countries, ideals of individualism typically prevail, and interpersonal ties, especially in business, can be described as rather rational, not based on kinship, rather depersonalized and usually more instrumental than sentimental (Li, 2007). In East Asian countries, by contrast, an often emotional orientation toward the community dominates the mind-set of an individual (Li, 2012). In Korea, "the individual was always viewed in the context of his affection network" (Hahm, 1986: 286; see also Lew, 2013). Affective ties and networks can be regarded as quasi-familial relations between those with whom affection is shared. Family-like networks have played an important role in Korea's rapid economic upturn since the 1960s. They have represented a platform for collaboration and have acted as a vehicle for informal information transfer between and among the government and businesses (Bell & Hahm, 2004; Lew, 2013). Since Korean economic development was state-directed, meaning that a few large corporations were put in charge of carrying out economic policy, it was necessary to build informal agreements and reliable relationships. These proceeded mostly through affective ties and networks (Hahm, 1986; Horak, 2014a, 2014b, 2015; Lew, 2013; Lew et al., 2003; Yee, 2000a, 2000b). Affective networks also supported economic development, especially in two respects: they reduced "transaction costs and solved the free-rider problem" (Kim, 2000: 178). Affective ties and networks still play an important role in contemporary Korea. They are not few in number and not limited to a single elite circle; they are numerous society-spanning networks. According to Lee (2000), Korean civil society has been replaced by these networks. However, affective ties in Korea, despite the country's importance in international business activities today, have largely been overlooked so far in international business and management studies (Bstieler & Hemmert, 2008; Horak, 2014, 2015). How can affective ties and networks in Korea be defined? Based on expert interviews conducted in Korea among leaders in business and society, Horak (2014) suggests a general categorization consisting of *Inmaek* (인맥), *Yongo* (연고) and *Yonjul* (연줄) ties.

## Inmaek, Yongo *and* Yonjul

*Inmaek* can be translated simply as "network." *Inmaek* describes the affection-based informal relationships that one establishes in the course of one's life. Some examples are relationships and friendships that are formed in the workplace or while pursuing a hobby or leisure activity.

*Yongo* ties are established due to similarities, because of shared backgrounds between actors. The syllable *yon* can be translated as "tie" and the syllable *go* means that the tie exists for a reason, and that reason is the shared common background. Traditionally, three backgrounds are distinguished: (1) the same place of birth or regional origin (in Korean: *Jiyon* [지연]), (2) attendance at the same school or having the same alma mater (*Hakyon* [학연]) and/or (3) kinship or blood ties (*Hyulyon* [혈연]). *Yongo* ties based on *Jiyon* (the same regional origin) or on *Hakyon* (alma mater) are influential in the political sphere. For instance, when elections are held, "many Koreans will vote for a political candidate, even if the person is less qualified, just because he or she attended the same school or came from the same region of the country" (Shim et al., 2008: 85). As of 2014, Korea has had ten presidents since 1948; half of these presidents originated from the same region (Gyeongsang province in the southeast of Korea). About 30 percent of chaebol founders, business executives and government ministers were born in that same region (Kim, 2007). Furthermore, *Hakyon* (alma mater)-based *Yongo* ties are important. Korea has approximately 370 institutions that provide higher education (QS, 2015), but Seoul National University, along with Yonsei University and Korea University, is regarded as one of the most prestigious of them. The alma mater is the only source of *Yongo* that can be selected freely. Hence, the universities that promise the highest potential for *Yongo* acquisition through becoming an alumnus are opportunistic for many. According to Kim (2007), about 50 percent of Korean ministers and upper-government representatives and more than 30 percent of executives in the business sector graduated from a single university: Seoul National University. The ties between business and government are strengthened when former government officials enter the business field as consultants or managers. According to Kim (2007: 27), "the business community actively looks for retiring bureaucrats who have close personal connections within the relevant ministries." Moreover, *Hyulyon*-based *Yongo* ties (kinship ties) are formed between large businesses. Although the huge family–owned Korean *Chaebols* compete with each other, 23 of the top 30 *Chaebols* are connected through intermarriage ties among the leading families. Kim (2007) asserts that assimilation serves to align business interests.

*Yongo* ties are based on relationships that are established by at least one of these shared backgrounds. Consequently, *Yongo* has distinctive characteristics. Once ascribed, *Yongo* is immutable and irreversible; as it is *cause*-based, it is almost predefined by birth, and it cannot be chosen (with the exception of an alma mater). It exists naturally and does not imply any action, intention or purpose per se. *Yongo*-based ties can be and usually are maintained for life. Those who share *Yongo* engage in activities such as meeting regularly, exchanging information or sharing the costs of celebrations, anniversaries or funerals. Because of the shared background, *Yongo* networks are quite homogeneous. Moreover, they are closed and exclusive. One cannot become a member of a *Yongo* network. For instance, if one person graduated from university X and another from university Y, they cannot share *Hakyon*-based *Yongo* by definition. They can certainly have a close and trusting relationship, but that relationship would be defined as *Inmaek* rather than *Yongo*. Hence, different *Yongo* networks cannot easily be connected. Accordingly, "bridging" (Coleman, 1988) between different networks is very unusual. Bridging within a particular *Yongo* network, by contrast, works well, as a certain degree of ad hoc trust is ascribed to members who share *Yongo* but have not so far been in contact. Foreigners, such as expatriates, cannot easily establish original *Yongo*, since they have no genuine Korean ties. Different *Yongo* networks can be, and are often reported as being in competition with or hostile towards each other (Horak, 2014; Lee, 2000; Lew, 2013; Yee, 2000a). Within a *Yongo* network, there is "flexibility, tolerance, mutual understanding as well as trust. Outside the boundary, on the contrary, people are treated as 'non-persons' and there can be discrimination and even hostility" (Kim, 2000: 179; see Table 4.2 for further characteristics of *Yongo*).

The *Yongo*-based segmentation of Korean society has been found to have existed as early as the Choson dynasty (1392–1910), when the ruling class, the *Yangban*, "grouped itself into mutually exclusive factions and clans that engaged in fierce rivalry. The fragmentation of the *Yangban* society along the lines of scholarly association, kinship and region gave rise to purges and factional strife" (Sik, 2005: 84).

Furthermore, *Yonjul* relationships often, but not always, stem from a shared basis, for example preexisting as *Inmaek* or *Yongo*. While, for the formation of *Yongo* networks (which are *cause*-based), the cause is significant (i.e., there is a shared basis), for the development of *Yonjul* (which is *purpose*-based), intention is more important. *Yonjul* relationships can be interpreted as a "mutual patron–client network with a strong paternalistic tone" (Lee, 2000: 369). The *yon* here,

**TABLE 4.2** *Yongo* in descriptive terms

| *Characteristics of* Yongo *(selection)* |
| --- |
| • Partly preset, i.e., partly given by birth |
| • Immutable and irreversible |
| • Cause-based, it cannot be established, "it exists." It can be (further) developed |
| • Not purpose-based, it is a conventional social relationship in Korea |
| • Every Korean is a member of a *Yongo* network ("network society") |
| • Homogeneous and exclusive |
| • *Yongo* networks are often hostile towards each other and in competition |
| • Lifelong relationships |
| • Sometimes perceived as a burden |
| • Used for job acquisition, career progression, information gathering, government relations, etc. |

just as in the case of *Yongo*, can be interpreted as a "relationship" or "connection," whereas the *jul* means "rope" or "cord." *Yonjul* has a rather negative connotation. *Yonjul* relationships are often established to gain personal benefit in a situation in which there should be fair competition or equality. Unethical behavior, such as under-the-table transactions, cronyism, bribery, corruption and so on, are closely associated with *Yonjul* (Kim, 2000; Lee, 2000). Since *Yonjul* ties can be established through, and might be intertwined with, pre-existing *Inmaek* and *Yongo*, it is difficult to delineate them precisely. However, since *Yonjul* is purpose-based, has a negative connotation and is clearly perceived as negative in Korea and *Inmaek* and *Yongo* are, by definition, value-neutral terms, it is important to draw a definitive demarcation line (Figure 4.1).

## Alternative views of the Korean cultural context

### Collectivism? Contextuals in a network society

Classifying cultures into rather static categories was a popular approach during the 1980s and 1990s (Hofstede, 1980, 1991; Inglehart, 1998; Trompenaars & Hampden-Turner, 1998). However, since then, Asian countries, in particular, have developed dynamically (Froese, 2013; Jöns et al., 2007). The conventional approach has been criticized as no longer sufficient for explaining national cultures in a satisfactory way (Fang, 2012; Van de Ven & Jing, 2012) because it treats national cultures as static constructs. Thus, there is a need for reevaluation (Lim et al., 2011) and the inclusion of a dynamic view of culture. In particular, the Korean economy and society experienced drastic changes in the aftermath of the Asian financial crisis of 1997/98 and the restructuring measures directed by the IMF (International Monetary Fund; Hutchison, 2003). Similarly, when compared with Japan or China, Korea has conventionally been classified as a typical collectivist country, in which group norms prevail, influencing social interaction at the group

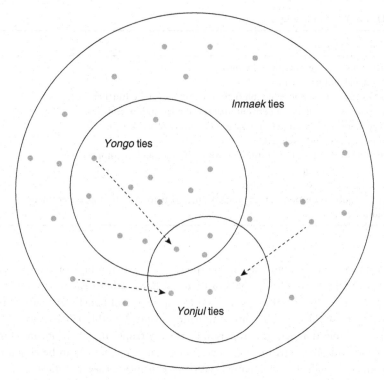

**FIGURE 4.1** *Inmaek, Yongo,* and *Yonjul* – interrelatedness and the possible development path of a relational tie

*Source:* Horak (2014: 90).

and community levels (Ali & Jung, 2017; Park & Lunt, 2015). However, fewer empirical studies in this field have been conducted in Korea, making it difficult to challenge this view. Those studying collectivism more deeply are for instance studies by Chang (2006) and Cho and Yoon (2001). Chang (2006) studies the effect of individual pay-for-performance systems on employee attitudes toward organizational commitment. Because Korea is regarded as a highly collectivistic culture that values seniority and group culture over individual performance (Bae, 2012; Hofstede, 1991), it is assumed that rewarding a better-performing individual and ignoring group collectivism will cause tension because of the violation of prevailing social group norms. Surprisingly, the research by Chang (2006) does not confirm the existence of a negative effect on organizational commitment. Chang (2006) explains this result by suggesting that the general basic assumption that Korea is a purely collectivistic culture is incorrect. In fact, norms of collectivism and individualism both prevail in Korea (Chang, 2006; Lee et al., 2014; Ungson et al., 1997).

These results indicate, first, that the implications of the conventional dimensions of the classification of the national culture should be treated with caution, as their explanatory scope is limited, and, second, that individual behavior and group behavior are determined situationally and are context-specific. Following the preceding discussion, we suggest that Koreans can, depending on situational context, be both individualistic and collectivistic, making the relational context, rather than the overall societal configuration, pivotal. Cho and Yoon (2001) propose an identical distinction, as do Hamaguchi et al. (1985) in an earlier attempt to describe relationships in East Asia. These latter authors distinguish between the interactions of individuals, whom they describe metaphorically as atoms, and those of contextuals, who are shaped more like molecules. In individual interactions, actors are simply subjects outside the life space of each other. By comparison, contextuals share life spaces by being embedded in them and by their relational ties, making them dependent on each other. Hence, contextuals can be described as relational actors. As the sharing of life spaces can have different degrees of importance between different actors, the relational context determines whether individual or contextual interaction dominates (Figure 4.2).

As described initially, affective ties of *Yongo* and *Inmaek* relationships embedded in a Confucian value frame largely determine relationships between actors in Korea. Thus, affective ties can be regarded as an important contextual dimension or life space. To develop the collectivism paradigm further, we suggest that collectivism depends on the context. To simplify, if affective ties exist, Koreans act as contextuals; if not, they act in rather individualistic ways.

## Can Korea still be regarded as a low-trust society?

Trust is widely regarded as a crucial element of business transactions (Nee et al., 2018) and is important for a stable democracy and political landscape (Ostrom & Walker, 2003). In social transactions, trust can be defined as the confidence in

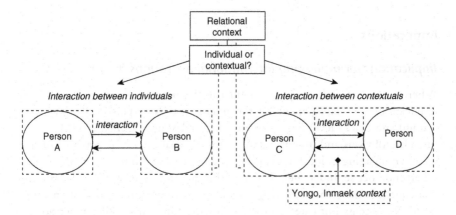

**FIGURE 4.2** Relational interaction context of individuals and contextuals

*Source:* Adopted (modified and extended) from Hamaguchi et al. (1985), in Horak and Yang (2017a: 9).

or likelihood of a predictable positive result of one actor's assessment of another before the action can be monitored (Gambetta, 2000). In societies in which Confucian norms of behavior are exercised, trust in strangers is often said to be weak. Korea, a country where Confucian norms are strongly influential, is conventionally considered to be a low-trust society (Chang & Chang, 1994; Fukuyama, 1995; Kim & Son, 1998). Prominent large-scale surveys, such as the World Values Survey (WVS), underpin the belief that general trust is weak in Korea (WVS, 2009, fifth wave). However, this view may need to be revised, as today it seems to be outdated or to fail to consider a specific aspect of Korean society, namely informal networks that are built on affective ties, as presented earlier. If informal networks are taken into consideration, Korea might, in fact, be classified as a society in which the level of social cohesion is quite high. Other surveys, such as the Korean General Social Survey (Seok & Kim, 2004), suggest that a description of Korea as simply a low-trust country cannot easily be maintained or is just one side of the coin. Even though institutional trust might be low, interpersonal trust facilitated by affective ties is, in fact, exceptionally high. More recent studies seem to confirm these results, so the conventional view of the state of trust in Korea should be adjusted. Based on data gathered between 2001 and 2003, the East Asian Barometer (EAB) has concluded that trust is stronger in Korea than in Japan, Hong Kong, Mongolia, the Philippines and Thailand and that Korea ranks in the top cluster for trust along with Mainland China and Taiwan (EAB, 2003). A recent international trust survey conducted by the Edelman Global Trust Barometer (Edelman, 2014), although observing a decline in trust in 26 countries, including the US and France, surprisingly finds a reverse trend in the case of Korea. Korea is placed with Sweden, Germany, the UK and Australia (among others) in the cluster in which trust is at a medium level. Compared with the views that were popular in the 1990s and at the beginning of this century, today we find less evidence portraying Korea as a typical low-trust society. While general trust was low in the past, it is higher today.

## Implications

### Implications for managing international operations in Korea

Whereas the network view of conducting business in Korea has multilevel implications for management on the micro level (interpersonal), meso level (group) and macro level (government – firm relations) (Horak, 2014b), one of the more obvious and urgent questions for international managers in Korea is whether engaging in local networking is achievable and in line with their ethical attitude per se. Independent of how this question is answered, what are the consequences that especially *Yongo* ties have for the life and work of an expatriate? We discuss both items in the following through a rather practitioner-oriented lens.

## Networking Korean style: is it ethical to engage in local networking?

Should a manager abroad network? While this question may appear to be rhetorical, prior studies tend to confirm positive effects from an expatriate being integrated into a social network, with positive effects on well-being (Johnson et al., 2003; Kashima & Loh, 2006; Wang & Nayir, 2006) and job performance (Liu & Shaffer, 2005). Being a successful networker is usually assumed to depend on prior international experience and intercultural competence (Leung et al., 2014; Wang, 2002) or traits such as extraversion and openness (Froese & Peltokorpi, 2012). Since networking is not a one-way street, Horak and Yang (2016), as well as Osman-Gani and Rockstuhl (2008), recognize a lack of integration of the external dimension into the current research models and suggest paying more attention to the foreign social environment into which an expatriate is embedded. The so-called *environmental receptiveness* (Horak & Yang, 2016) becomes an important variable because it finally determines whether a social environment is generally receptive to integrating a foreign expatriate *independently* of the person being empathic, talkative, open and so on. In other words, the environment determines whether social network integration is possible per se. Whereas personal traits may be regarded as a suitable predictor of social network integration in many Western countries, this logic does not work so well in Korea, and for foreigners who are unfamiliar with the Korean social environment, it can be risky (and naïve) to assume that sociability follows the same pattern as in Western countries. The decision regarding whether to be willing to network and, if so, what kind of tie to conclude is important, and this makes an understanding of the nature of the informal ties in Korea important. Assuming an actor prefers to conclude ethical ties, relevant ties can be distinguished into *Yongo*, *Inmaek* and *Yonjul* ties, as defined earlier.

All three ties, *Yongo, Inmaek* and *Yonjul*, are in principle useful and exploitable for business purposes. *Yonjul* is typically instrumental by nature, as it serves a purpose. *Yonjul* has a negative connotation in Korean since it refers to a string or rope that attaches someone to others. Usually, selfish actions are connected to *Yonjul* that lead to personal gains, and "under the table" activities are described as *Yonjul* action even up to bribery, cronyism or corruption in any form (Kim, 2000; Lee, 2000). While *Yonjul* actions can be established based on *Yongo* or *Inmaek* ties, most people would describe *Yonjul* as clearly unethical.

As described earlier, *Yongo* is to a great extent preset; hence, it is cause-based, as it does not imply any purpose. Thus, by its very nature, it is not instrumental, but it can certainly become instrumental, and in practice, it often is, especially in business and politics. This ambivalent nature of *Yongo* is important to recognize. It is in principle a very positive social tie unless it is used for *Yonjul* actions. It binds people and provides ad hoc prescriptions of trust that can be developed further if desired by the parties involved. Since virtually every Korean person (in Korea) possesses *Yongo* of different intensities and qualities, it can be seen as a reciprocal social asset that can be activated anytime and converted into backup, help, support or care. However, this means in consequence that becoming deeply integrated into *Yongo* networks is nearly impossible for non-Korean international expatriates. Theoretically, there is a chance to acquire *Hakyon*-based *Yongo* by attending and graduating from a Korean high school or university. However, realistically, this is very seldom the case for typical expatriates on a business mission based in Korea. Still, it would be interesting to understand better and in detail whether the named scenario would lead to influential *Yongo* ties even for non-Korean expatriates. Assessing the ethicality of *Yongo* depends on the point of view. Originally, by its very nature, when accepting that *Yongo* is a cultural product, is not purpose-based and is not used instrumentally, it can be regarded as very ethical; when it turns into *Yonjul* actions, however, it is certainly not very ethical.

*Inmaek* is rather straightforward to assess, since it is a rather broad term with the same meaning as *network* in English. It is potentially purpose-based and potentially instrumental, but it is definitely not cause-based, as *Yongo* is. Since networking is in general not regarded as an unethical activity, engaging in *Inmaek* can under normal circumstances be regarded as ethical. Table 4.3 summarizes the assessment. Overall, since *Yongo* ties cannot be established by expatriates and *Yonjul* is most often connected to unethical conduct, expats may focus on *Inmaek* and develop high-trust *Inmaek*-based ties to compete with the *Yongo* ties that are prevalent in the same business environment.

### Expatriates and Yongo

Since, for expatriates, based on the preceding assessment, *Inmaek* ties remain the best option to focus on when developing a social network, it would still be in a relational competition with *Yongo* networks. Hence, it is important to understand the characteristics and consequences of *Yongo*-based relationships since others, for example. colleagues, friends, inferiors, superiors, competitors and so on rely on them anyway or are voluntarily or involuntary involved in them to certain extents. However, they do not talk about *Yongo*-based ties since they are often regarded as a taboo, something very personal or the joker that one possesses in competing for jobs, information or career advancement.

**TABLE 4.3** Ethical assessment of engaging in local networking

| | Purpose-*based by nature?* | Cause-*based by nature?* | *Instrumental by nature?* | *Exploitable for business purposes?* | *In principle ethical?* |
|---|---|---|---|---|---|
| *Yongo* | No | Yes | No | Yes | Yes |
| *Inmaek* | Possible | No | Possible | Yes | Yes |
| *Yonjul* | Yes | No | Yes | Yes | No |

*Source:* Horak (2016: 11; slightly modified).

One important aspect to keep in mind is that *Yongo* networks are embedded in a Confucian value frame that shapes the behavioral norms that apply between persons. What often looks to cultural outsiders like a top-down command master–slave relationship is, in fact, a reciprocal give and take relationship, in which the younger "serves" the elder and the elder fully supports the younger when it comes to promotions, recommendations or other benefits. Often professional competence is secondary; loyalty to relational ties is a core competence. In *Yongo* networks, loyalty to persons with whom one shares *Yongo* is greater than that to a company's code of conduct. If, for example, a senior from university days calls a younger person asking for company internal information but they work for competing companies, *Yongo* ethics would prevent the younger from refusing. *Yongo* is a higher power superseding this. It is regarded neither as odd to ask nor as odd to deliver in this context, as it likely would be judged in a typical Western context. Expatriates perceive this as hard to deal with, as the example of a president and CEO of an automotive firm shows; he reports that, because of *Yongo*,

> you can hardly keep information confidential. I was quite shocked in the beginning. You cannot keep anything confidential and that's what makes it difficult to establish a relationship with your colleagues.
>
> *(interview ID30–09expat, in Horak & Yang, 2016: 1038)*

This statement, next to the challenges concerning how to compete fairly that it implies, also draws attention to working with colleagues and establishing trust with them. If loyalty to *Yongo* networks supersedes conventional corporate citizenship morals of not telling competitors internal secrets, how can expatriates establish trustful intrafirm ties?

Besides that, an expatriate who is sent as a leader to Korea may face difficulties in determining how to lead a Korean team when *Yongo* comes into play. Informal groups based on *Hakyon* can be widespread within the firm. It is recommendable to find out from which university host country nationals within the team graduated, because, if many graduated from the same university, the most senior of them is likely to be the informal leader. This can lead to firm–intern fragmentation and camp building with different *Hakyon*-based camps that do not communicate with each other, that compete against each other or that just do not support each other.

In sum, there are several challenges for expatriate managers to master when taking *Yongo* into account. Most importantly, managers and firms must find ways to prevent *Yongo*-based information transfer, since this has a direct influence on competition and costly developed knowledge. Second, teams need to be organized in such a way that considers heterogeneity in terms of personal background so that *Yongo* fragmentation within a team or firm would not take effect. Third, since expatriate managers can hardly establish *Yongo*, it may be a viable solution to hire local managers with high *Yongo* endowment and place them inside the company in positions in which they can take full advantage of the existing *Yongo* ties or ties that can easily be activated. Expatriate managers themselves may consider splitting their position and establishing a management tandem including a vice manager who handles local *Yongo*-based affairs. This is an approach to consider for instance in local sales and key account management, project acquisition and business development, functions dealing mainly with dispute and crisis management or interactions between the firm and the government. Finally, approaching management in Korea through the lens of *Yongo* can work better in practice than relying on the conventional paradigms of a low-trust society, collectivism and group harmony.

## Conclusion

As this chapter has shown, the network view of the Korean society and business environment can supersede the low-trust and collectivist society paradigm and bring new phenomena to the surface that advance the current knowledge on Korea's cultural environment. First and foremost, the discussion about the characteristics of informal ties and networks, namely, *Inmaek, Yongo* and *Yonjul*, revealed how challenging or nearly impossible it is for international managers to establish *Yongo*, which is very important when conducting business in Korea. Whether establishing *Inmaek* will produce the same result for expatriates is difficult to answer given the current absence of research into that area. Clearly, knowledge about informal networking in Korea, including (1) detailed knowledge about its character, (2) its exclusive and partly predefined nature, (3) the loyalty that people attach to informal ties that are stronger than those to a firm's code of conduct and (4) consequently the potential risk of a free flow of strategically relevant and therefore secret information to competitors, needs to be taken seriously and should be available to every international manager expatriated to Korea. Thus, it should be an essential part of or addition to any corporate expatriate preparation program.

## Bibliography

### Key references

Hemmert, M. 2012. *Tiger Management: Korean Companies on World Markets*. London, New York: Routledge.

Horak, S. 2014. Antecedents and characteristics of informal relation-based networks in Korea: Yongo, Yonjul and Inmaek. *Asia Pacific Business Review*, 20(1): 78–108.

Horak, S., Taube, M., Yang, I., & Restel, K. 2019. Two not of a kind: Social network theory and informal social networks in East Asia. *Asia Pacific Journal of Management*, 36(2): 349–372.

Horak, S., & Yang, I. 2016. Affective networks, informal ties, and the limits of expatriate effectiveness. *International Business Review*, 25(5): 1030–1042.

Kim, D. O., & Bae, J. S. 2004. *Employment relations and HRM in South Korea*. Burlington: Ashgate.

Rowley, C., & Warner, M. 2014. *Management in South Korea revisited*. London, New York: Routledge.

Yang, I., & Horak, S. 2018. Emotions, indigenous affective ties, and social network theory – The case of South Korea. *Asia Pacific Journal of Management*, 36(2): 395–414.

## Online sources

Worldbank: www.worldbank.org/en/country/korea
World Business Culture: www.worldbusinessculture.com/country-profiles/south-korea/

## References

Ali, M. A., & Jung, H. J. 2017. CSR and the workplace attitudes of irregular employees: The case of subcontracted workers in Korea. *Business Ethics: A European Review*, 26(2): 130–146.

Bae, J. 2012. Self-fulfilling processes at a global level: The evolution of human resource management practices in Korea, 1987–2007. *Management Learning*, 43(5): 579–607.

Bell, D. A., & Hahm, C. 2004. The politics of affective relations in East Asia. In D. A. Bell & C. Hahm (Eds.), *The politics of affective relations: East Asia and beyond*: 1–16. Oxford: Lexington Books.

Bstieler, L., & Hemmert, M. 2008. Trust formation in Korean new product alliances: How important are pre-existing social ties? *Asia Pacific Journal of Management*, 27(2): 299–319.

Chang, E. 2006. Individual pay for performance and commitment HR practices in South Korea. *Journal of World Business*, 41(4): 368–381.

Chang, C. S., & Chang, N. J. 1994. *The Korean Management System: Cultural, Political, Economic Foundations*. Westport: Quorum.

Cho, Y. H., & Yoon, J. 2001. The origin and function of dynamic collectivism: An analysis of Korean corporate culture. *Asia Pacific Business Review*, 7(4): 70–88.

Coleman, J. S. 1988. Social capital in the creation of human capital. *American Journal of Sociology*, 94: 95–120.

EAB (East-Asian Barometer). 2003. East Asian Barometer 2001–2003. www.jdsurvey.net/jds/jdsurveyAnalisis.jsp?Idioma=I&ES_COL=101. Accessed 2 June 2016.

Edelman. 2014. 2014 Edelman trust barometer executive summary. http://edelmaneditions.com/wp-content/uploads/2014/01/FINAL-BROCHURE-2014.pdf. Accessed 10 July 2017.

Fang, T. 2012. Yin Yang: A new perspective on culture. *Management and Organization Review*, 8(1): 25–50.

Froese, F. J. 2013. Work values of the next generation of business leaders in Shanghai, Tokyo, and Seoul. *Asia Pacific Journal of Management*, 30(1): 297–315.

Froese, F. J., & Peltokorpi, V. 2012. The impact of expatriate personality traits on cross-cultural adjustment: A study with expatriates in Japan. *International Business Review*, 21(4): 734–746.

Fukuyama, F. 1995. *Trust: The Social Virtues and the Creation of Prosperity*. New York: The Free Press.

Gambetta, D. 2000. Can We Trust Trust? In D. Gambetta (Ed.), *Making and Breaking Cooperative Relations* (Electronic Edition): 213–237. Oxford: Trust Department of Sociology, University of Oxford. Retrieved from www.sociology.ox.ac.uk/papers/

Hahm, P. C. 1986. *Korean Jurisprudence politics and culture*. Seoul: Yonsei University Press.

Hamaguchi, E., Kumon, S., & Creighton, M. R. 1985. A contextual model of the Japanese: Toward a methodological innovation in Japan studies. *Journal of Japanese Studies*, 11(2): 289–321.

Hofstede, G. 1980. *Culture's consequences – International differences in work related values*. Newbury Park, London, New Delhi: Sage.

Hofstede, G. 1991. *Culture and organizations: Software of the mind*. New York: McGraw-Hil.

Holcombe, C. 2017. *A history of East Asia. From the origins of civilization to the twenty-first century.* Cambridge: Cambridge University Press.

Horak, S. 2014a. Antecedents and characteristics of informal relation-based networks in Korea: Yongo, Yonjul and Inmaek. *Asia Pacific Business Review,* 20(1): 78–108.

Horak, S. 2014b. The multi-dimensional influence of informal social networks in Korea – propositions for future management research. *Journal of General Management,* 40(2): 47–65.

Horak, S. 2015. Approaching Korean business and management ideals through the lens of Yongo. A scholar-practitioner perspective. *Journal of Asia-Pacific Business,* 16(3): 210–222.

Horak, S. 2016. Join In or Opt Out? A normative – Ethical analysis of affective Ties and networks in South Korea. *Journal of Business Ethics,* 149(1): 207–220.

Horak, S., & Yang, I. 2016. Affective networks, informal ties, and the limits of expatriate effectiveness. *International Business Review,* 25(5): 1030–1042.

Horak, S., & Yang, I. 2017a. A complementary perspective on business ethics in South Korea: Civil religion, common misconceptions, and overlooked social structures. *Business Ethics: A European Review,* 27(1): 1–14.

Horak, S., & Yang, I. 2017b. Whither seniority? Career progression and performance orientation in South Korea. *International Journal of Human Resource Management,* forthcoming. http://dx.doi.org/10.1080/09585192.2017.1362659

Hutchison, M. M. 2003. A cure worse than the disease? Currency crises and the output costs of IMF-supported stabilization programs. In M. P. Dooley & J. A. Frankel (Eds.), *Managing currency crises in emerging markets*: 321–359. Chicago: University of Chicago Press.

Inglehart, R. 1998. *Modernization and post-modernization: Cultural, economic, and political change in 43 societies.* Princeton, NJ: Princeton University Press.

Johnson, E. C., Kristof-Brown, A. L., Van Vianen, A. E. M., De Pater, I. E., & Klein, M. R. 2003. Expatriate social Ties: Personality antecedents and consequences for adjustment. *International Journal of Selection and Assessment,* 11(4): 277–288.

Jöns, I., Froese, F. J., & Pak, Y. S. 2007. Cultural changes during the integration process of acquisitions: A comparative study between German and German – Korean acquisitions. *International Journal of Intercultural Relations,* 31(5): 591–604.

Jun, W., & Rowley, C. 2014. Change and continuity in management systems and corporate performance: Human resource management, corporate culture, risk management and corporate strategy in South Korea. *Business History,* 56(3): 485–508.

Kashima, E. S., & Loh, E. 2006. International students' acculturation: Effects of international, conational, and local ties and need for closure. *International Journal of Intercultural Relations,* 30(4): 471–485.

Kim, Y. H. 2000. Emergence of the network society: Trends, new challenges, and an implication for network capitalism. *Korea Journal,* 40(3): 161–184.

Kim, Y. T. 2007. Korean elites: Social networks and power. *Journal of Contemporary Asia,* 37(1): 19–37.

Kim, Y., & Son, J. 1998. Trust, cooperation, and social risk: A cross-cultural comparison. *Korea Journal,* 38(1): 131–153.

KOSTAT (Statistics Korea) 2015. *Population and housing census 2015. Statistics Korea, Daejeon.* http://kostat.go.kr/portal/korea/index.action. Accessed 10 August 2016.

Koh, B. I. 1996. Confucianism in Contemporary Korea. In W. M. Tu (Ed.), *Confucian traditions in East Asian Modernity: Moral education and economic culture in Japan and the Four Mini-Dragons*: 191–201. Cambridge, MA: Harvard University Press.

Lee, J. 2000. Society in a Vortex? Yonjul network and civil society in Korea. *Korea Journal,* 40(1): 366–391.

Lee, K., Scandura, T. A., & Sharif, M. M. 2014. Cultures have consequences: A configural approach to leadership across two cultures. *The Leadership Quarterly,* 25(4): 692–710.

Leung, K., Ang, S., & Tan, M. L. 2014. Intercultural competence. *Annual Review of Organizational Psychology and Organizational Behavior*, 1: 489–519.

Lew, S. C. 2013. Missing Links in Understanding Korean Development. In S. C. Lew (Ed.), *The Korean economic development path – Confucian tradition, affective network*: 3–24. New York: Palgrave Macmillan.

Lew, S. C., Chang, M. H., & Kim, T. E. 2003. Affective networks and modernity – The case of Korea. In D. A. Bell & C. Hahm (Eds.), *Confucianism for the modern world*: 201–217. Cambridge, NY: Cambridge University Press.

Li, P. P. 2007. Social tie, social capital, and social behavior: Toward an integrative model of informal exchange. *Asia Pacific Journal of Management*, 24(2): 227–246.

Li, P. P. 2012. Toward an integrative framework of indigenous research: The geocentric implications of Yin-Yang Balance. *Asia Pacific Journal of Management*, 29(4): 849–872.

Lim, T. S., Kim, S. Y., & Kim, J. 2011. Holism: A missing link in individualism-collectivism research. *Journal of Intercultural Communication Research*, 40(1): 21–38.

Liu, X., & Shaffer, M. A. 2005. An investigation of expatriate adjustment and performance: A social capital perspective. *International Journal of Cross Cultural Management*, 5(3): 235–254.

Milliman, J. F., Kim, Y. M., & Von Glinow, M. A. 1993. Hierarchical advancement in Korean chaebols: A model and research agenda. *Human Resource Management Review*, 3(4): 293–320.

Nee, V., Holm, H. J., & Opper, S. 2018. Learning to trust: From relational exchange to generalized trust in China. *Organization Science*, 29(5): 969–986.

Osman-Gani, A. M., & Rockstuhl, T. 2008. Antecedents and consequences of social network characteristics for expatriate adjustment and performance in overseas assignments: Implications for HRD. *Human Resource Development Review*, 7(1): 32–57.

Ostrom, E., & Walker, J. (Eds.) 2003. *Trust and reciprocity: Interdisciplinary lessons for experimental research*. New York: Russell Sage Foundation.

Park, S., & Lunt, N. 2015. Confucianism and qualitative interviewing: Working Seoul to soul. *Forum Qualitative Sozialforschung/Forum: Qualitative Social Research*, 16(2). www.qualitative-esearch.net/index.php/fqs/article/view/2166/3792. Accessed 15 August 2015.

QS. 2015. *Country Guides – Study in South Korea*. www.topuniversities.com/where-to-study/asia/south-korea/guide. Accessed 15 August 2015.

Seok, H., & Kim, S. 2004. *Korea general social survey*. Retrieved from the Korean Social Science Data Archive, Korean Social Science Library. www.kossda.or.kr. Accessed 10 July 2014.

Shim, H. J. 2004. *Die Herausforderung der koreanischen Kultur durch die hegemoniale Globalisierung*. Frankfurt am Main: IKO.

Shim, T. Y., Kim, M. S., & Martin, J. 2008. *Changing Korea – Understanding culture and communication*. New York: Peter Lang.

Sik, S. H. 2005. *A brief history of Korea: The spirit of Korean cultural roots*. Seoul: Ewha Womens University Press.

Trompenaars, F., & Hampden-Turner, C. 1998. *Riding the Waves of culture: Understanding cultural diversity in global business*. New York: McGraw-Hill.

Ungson, G., Steers, R., & Park, S. 1997. *Korean enterprise: The quest for globalization*. Boston: Harvard Business School Press.

Van de Ven, A. H., & Jing, R. 2012. Indigenous management research in China from an engaged scholarship perspective. *Management and Organization Review*, 8(1): 123–137.

Wang, X. 2002. Expatriate adjustment from a social network perspective: Theoretical examination and a conceptual model. *International Journal of Cross Cultural Management*, 2(3): 321–337.

Wang, X., & Nayir, D. Z. 2006. How and when is social networking important? Comparing European expatriate adjustment in China and Turkey. *Journal of International Management*, 12(4): 449–472.

Warner, M., & Rowley, C. 2014. Context and implications for Korean management and business. *Asia Pacific Business Review*, 20(1): 197–207.

WVS (World Values Survey) 2009. *World values survey 1981–2008, official aggregate v.20090901, 2009*. www.wvsevsdb.com/wvs/WVSData.jsp. Accessed 12 August 2014.

Yang, I. 2014. The informal organization of Korean companies: Implications for Korean MNCs. *Thunderbird International Business Review*, 56(6): 577–588.

Yee, J. 2000a. The social networks of Koreans. *Korea Journal*, 40(1): 325–352.

Yee, J. 2000b. Too modern too soon? Dualism in civil society, everyday life, and social relations in contemporary Korea. *Korea Journal*, 40(1): 282–284.

Yee, J. 2015. Social capital in Korea: Relational capital, trust, and transparency. *International Journal of Japanese Sociology*, 24(1): 30–47.

# PART II
# Market access

# 5

# MARKET ENTRY

## Inbound FDI into Korea

*In Hyeock (Ian) Lee*

## Introduction

MNEs are commercial organizations conducting overseas operations across national borders with an aim to serve foreign local customers, and, as a result, gain market entry into foreign countries using diverse entry modes, which is a prerequisite for the achievement of MNEs' profit maximization from overseas operations. According to the Uppsala process theory of internationalization (Johanson & Vahlne, 1977, 1990), there is a sequence of entry modes that are chosen by MNEs when entering foreign markets. This is because foreign markets are perceived as risky and uncertain to MNEs, and MNEs are willing to choose market entry modes that increase the levels of their resource commitment into foreign countries step by step as they accumulate enough knowledge and experience about the foreign markets with the passage of time. This rationale delineates the incremental process of MNEs' choosing license first, followed by exporting using either local distributors or sales agents, local packaging or assembly, and eventually FDI as their entry modes into foreign markets (Johanson & Vahlne, 1977, 1990).

Among the diverse modes of market entry available to MNEs, FDI is unique from the others in the sense that it represents MNEs' control and ownership over foreign subsidiaries established in foreign countries with the highest level of resource commitment therein. It has been reported that MNEs are the main investors that drive the integration of both production and markets worldwide using FDI and that the largest MNEs on the list of Fortune Global 500 account for nearly 90% of the stock of world FDI (Rugman, 2005; Lee & Rugman, 2009). Considering that MNEs' foreign market entry using FDI signifies their achievement of deep and successful integration into local contexts with control and ownership in host countries, evaluating a country in terms of attracting direct investment projects from MNEs using FDI would provide prospective foreign investors with useful insights on doing their future business in the country.

As such, this chapter has two main objectives. First, built on Lee and Rugman (2009), it presents the overview of inbound FDI statistics in the context of Korea over the period of 2005–2017. For this purpose, I analyze the vast firm-level data on 39,423 inbound FDI notifications to Korea that have been accumulated in the Korean government database over thirteen years (http://insc.kisc.org/). The chapter provides details on inbound FDI into Korea by region, industry, country of origin, subnational region of destination, foreign ownership, and investment purposes in terms of their counts and amounts. Second, I discuss the main observations and findings from the inbound FDI statistics in terms of modern theories and arguments on MNEs and FDI. For this purpose, I exploit prior research on MNEs and FDI from the IB literature, including both conceptual and empirical studies, to highlight the meaning and importance of the observed phenomena from the data to prospective foreign investors considering direct investment plans into Korea. In addition, I also gather archival data from a diverse source of information, including unpublished reports by the Korean government and analyses by Korea's trade and investment promotion agency to hint on policy implications for host-country governments in need of attracting inbound FDI from foreign investors.

## Analyses on inbound FDI into Korea: 2005–2017

### Overview of inbound FDI into Korea

Table 5.1 shows the overview of inbound FDI notifications to Korea over thirteen years (2005–2017) in terms of their counts and amounts. Korea attracted a total of 39,423 notifications amounting to US$198 billion in inbound FDI over the period. This evidence seems to verify the increasing trends of inbound FDI into Korea, because the total amounts are more than twice the total of US$96.8 billion made during the previous fifteen years, from 1990 to 2004 (Lee & Rugman, 2009). It should be noted in the table that the average size of the inbound FDI notifications has more than doubled for the past decade from US$3.2 million to US$7.7 million per each FDI project.

As has been highlighted in the traditional FSAs and CSAs framework for explaining the internationalization of MNEs, foreign investors keep attempting to

**TABLE 5.1** Inbound FDI into Korea[†]

|  | 2005–2009 | 2010–2014 | 2015–2017 | Total |
| --- | --- | --- | --- | --- |
| # of counts | 17,215 | 13,754 | 8,454 | 39,423 |
| Amounts[††] | 56.5 | 76.6 | 65.1 | 198 |
| Average size[†††] | 3.2 | 5.6 | 7.7 | 5.0 |

[†] Author's calculation based on inbound FDI statistics from the Investment Notification Statistics Center in Korea (http://insc.kisc.org/).

[††] In billion US$.

[†††] In million US$.

exploit and/or upgrade their FSAs by searching for complementary CSAs to the FSAs from host countries where they invest (Rugman, 1981, 2005; Rugman & Verbeke, 2001, 2004). The evidence in Table 5.1 signifies that the host CSAs of Korea have persistently been upgraded in such a way that appeals to the diverse investment motivations of MNEs formulating and implementing direct investment plans in Korea. After shifting the main focus of economic development policies from foreign loans to foreign investors' direct investments during the late 1990s and early 2000s (Lee & Rugman, 2009), the Korean governments have implemented a series of strong policy measures to attract sophisticated foreign investors and their MNEs within their national jurisdiction, including but not limited to preferential tax treatment and provision of locational support for greenfield FDI in high-tech manufacturing sectors (Korea, MOCIE, 2003), awarding direct cash grants to greenfield FDI with over 30% of foreign ownership and total invested amounts of US$10 million in high-tech industries (Invest Korea, 2006), and establishing one-stop grievance resolution systems to any foreign investors (Korea, MOTIE, 2016). In addition to these examples of governmental endeavors, Korea has steadily improved in terms of both market powers and knowledge-intensive resources with US$1.4 trillion of GDP and US$7 billion of joint R&D projects in 2016, respectively (Korea, MOTIE, 2016).

## Inbound FDI into Korea by region

Table 5.2 summarizes inbound FDI notifications to Korea over the period from 2005 to 2017 from each of the world geographic regions in three categories of time series. In terms of their counts, Korea has consistently attracted about 60% of total 39,423 notifications from Asia-Pacific throughout the time series, with Europe and North America competing for the second place in the race. In terms of their amounts, on the other hand, the table shows that the largest source region was Europe with 47.4% until the late 2000s, changing to Asia-Pacific with around 40% after 2010. Europe still maintains the status of the second-largest investors into Korea with 26.9% in the most recent three years: however, North America is threatening that status with 24.5% of inbound FDI into Korea.

These statistical observations on the powers of Asia-Pacific in the inbound FDI notifications to Korea are in line with the perspective of regional MNEs put forward by Rugman and Verbeke (2004) and Rugman (2005). According to this path-breaking paradigm criticizing the phenomenon of globalization, they argue that successful MNEs on the list of Fortune Global 500 possess a strong tendency to conduct over the majority of their annual sales activities within their home regions of the triad (i.e., North America, Europe, and Asia-Pacific), making themselves regionalized MNEs rather than globalized MNEs. Abundant empirical studies afterwards demonstrated the validity of this argument using diverse data and samples (e.g., Arregle et al., 2009; Lopez et al., 2009; Almodóvar & Rugman, 2015) and even performance implications of regional MNEs compared to global MNEs (Lee & Marvel, 2009; Lee, 2010, 2013; Lee & Rugman, 2012; Almodóvar &

**TABLE 5.2** Inbound FDI into Korea by region[†]

| | 2005–2009 | | 2010–2014 | | 2015–2017 | | Total |
|---|---|---|---|---|---|---|---|
| # of counts | | | | | | | |
| Asia-Pacific | 9,962 | 57.9% | 8,223 | 59.8% | 5,099 | 60.3% | 23,284 |
| Europe | 2,569 | 14.9% | 2,237 | 16.3% | 1,293 | 15.3% | 6,099 |
| North America | 2,539 | 14.7% | 1,817 | 13.2% | 1,370 | 16.2% | 5,726 |
| South America | 596 | 3.5% | 474 | 3.4% | 327 | 3.9% | 1,397 |
| Africa–M. East | 1,544 | 9.0% | 976 | 7.1% | 361 | 4.3% | 2,881 |
| Others | 5 | 0.03% | 27 | 0.2% | 4 | 0.05% | 36 |
| Total | 17,215 | 100.0% | 13,754 | 100.0% | 8,454 | 100.0% | 39,423 |
| Amounts[††] | | | | | | | |
| Asia-Pacific | 16.7 | 29.5% | 32.1 | 41.9% | 24.9 | 38.2% | 73.7 |
| Europe | 26.8 | 47.4% | 23.2 | 30.3% | 17.5 | 26.9% | 67.5 |
| North America | 10.3 | 18.2% | 17.7 | 23.1% | 16.0 | 24.5% | 44.0 |
| South America | 2.0 | 3.5% | 2.6 | 3.4% | 3.8 | 5.9% | 8.4 |
| Africa–M. East | 0.8 | 1.4% | 1.0 | 1.3% | 2.9 | 4.5% | 4.7 |
| Others[†††] | 1.2 | 0.002% | 6.5 | 0.01% | 0.6 | 0.001% | 8.2 |
| Total | 56.5 | 100.0% | 76.6 | 100.0% | 65.1 | 100.0% | 198.0 |

[†] Author's calculation based on inbound FDI statistics from the Investment Notification Statistics Center in Korea (http://insc.kisc.org/).
[††] In billion US$
[†††] In million US$

Rugman, 2015). As such, it is natural to observe in Table 5.2 that Asia-Pacific has been salient as the largest source region in the inbound FDI notifications to Korea especially in the recent years in terms of both counts and amounts.

Table 5.3 breaks down Table 5.2 by key source countries per each of Asia-Pacific, Europe, and North America. In terms of their counts, China and Japan in Asia-Pacific and U.S. in North America have been the top three countries from which Korea has attracted about 44.4% of total 39,423 notifications throughout the time series. In terms of their amounts, on the other hand, the table shows that the largest source country was the U.S. in North America with 19.6% over the period, followed by Japan in Asia-Pacific and Netherlands in Europe with 13.8% and 8.4%, respectively, of total inbound FDI amounts made into Korea.

## Inbound FDI into Korea by industry

Table 5.4 reports data on inbound FDI notifications to Korea by industrial sectors for the same thirteen years. It is evident from the table that foreign investors' market entry into Korea has been dominating in service industries in terms of both their counts and amounts. More than 78% of the total counts of inbound FDI notifications have been consistently made in service industries for the past decade. In terms of their total amounts, the proportion of service industries was reduced from 68.1%

**TABLE 5.3** Inbound FDI into Korea by key countries[†]

|  | 2005–2009 | | 2010–2014 | | 2015–2017 | | Total |
|---|---|---|---|---|---|---|---|
| **# of counts** | | | | | | | |
| **Asia-Pacific** | | | | | | | |
| Japan | 2,483 | 14.4% | 2,276 | 16.5% | 932 | 11.0% | 5,691 |
| Singapore | 469 | 2.7% | 639 | 4.6% | 483 | 5.7% | 1,591 |
| Hong Kong | 422 | 2.5% | 593 | 4.3% | 771 | 9.1% | 1,786 |
| China | 2,287 | 13.3% | 2,451 | 17.8% | 2,012 | 23.8% | 6,750 |
| **Europe** | | | | | | | |
| Netherlands | 398 | 2.3% | 326 | 2.4% | 221 | 2.6% | 945 |
| U.K. | 477 | 2.8% | 390 | 2.8% | 208 | 2.5% | 1,075 |
| Germany | 440 | 2.6% | 360 | 2.6% | 207 | 2.4% | 1,007 |
| **North America** | | | | | | | |
| U.S. | 2,286 | 13.3% | 1,563 | 11.4% | 1,165 | 13.8% | 5,014 |
| Canada | 250 | 1.5% | 238 | 1.7% | 202 | 2.4% | 690 |
| Total | 17,215 | 100.0% | 13,754 | 100.0% | 8,454 | 100.0% | 39,423 |
| **Amounts[††]** | | | | | | | |
| **Asia-Pacific** | | | | | | | |
| Japan | 8.4 | 14.9% | 14.1 | 18.4% | 4.8 | 7.4% | 27.3 |
| Singapore | 2.8 | 4.9% | 5.1 | 6.7% | 6.8 | 10.4% | 14.6 |
| Hong Kong | 2.3 | 4.0% | 4.4 | 5.7% | 5.5 | 8.4% | 12.1 |
| China | 1.0 | 1.7% | 3.4 | 4.5% | 4.8 | 7.4% | 9.2 |
| **Europe** | | | | | | | |
| Netherlands | 7.0 | 12.4% | 5.9 | 7.7% | 3.8 | 5.8% | 16.7 |
| U.K. | 6.6 | 11.7% | 2.5 | 3.2% | 2.9 | 4.5% | 12.0 |
| Germany | 2.9 | 5.1% | 2.8 | 3.6% | 1.6 | 2.4% | 7.2 |
| **North America** | | | | | | | |
| U.S. | 9.6 | 16.9% | 15.2 | 19.8% | 14.1 | 21.6% | 38.8 |
| Canada | 0.7 | 1.3% | 2.6 | 3.3% | 1.9 | 2.9% | 5.2 |
| Total | 56.5 | 100.0% | 76.6 | 100.0% | 65.1 | 100.0% | 198.0 |

[†] Author's calculation based on inbound FDI statistics from the Investment Notification Statistics Center in Korea (http://insc.kisc.org/).
[††] In billion US$.

**TABLE 5.4** Inbound FDI into Korea by industry[†]

|  | 2005–2009 | | 2010–2014 | | 2015–2017 | | Total |
|---|---|---|---|---|---|---|---|
| **# of counts** | | | | | | | |
| Manufacturing | 3,261 | 18.9% | 2,720 | 19.8% | 1,634 | 19.3% | 7,615 |
| Service | 13,576 | 78.9% | 10,742 | 78.1% | 6,645 | 78.6% | 30,963 |
| Others | 378 | 2.2% | 292 | 2.1% | 175 | 2.1% | 845 |
| Total | 17,215 | 100.0% | 13,754 | 100.0% | 8,454 | 100.0% | 39,423 |
| **Amounts[††]** | | | | | | | |
| Manufacturing | 16.6 | 29.4% | 30.5 | 39.8% | 16.8 | 25.8% | 63.9 |
| Service | 38.5 | 68.1% | 43.9 | 57.3% | 45.6 | 70.0% | 128.0 |
| Others | 1.4 | 2.5% | 2.2 | 2.9% | 2.7 | 4.2% | 6.3 |
| Total | 56.5 | 100.0% | 76.6 | 100.0% | 65.1 | 100.0% | 198.0 |

[†] Author's calculation based on inbound FDI statistics from the Investment Notification Statistics Center in Korea (http://insc.kisc.org/).
[††] In billion US$.

between 2005 and 2009 to 57.3% between 2010 and 2014: however, it has recovered back to 70.0% in the most recent three years. Concurrently, the proportion of other industrial sectors such as agriculture, mining, energy, and utilities has been increasing from 2.5% to 4.2% for the past decade, signifying Korea's greater openness to diverse foreign investors.

Tables 5.5 and 5.6 provide similar pictures to Table 5.2 when inbound FDI notifications to Korea from each of the world geographic regions are examined by different industrial sectors. In manufacturing industries, Asia-Pacific has been the largest source region of inbound FDI into Korea in terms of both total counts and amounts, although the region's impact seems to have become weaker with about 40% when its total invested amounts are considered in Table 5.5. In service industries, on the other hand, foreign investors from Asia-Pacific have been dominating in market entry into Korea with more than 60% of their proportion when their total counts are evaluated in Table 5.6. It should be noted in the same table that, when the total invested amounts are evaluated, the most important source region for inbound FDI in service industries has been Europe with 50.7% from 2005 to 2009: however, Asia-Pacific, Korea's home triad region, has become more important for inbound FDI in service industries after the period, with proportions of 45.2% for 2010 to 2014 and 39.1% for 2015 to 2017, respectively. In addition, Table 5.6 also shows that Europe lost the status of the second-largest investors in service

**TABLE 5.5** Inbound FDI into Korea by region in manufacturing[†]

|  | 2005–2009 | | 2010–2014 | | 2015–2017 | | Total |
|---|---|---|---|---|---|---|---|
| # of counts |  |  |  |  |  |  |  |
| Asia-Pacific | 1,594 | 48.9% | 1,543 | 56.7% | 886 | 54.2% | 4,023 |
| Europe | 703 | 21.6% | 572 | 21.0% | 342 | 20.9% | 1,617 |
| North America | 744 | 22.8% | 439 | 16.1% | 315 | 19.3% | 1,498 |
| South America | 183 | 5.6% | 122 | 4.5% | 67 | 4.1% | 372 |
| Africa–M. East | 36 | 1.1% | 41 | 1.5% | 21 | 1.3% | 98 |
| Others | 1 | 0.03% | 3 | 0.1% | 3 | 0.2% | 7 |
| Total | 3,261 | 100.0% | 2,720 | 100.0% | 1,634 | 100.0% | 7,615 |
| Amounts[††] |  |  |  |  |  |  |  |
| Asia-Pacific | 6.7 | 40.3% | 11.9 | 39.2% | 6.6 | 39.0% | 25.2 |
| Europe | 6.5 | 39.2% | 11.2 | 36.8% | 6.3 | 37.3% | 24.0 |
| North America | 2.7 | 15.9% | 6.0 | 19.8% | 3.5 | 20.6% | 12.2 |
| South America | 0.7 | 4.2% | 0.7 | 2.3% | 0.3 | 2.0% | 1.7 |
| Africa–M. East | 0.07 | 0.4% | 0.6 | 1.9% | 0.2 | 1.1% | 0.9 |
| Others[†††] | 1.0 | 0.01% | 1.9 | 0.01% | 0.5 | 0.003% | 3.4 |
| Total | 16.6 | 100.0% | 30.5 | 100.0% | 16.8 | 100.0% | 63.9 |

[†] Author's calculation based on inbound FDI statistics from the Investment Notification Statistics Center in Korea (http://insc.kisc.org/).
[††] In billion US$.
[†††] In million US$.

**TABLE 5.6** Inbound FDI into Korea by region in service[†]

|  | 2005–2009 |  | 2010–2014 |  | 2015–2017 |  | Total |
|---|---|---|---|---|---|---|---|
| # of counts |  |  |  |  |  |  |  |
| Asia-Pacific | 8,214 | 60.5% | 6,489 | 60.4% | 4,096 | 61.6% | 18,799 |
| Europe | 1,736 | 12.8% | 1,616 | 15.0% | 927 | 14.0% | 4,279 |
| North America | 1,727 | 12.7% | 1,337 | 12.4% | 1,039 | 15.6% | 4,103 |
| South America | 397 | 2.9% | 344 | 3.2% | 249 | 3.7% | 990 |
| Africa–M. East | 1,498 | 11.0% | 933 | 8.7% | 333 | 5.0% | 2,764 |
| Others | 4 | 0.03% | 23 | 0.2% | 1 | 0.02% | 28 |
| Total | 13,576 | 100.0% | 10,742 | 100.0% | 6,645 | 100.0% | 30,963 |
| Amounts[††] |  |  |  |  |  |  |  |
| Asia-Pacific | 9.9 | 25.6% | 19.8 | 45.2% | 17.8 | 39.1% | 47.5 |
| Europe | 19.5 | 50.7% | 11.1 | 25.3% | 10.6 | 23.4% | 41.3 |
| North America | 7.3 | 18.8% | 10.7 | 24.4% | 12.3 | 26.9% | 30.2 |
| South America | 1.2 | 3.2% | 1.9 | 4.2% | 3.4 | 7.5% | 6.5 |
| Africa–M. East | 0.7 | 1.7% | 0.4 | 0.9% | 1.5 | 3.2% | 2.5 |
| Others[†††] | 0.2 | 0.0004% | 3.6 | 0.01% | 0.1 | 0.0002% | 3.9 |
| Total | 38.5 | 100.0% | 43.9 | 100.0% | 45.6 | 100.0% | 128.0 |

[†] Author's calculation based on inbound FDI statistics from the Investment Notification Statistics Center in Korea (http://insc.kisc.org/).
[††] In billion US$.
[†††] In million US$.

industries to North America in the recent three years in terms of both counts and amounts. It is partly due to the U.S.–Korea Free Trade Agreement (KORUS FTA) signed on June 30, 2007, and entered into force on March 15, 2012, which brought the U.S. services trade surplus with Korea.

The salience of inbound FDI notifications to Korea in service industries from Asia-Pacific, Korea's home region of the triad, is related to the main characteristics of service sectors that may be different from those of manufacturing sectors. First of all, services that MNEs provide to their customers in foreign markets can neither be stored nor are unperishable for a long time, and, as a result, it is indispensable for MNEs to locate close to foreign customers to serve them effectively and efficiently (Anand & Delios, 1997; Capar & Kotabe, 2003; Contractor et al., 2003; Goerzen & Makino, 2007). Second, partly due to the first feature of service sectors, service MNEs conducting FDI projects in foreign countries have to work on intensive localization and adaptation strategies to better understand heterogeneous tastes and preferences possessed by local foreign customers (Asakawa et al., 2013; Capar & Kotabe, 2003; Contractor et al., 2003; Goerzen & Makino, 2007; Rugman & Verbeke, 2008a). Both of these unique features in service sectors may provide stronger competitive advantages to MNEs from nearby home-region countries of the triad versus those from remote host-region countries in conducting service-related outbound FDI activities.

## Inbound FDI into Korea by country of origin

Table 5.7 reports data on inbound FDI notifications to Korea by OECD versus non-OECD countries of origin where foreign investors are headquartered. Foreign investors from OECD countries invested in 17,281 projects with total amounts of US$129.0 billion for thirteen years from 2005 to 2017. Foreign investors from non-OECD countries are shown to have been undertaking more than 55% of inbound FDI notifications to Korea over the same period in terms of counts: however, their proportions in amounts are far below one third the total amounts of inbound FDI from 2005 to 2014. A notable observation from the same table is that the role of non-OECD investors has been incomparable to that of OECD investors until the most recent three years: both groups of foreign investors are shown to become even in the proportions of their invested amounts in Korea only for 2015 to 2017.

The statistical evidence in Table 5.7 reinforces the meaning and importance of country-of-origin effects on inbound FDI projects in host countries. Considering that the possession of advanced FSAs in either upstream technological value chains or downstream marketing/distribution channels may enable foreign investors to conduct direct investment projects in unfamiliar host countries (Hymer, 1976; Rugman, 1981, 2005), foreign investors and their MNEs that have originated from advanced economies are equipped with stronger manufacturing technology, innovation capabilities, management skills, and brand recognition than their counterparts that have home country origins in developing and/or underdeveloped economies. It is because, as Nachum (2003) argues, the competitive advantages of MNEs are partly shaped by the resources from their home countries (Wang et al., 2009), and the home country-based advantages endow MNEs with superior FSAs, especially when the home countries concerned possess superior CSAs compared to the host countries where MNEs invest. As such, when MNEs are equipped with strong upstream and downstream FSAs accumulated in their competitive home

**TABLE 5.7** Inbound FDI into Korea by country of origin[†]

|  | 2005–2009 | | 2010–2014 | | 2015–2017 | | Total |
|---|---|---|---|---|---|---|---|
| # of counts |  |  |  |  |  |  |  |
| OECD countries | 7,501 | 43.6% | 6,177 | 44.9% | 3,603 | 42.6% | 17,281 |
| Non-OECD countries | 9,714 | 56.4% | 7,577 | 55.1% | 4,851 | 57.4% | 22,142 |
| Total | 17,215 | 100.0% | 13,754 | 100.0% | 8,454 | 100.0% | 39,423 |
| Amounts[††] |  |  |  |  |  |  |  |
| OECD countries | 44.0 | 77.9% | 51.7 | 67.6% | 32.8 | 50.4% | 129.0 |
| Non-OECD countries | 12.5 | 22.1% | 24.8 | 32.4% | 32.3 | 49.6% | 69.7 |
| Total | 56.5 | 100.0% | 76.6 | 100.0% | 65.1 | 100.0% | 198.0 |

[†] Author's calculation based on inbound FDI statistics from the Investment Notification Statistics Center in Korea (http://insc.kisc.org/).
[††] In billion US$.

country environments, they are able to access local customers of foreign markets better and more effectively than those unequipped with such FSAs. This argument of country-of-origin effects supports the observation that foreign investors from OECD member countries have been undertaking substantial inbound FDI projects of bulky sizes in Korea in terms of their invested amounts.

## Inbound FDI into Korea by subnational region of destination

It is useful and meaningful to examine the final destinations of MNEs' inbound FDI projects within a host country after they decide to enter the foreign market. Although most empirical studies on MNE and FDI location choices have utilized a country as a unit of their analyses, it is the subnational regions within a host country where FDI projects are finally implemented (Chan et al., 2010). It is because subnational regions provide foreign investors with diverse but unique opportunities due to heterogeneous political, institutional, and governmental rules and regulations across neighboring regions (Chan et al., 2010; Meyer & Nguyen, 2005; Sethi et al., 2011), social values and/or cultural traditions that are unique to insiders within the regions (Chan et al., 2010; Tung, 2008), and different developmental stages of economic infrastructure, resource availability, and transactional and congestion costs (Chan et al., 2010; Chung & Alcácer, 2002). That is not an exception to the common classification of metropolitan versus non-metropolitan Seoul areas often attempted in the Korean context, because the majority of the Korean population, firms, financial institutions, labor forces, job opportunities, universities, R&D institutes, and so on have been concentrated in three subnational regions of Seoul, Gyeonggi, and Incheon in Korea, which have been referred to as the metropolitan Seoul areas.

Table 5.8 summarizes data on inbound FDI notifications to Korea for the same period of thirteen years by subnational regions of destination where the direct investment projects are to be located in Korea. It is evident from the table that foreign investors' market entry into Korea have concentrated in the metropolitan Seoul areas of Seoul, Gyeonggi, and Incheon in terms of both their counts and amounts: more than two thirds the total counts and about 60% to 70% of the total amounts of inbound FDI notifications have been consistently located in the three subnational regions of Korea for the periods. It is because foreign investors often would like to exploit agglomeration benefits from their location sites to their overseas business advantages, and as a result, they may recognize that the metropolitan Seoul areas are expected to help the foreign investors gain easy access to downstream customers, upstream intermediary providers, business and research infrastructure, local governments' support, and so on in close proximity. Nevertheless, the same table provides two notable observations on the subnational location choices of inbound FDI into Korea: first, foreign investors' preference for the metropolitan Seoul areas has been in an overall decreasing trend for the past decade, and, second, foreign investors tend to become cautious in choosing subnational location selection at the time of their investment notification because the proportions of those not yet decided about it have been increasing from 4.9% to 17.2% for the past decade.

**TABLE 5.8** Inbound FDI into Korea by subnational region of destination[†]

|  | 2005–2009 |  | 2010–2014 |  | 2015–2017 |  | Total |
|---|---|---|---|---|---|---|---|
| # of counts |  |  |  |  |  |  |  |
| Metropolitan Seoul areas | 12,915 | 75.0% | 9,560 | 69.5% | 5,806 | 68.7% | 28,281 |
| Non-metropolitan Seoul areas | 2,975 | 17.3% | 2,889 | 21.0% | 1,652 | 19.5% | 7,516 |
| Not decided | 1,325 | 7.7% | 1,305 | 9.5% | 996 | 11.8% | 3,626 |
| Total | 17,215 | 100.0% | 13,754 | 100.0% | 8,454 | 100.0% | 39,423 |
| Amounts[††] |  |  |  |  |  |  |  |
| Metropolitan Seoul areas | 39.4 | 69.8% | 43.5 | 56.8% | 39.6 | 60.8% | 122.0 |
| Non-metropolitan Seoul areas | 14.3 | 25.3% | 22.7 | 29.7% | 14.3 | 22.0% | 51.3 |
| Not decided | 2.8 | 4.9% | 10.4 | 13.5% | 11.2 | 17.2% | 24.4 |
| Total | 56.4 | 100.0% | 76.6 | 100.0% | 65.1 | 100.0% | 198.0 |

[†] Author's calculation based on inbound FDI statistics from the Investment Notification Statistics Center in Korea (http://insc.kisc.org/).
[††] In billion US$.

## Inbound FDI into Korea by ownership

According to modern theories of MNEs that have been established in the international business literature, MNEs and foreign investors who own them commonly try to transfer, exploit, and replicate their FSAs in foreign markets resulting in economic integration benefits from their internationalization (Hymer, 1976; Rugman, 1981, 2005). In the internationalization process, MNEs and foreign investors also keep trying to achieve an optimal combination between FSAs and CSAs by accessing immobile county-level resources and capabilities in host countries, such as natural or labor resources, new foreign customers with strong purchasing powers and/or sophisticated scientific knowledge, and know-how that is instrumental for their successful foreign operations therein (Dunning, 1998). When MNEs' attempts to access such immobile country-level resources and capabilities in foreign countries are constrained due to transborder regulations and market imperfections therein, MNEs commonly consider obtaining control and ownership over immobile host CSAs using outbound FDI projects into the host countries (Buckley & Casson, 1976; Rugman, 1981) to minimize potential transaction costs involved in accessing scarce country-level resources in foreign markets (Hennart, 1982, 2009). As such, 100% full ownership of FDI represents that foreign investors and their MNEs undertake both control/decision-making power and potential risks/uncertainties under their full responsibility by setting up wholly owned subsidiaries. On the other hand, a partial ownership structure of FDI in either majority or minority ownership means that foreign investors agree to share with domestic investment partners in host countries both control and risks of their foreign operations, with the former granting MNEs with important decision-making powers.

Table 5.9 reports data on inbound FDI notifications to Korea by the levels of foreign investors' ownership in their FDI projects. In terms of their counts,

**TABLE 5.9** Inbound FDI into Korea by ownership[†]

|  | 2005–2009 | | 2010–2014 | | 2015–2017 | | Total |
|---|---|---|---|---|---|---|---|
| # of counts | | | | | | | |
| Full | 11,029 | 64.1% | 8,831 | 64.2% | 5,197 | 61.5% | 25,057 |
| Majority | 3,129 | 18.2% | 2,692 | 19.6% | 1,788 | 21.1% | 7,609 |
| Minority | 2,945 | 17.1% | 2,149 | 15.6% | 1,401 | 16.6% | 6,495 |
| N/A | 112 | 0.7% | 82 | 0.6% | 68 | 0.8% | 262 |
| Total | 17,215 | 100.0% | 13,754 | 100.0% | 8,454 | 100.0% | 39,423 |
| Amounts[††] | | | | | | | |
| Full | 21.3 | 37.7% | 36.3 | 47.4% | 35.3 | 54.2% | 92.9 |
| Majority | 17.4 | 30.9% | 25.9 | 33.8% | 16.2 | 24.9% | 59.6 |
| Minority | 16.1 | 28.6% | 11.9 | 15.6% | 12.0 | 18.4% | 40.1 |
| N/A | 1.6 | 2.8% | 2.4 | 3.1% | 1.7 | 2.5% | 5.6 |
| Total | 56.4 | 100.0% | 76.6 | 100.0% | 65.1 | 100.0% | 198.0 |

[†] Author's calculation based on inbound FDI statistics from the Investment Notification Statistics Center in Korea (http://insc.kisc.org/).
[††] In billion US$

foreign investors seem to prefer to establish wholly owned subsidiaries when entering Korea, because they invested in 25,057 projects with 100% ownership out of the total 39,423 projects, which constitutes consistently over 60% of inbound FDI notifications to Korea throughout the time series from 2005 to 2017. In terms of their amounts, however, the table shows that foreign investors preferred to share ownership of their FDI projects with domestic investors in Korea until the recent three years from 2015 to 2017. This is because the invested amounts for partially owned subsidiaries using either majority or minority ownership in their FDI projects were greater than those for wholly owned subsidiaries with 59.5% and 49.4% between 2005 and 2009 and between 2010 and 2014, respectively. Both pieces of evidence signify that MNEs conducting inbound FDI into Korea would like to spread potential risks and uncertainties in the form of shared ownership with indigenous Korean partners as they implement their direct investment projects of bulky sizes with high invested amounts.

Table 5.10 shows the world geographic breakdowns in the data on inbound FDI notifications to Korea with foreign investors' full ownership. The table confirms that Asia-Pacific has been the largest source region of inbound FDI into Korea across the thirteen years in terms of total counts when foreign investors use full ownership in their FDI projects. When the total invested amounts are evaluated, on the other hand, the same table also shows that the home triad power from Asia-Pacific seems to become weaker. For example, the most important source region for inbound FDI using full ownership has been Europe with total invested amounts of US$8.8 billion between 2005 and 2009, which are greater than US$6.4 billion that Asia-Pacific, Korea's home triad region, has put into the Korean markets over

**TABLE 5.10** Inbound FDI into Korea with full ownership by region[†]

|  | 2005–2009 | | 2010–2014 | | 2015–2017 | | Total |
|---|---|---|---|---|---|---|---|
| # of counts | | | | | | | |
| Asia-Pacific | 6,822 | 61.9% | 5,413 | 61.3% | 3,124 | 60.1% | 15,359 |
| Europe | 1,369 | 12.4% | 1,431 | 16.2% | 862 | 16.6% | 3,662 |
| North America | 1,360 | 12.3% | 1,000 | 11.3% | 800 | 15.4% | 3,160 |
| South America | 168 | 1.5% | 150 | 1.7% | 114 | 2.2% | 432 |
| Africa–M. East | 1,308 | 11.9% | 817 | 9.3% | 296 | 5.7% | 2,421 |
| Others | 2 | 0.02% | 20 | 0.2% | 1 | 0.02% | 23 |
| Total | 11,029 | 100.0% | 8,831 | 100.0% | 5,197 | 100.0% | 25,057 |
| Amounts[††] | | | | | | | |
| Asia-Pacific | 6.4 | 30.0% | 16.3 | 44.8% | 13.2 | 37.5% | 35.9 |
| Europe | 8.8 | 41.4% | 8.5 | 23.5% | 7.8 | 22.2% | 25.2 |
| North America | 5.7 | 26.5% | 10.8 | 29.8% | 10.4 | 29.4% | 26.9 |
| South America | 0.3 | 1.5% | 0.5 | 1.5% | 2.6 | 7.3% | 3.5 |
| Africa–M. East | 0.1 | 0.5% | 0.2 | 0.5% | 1.3 | 3.6% | 1.5 |
| Others[†††] | 0.080 | 0.0004% | 2.8 | 0.008% | 0.1 | 0.0003% | 3.0 |
| Total | 21.3 | 100.0% | 36.3 | 100.0% | 35.3 | 100.0% | 92.9 |

[†] Author's calculation based on inbound FDI statistics from the Investment Notification Statistics Center in Korea (http://insc.kisc.org/).
[††] In billion US$.
[†††] In million US$.

the same period. However, Asia-Pacific recovered its top status for the periods from 2010 to 2014 and 2015 to 2017 with 44.8% and 37.5%, respectively, of the total amounts invested in each period.

Such observed phenomena in the world geographic breakdowns of inbound FDI may be due to different costs that foreign investors have to pay for when internalizing country-level resources in Korea using inbound FDI. For inbound FDI projects to Korea with full ownership, foreign investors are supposed to take over both business control and risks, and as a result, those from Asia-Pacific are more willing to establish wholly owned subsidiaries than their counterparts from remote regions when entering Korean markets, because they suffer from low levels of cultural, administrative, geographic, and/or economic distances between Korea and their home country within the same triad region (Ghemawat, 2001). As such, the statistical observations in Table 5.10 confirm that the liability of intraregional foreignness is smaller than that of interregional foreignness when foreign investors enter Korean markets using inbound FDI (Rugman & Verbeke, 2007, 2008b).

## Inbound FDI into Korea by investment purpose

Investment purposes of foreign investors are important considerations when evaluating MNEs' inbound FDI projects, because they represent different motivations of FDI that lead to variations in MNEs' decision-making, and the motivations are endogenous to MNEs' strategic decisions about FDI (Hong et al., 2019; Makino et al., 2002). Dunning (1998) suggested four key motivations of FDI that might encourage MNEs to conduct direct investment in host countries. They are (1) resource-seeking motivation, whereby MNEs look for immobile and scarce country-level input resources such as natural or labor resources; (2) market-seeking motivation, whereby MNEs search for local customers who are willing and able to purchase their products and services; (3) efficiency-seeking motivation, whereby MNEs attempt to enhance their production efficiency and/or to further reduce manufacturing costs; and (4) strategic asset-seeking motivation whereby MNEs source sophisticated knowledge assets from foreign countries. Although not perfectly clear-cut, the market-seeking motivation of FDI is often implemented by establishing business offices in the areas of a large number of customers with strong purchasing powers. Establishing factories in host countries are often to achieve such motivations of resource, efficiency, and strategic asset seeking. Mergers and acquisitions are often used as one way for MNEs to upgrade their current scientific and innovative capabilities by purchasing capable local firms with knowledge assets in foreign countries.

Table 5.11 summarizes data on inbound FDI notifications to Korea over the period between 2005 and 2017 by foreign investors' investment purposes into Korea. It is evident from the table that foreign investors would like to use Korea for conducting downstream-side business activities in terms of both their counts and amounts. More than 80% of foreign investors consistently reported establishing business offices as their main investment purposes into Korea, which

**TABLE 5.11** Inbound FDI into Korea by investment purpose[†]

|  | 2005–2009 | | 2010–2014 | | 2015–2017 | | Total |
|---|---|---|---|---|---|---|---|
| # of counts |  |  |  |  |  |  |  |
| Establishing offices | 14,545 | 84.5% | 11,540 | 83.9% | 7,069 | 83.6% | 33,154 |
| Establishing factories | 998 | 5.8% | 942 | 6.8% | 447 | 5.3% | 2,387 |
| Mergers & acquisitions | 82 | 0.5% | 139 | 1.0% | 169 | 2.0% | 390 |
| N/A | 1,590 | 9.2% | 1,133 | 8.2% | 769 | 9.1% | 3,492 |
| Total | 17,215 | 100.0% | 13,754 | 100.0% | 8,454 | 100.0% | 39,423 |
| Amounts[††] |  |  |  |  |  |  |  |
| Establishing offices | 28.9 | 51.1% | 39.6 | 51.7% | 39.3 | 60.3% | 108.0 |
| Establishing factories | 8.4 | 14.9% | 16.3 | 21.3% | 5.5 | 8.5% | 30.2 |
| Mergers & acquisitions | 4.3 | 7.7% | 9.1 | 11.9% | 9.7 | 14.9% | 23.1 |
| N/A | 14.8 | 26.3% | 11.6 | 15.1% | 10.7 | 16.4% | 37.1 |
| Total | 56.4 | 100.0% | 76.6 | 100.0% | 65.1 | 100.0% | 198.0 |

[†] Author's calculation based on inbound FDI statistics from the Investment Notification Statistics Center in Korea (http://insc.kisc.org/).
[††] In billion US$.

constitutes over the majority of their total invested amounts made in the same period. In addition, two observations are worth being noted from the same table: first, the attractiveness of Korea for efficient manufacturing sites seems to have been reduced in recent years, because the proportion of establishing factories as foreign investors' main investment purposes has decreased substantially from 21.3% between 2010 and 2014 to 8.5% between 2015 and 2017 in terms of their amounts, and second, Korean firms seem to have been more attractive targets for foreign investors' M&As for the past decade, because the proportion of foreign investors' citing that purpose has increased substantially from 7.7% between 2005 and 2009 to 14.9% between 2015 and 2017 in terms of their invested amounts.

Tables 5.12 through 5.14 report data on inbound FDI notifications to Korea by subnational regions of their final destinations per each of the three investment purposes into Korea. It is evident from Table 5.12 that foreign investors' market entry into Korea for the purpose of establishing business offices has been concentrating in the metropolitan Seoul areas of Seoul, Gyeonggi, and Incheon in terms of both their counts and amounts. From Table 5.13, on the other hand, foreign investors seem to have been moving toward the non-metropolitan areas outside Seoul, Gyeonggi, and Incheon to look for manufacturing sites to establish factories. However, foreign investors are returning to the metropolitan Seoul areas for hunting their mergers and acquisitions targets, especially in recent years. Reflecting this, Table 5.14 shows that the proportions of inbound FDI into Korea with the purpose of M&As in the metropolitan Seoul areas are 82.2% in terms of their counts and 85.2% in terms of their amounts over the recent period between 2015 and 2017.

**TABLE 5.12** Inbound FDI into Korea for establishing offices by subnational region[†]

| | 2005–2009 | | 2010–2014 | | 2015–2017 | | Total |
|---|---|---|---|---|---|---|---|
| # of counts | | | | | | | |
| Metropolitan Seoul areas | 11,214 | 77.1% | 8,190 | 71.0% | 4,927 | 69.7% | 24,331 |
| Non-metropolitan Seoul areas | 2,042 | 14.0% | 2,115 | 18.3% | 1,196 | 16.9% | 5,353 |
| Not decided | 1,289 | 8.9% | 1,235 | 10.7% | 946 | 13.4% | 3,470 |
| Total | 14,545 | 100.0% | 11,540 | 100.0% | 7,069 | 100.0% | 33,154 |
| Amounts[††] | | | | | | | |
| Metropolitan Seoul areas | 20.6 | 71.5% | 23.3 | 59.0% | 22.6 | 57.6% | 66.6 |
| Non-metropolitan Seoul areas | 6.0 | 20.7% | 8.8 | 22.3% | 7.2 | 18.2% | 22.0 |
| Not decided | 2.3 | 7.8% | 7.4 | 18.7% | 9.5 | 24.2% | 19.2 |
| Total | 28.9 | 100.0% | 39.6 | 100.0% | 39.3 | 100.0% | 108.0 |

[†] Author's calculation based on inbound FDI statistics from the Investment Notification Statistics Center in Korea (http://insc.kisc.org/).

[††] In billion US$.

**TABLE 5.13** Inbound FDI into Korea for establishing factories by subnational region[†]

|  | 2005–2009 | | 2010–2014 | | 2015–2017 | | Total |
|---|---|---|---|---|---|---|---|
| **# of counts** | | | | | | | |
| Metropolitan Seoul areas | 459 | 46.0% | 434 | 46.1% | 169 | 37.8% | 1,062 |
| Non-metropolitan Seoul areas | 506 | 50.7% | 448 | 47.6% | 238 | 53.2% | 1,192 |
| Not decided | 33 | 3.3% | 60 | 6.4% | 40 | 8.9% | 133 |
| Total | 998 | 100.0% | 942 | 100.0% | 447 | 100.0% | 2,387 |
| **Amounts[††]** | | | | | | | |
| Metropolitan Seoul areas | 3.3 | 39.2% | 4.9 | 30.1% | 1.7 | 31.3% | 9.9 |
| Non-metropolitan Seoul areas | 4.6 | 54.5% | 8.7 | 53.5% | 3.2 | 58.1% | 16.5 |
| Not decided | 0.5 | 6.2% | 2.7 | 16.4% | 0.6 | 10.6% | 3.8 |
| Total | 8.4 | 100.0% | 16.3 | 100.0% | 5.5 | 100.0% | 30.2 |

[†] Author's calculation based on inbound FDI statistics from the Investment Notification Statistics Center in Korea (http://insc.kisc.org/).
[††] In billion US$.

**TABLE 5.14** Inbound FDI into Korea for M&As by subnational region[†]

|  | 2005–2009 | | 2010–2014 | | 2015–2017 | | Total |
|---|---|---|---|---|---|---|---|
| **# of counts** | | | | | | | |
| Metropolitan Seoul areas | 62 | 75.6% | 111 | 79.9% | 139 | 82.2% | 312 |
| Non-metropolitan Seoul areas | 17 | 20.7% | 20 | 14.4% | 21 | 12.4% | 58 |
| Not decided | 3 | 3.7% | 8 | 5.8% | 9 | 5.3% | 20 |
| Total | 82 | 100.0% | 139 | 100.0% | 169 | 100.0% | 390 |
| **Amounts[††]** | | | | | | | |
| Metropolitan Seoul areas | 3.2 | 74.1% | 6.6 | 72.6% | 8.3 | 85.2% | 18.1 |
| Non-metropolitan Seoul areas | 1.1 | 25.8% | 2.2 | 24.2% | 0.3 | 3.1% | 3.6 |
| Not decided | 0.001 | 0.01% | 0.3 | 3.2% | 1.1 | 11.7% | 1.4 |
| Total | 4.3 | 100.0% | 9.1 | 100.0% | 9.7 | 100.0% | 23.1 |

[†] Author's calculation based on inbound FDI statistics from the Investment Notification Statistics Center in Korea (http://insc.kisc.org/).
[††] In billion US$.

## Mini-case study on inbound FDI into Korea[1]

### Yuzhen from China: resource-seeking and market-seeking FDI

Having made trade transactions with the top steelmaker POSCO in Korea since 2010, Gansu Yuzhen Logistics Group Co. Ltd. in China identified an unexplored business opportunity in Korea and decided to conduct FDI projects by establishing Yuzhen International Korea in Pohang, Korea in 2015. Yuzhen International Korea is a manufacturing subsidiary producing silicon metal that is a key material for making semiconductors and solar cells. Yuzhen International Korea chose Pohang as its optimal location to exploit several CSAs of the Pohang area to enhance their business advantage. First, as a home to the Korean steelmaker POSCO, and as a significant industrial and coastal city of Korea, Pohang is already equipped with well-developed manufacturing and scientific infrastructure for producing silicon metal, such as geographic proximity to the seaport in the city, highly skilled retired employees from POSCO, and technical support from the renowned physical sciences university POSTECH. Second, Yuzhen International Korea could use land for its manufacturing facility free of charge for fifty years as a part of foreign-invested businesses. Last, sludge from the silicon metal production process can be purchased and recycled by POSCO, because this sludge prevents the sulfur smoke that is accompanied in the manufacturing process of steel and steel strips: in addition, Yuzhen International Korea can utilize the liquefied carbon dioxide and oxygen from the POSCO's steel mills, which are indispensable for manufacturing silicon metal.

Yuzhen International Korea is a type of (natural) resource-seeking FDI in Korea, because they secure their access to quartzite, the main raw material for silicon metal, from another mining subsidiary established by Gansu Yuzhen Logistics Group Co. Ltd. in Jangsu, Jeolla Province. Yuzhen International Korea also contains a feature of market-seeking FDI in Korea, because despite Korea's high demand for 70,000 tons of silicon metal every year, there has been no domestic production of silicon metal in the country until Yuzhen International Korea initiated this FDI project in 2015. As such, Yuzhen International Korea is expected not only to substitute for the import of silicon metal from foreign countries using their own domestic production in Pohang, Korea but also to contribute to the development of regional economies in Jangsu, Jeolla Province, with their FDI projects.

## Conclusion

After analyzing the statistical data on inbound FDI notifications to Korea over the thirteen years between 2005 and 2017, I discussed the main observations from the data in terms of theoretical and empirical aspects from the previous IB literature. The data suggest that inbound FDI into Korean markets have consistently increased over the period with a strong regional dimension from Asia-Pacific, especially in service industries, with the country of origin in OECD member countries, toward the metropolitan Seoul areas within Korea, using full ownership, and for the investment purpose of establishing business offices. In addition, this chapter confirms that the main observations from the data are in line with theoretical predictions and empirical evidence from previous studies in the IB literature.

Overall, it seems that three main shifts in the relationship between MNEs and host-country governments, identified by Rugman et al. (2005) and confirmed in Lee and Rugman (2009), are still valid in the Korean context of inbound FDI into the country. First, the increased counts and amounts of inbound FDI into Korea, in connection with the Korean government's incentive measures for foreign investors, demonstrate the goal complementarity between MNEs and the Korean government even after the early 2000s. Second, the proliferation of inbound FDI with full ownership for business offices established in the metropolitan Seoul areas by service MNEs from nearby Asia-Pacific countries signifies MNEs' achievement of national responsiveness in Korea by making successful local market penetration. Third, it is evident that a series of government policies played a pivotal role in supporting the bargaining process between MNEs and the Korean government policy in the process of the country's attracting sophisticated foreign investors.

The managerial and policy implications from this chapter are twofold. For prospective managers of MNEs considering market entry, especially using direct investment, into Korea, they are advised to scrutinize the firm-, industry-, home country-, host country-, and region-level profiles of their precedent investors' inbound FDI projects implemented in the country. This is because MNEs' FDI strategy is to search for the best and optimal complementarity between their FSAs and CSAs and to find the best fit between their overseas business and customers in the context of subnational regions within a host country. For public policy makers of host-country governments in charge of attracting foreign investors, it is important to recognize the meaning of the strong regional nature of the inbound FDI notifications to Korea: although they may be tempted to lure all potential investors from every corner of the world, MNEs' foreign operations and especially their direct investment plans are a highly regional rather than global phenomena. As such, they are advised to select relevant strategic regions when customizing public policy measures to attract inbound FDI within their national border.

## Acknowledgments

I would like to thank Director General H.-K. Yeo at the Korean Ministry of Trade, Industry & Energy (MOTIE) for granting me access to the inbound FDI statistics in Korea for this chapter.

## Note

1  The case study was selected and reorganized from Invest Korea (2017) in which a total of twenty cases of successful inbound FDI into Korea are available for further interested readers.

## Bibliography

### Key references

Dunning, J. H. 1998. Location and the multinational enterprise: A neglected factor? *Journal of International Business Studies*, 29(1): 45–66.
Ghemawat, P. 2001. Distance still matters: The hard reality of global expansion. *Harvard Business Review*, 79(8): 137–147.

Lee, I. H., & Rugman, A. M. 2009. Multinationals and public policy in Korea. *Asian Business & Management*, 8(1): 59–82.

Rugman, A. M. 2005. *The regional multinationals*. Cambridge: Cambridge University Press.

Rugman, A. M., & Verbeke, A. 2004. A perspective on regional and global strategies of multinational enterprises. *Journal of International Business Studies*, 35(1): 3–18.

## Online sources

Invest Korea: www.investkorea.org/kr/index.do/

Investment Notification Statistics Center in Korea: http://insc.kisc.org/

Korean Statistical Information Service: http://kosis.kr/index/index.do/

## References

Almodóvar, P., & Rugman, A. M. 2015. Testing the revisited Uppsala model: Does insidership improve international performance? *International Marketing Review*, 32(6): 686–712.

Anand, J., & Delios, A. 1997. Location specificity and the transferability of downstream assets to foreign subsidiaries. *Journal of International Business Studies*, 28: 579–603.

Arregle, J. L., Beamish, P. W., & Hébert, L. 2009. The regional dimension of MNEs' foreign subsidiary localization. *Journal of International Business Studies*, 40(1): 86–107.

Asakawa, K., Ito, K., Rose, E., & Westney, D. E. 2013. Internationalization in Japan's service industries. *Asia Pacific Journal of Management*, 30(4): 1155–1168.

Buckley, P. J., & Casson, M. 1976. *The future of the multinational enterprise*. London: Holmes and Meier.

Capar, N., & Kotabe, M. 2003. The relationship between international diversification and performance in service firms. *Journal of International Business Studies*, 34: 345–355.

Chan, C. M., Makino, S., & Isobe, T. 2010. Does subnational region matter? Foreign affiliate performance in the United States and China. *Strategic Management Journal*, 31: 1226–1243.

Chung, W., & Alcácer, J. 2002. Knowledge seeking and location choice of foreign direct investment in the United States. *Management Science*, 48(12): 1534–1554.

Contractor, F. J., Kundu, S. K., & Hsu, C. 2003. A three-stage theory of international expansion: The link between multinationality and performance in the service sector. *Journal of International Business Studies*, 34: 5–18.

Dunning, J. H. 1998. Location and the multinational enterprise: A neglected factor? *Journal of International Business Studies*, 29(1): 45–66.

Ghemawat, P. 2001. Distance still matters: The hard reality of global expansion. *Harvard Business Review*, 79(8): 137–147.

Goerzen, A., & Makino, S. 2007. Multinational corporation internationalization in the service sector: A study of Japanese trading companies. *Journal of International Business Studies*, 38: 1149–1169.

Hennart, J. F. 1982. *A theory of multinational enterprise*. Ann Arbor: University of Michigan Press.

Hennart, J. F. 2009. The theories of the multinational enterprise. In A.M. Rugman (Ed.), *The Oxford handbook of international business* (2nd Edition): 125–145. Oxford: Oxford University Press.

Hong, E., Lee, I. H., & Makino, S. 2019. Outbound Foreign Direct Investment (FDI) Motivation and Domestic Employment by Multinational Enterprises (MNEs). *Journal of International Management*, https://doi.org/10.1016/j.intman.2018.11.003.

Hymer, S. H. 1976. *The international operations of national firms: A study of direct foreign investment*. Cambridge, MA: MIT Press.

Invest Korea. 2006. *How to take cash grants*. Seoul, Korea, IK: KOTRA.

Invest Korea. 2017. *2017 KOTRA success cases of foreign-invested companies*. Seoul, Korea, IK: KOTRA.

Johanson, J., & Vahlne, J. E. 1977. The internationalization process of the firm: A model of knowledge development and increasing foreign market commitments. *Journal of International Business Studies*, 8(1): 23–32.

Johanson, J., & Vahlne, J. E. 1990. The mechanism of internationalization. *International Marketing Review*, 7(4): 11–24.

Korea, Ministry of Commerce, Industry and Energy. 2003. *Performance of the attraction of inward FDI for the past 5 years: Special report to the minister*. Seoul, Korea, IK: MOTIE.

Korea, Ministry of Trade, Industry and Energy. 2016. *Directions for FDI*. Seoul, Korea, IK: MOTIE.

Lee, I. H. 2010. The M Curve: The performance of born regional firms from Korea. *Multinational Business Review*, 18(4): 1–22.

Lee, I. H. 2013. The M Curve and the multinationality-performance relationship of Korean INVs. *Multinational Business Review*, 21(3): 214–231.

Lee, I. H., & Marvel, M. R. 2009. The moderating effects of home region orientation on R&D investment and international SME performance: Lessons from Korea. *European Management Journal*, 27(5): 316–326.

Lee, I. H., & Rugman, A. M. 2009. Multinationals and public policy in Korea. *Asian Business & Management*, 8(1): 59–82.

Lee, I. H., & Rugman, A. M. 2012. Firm-specific advantages, inward FDI origins, and performance of multinational enterprises. *Journal of International Management*, 18(2): 132–146.

Lopez, L. E., Kundu, S. K., & Ciravegna, L. 2009. Born global or born regional? Evidence from an exploratory study in the Costa Rican software industry. *Journal of International Business Studies*, 40(7): 1228–1238.

Makino, S., Lau, C. M., & Yeh, R. S. 2002. Asset exploitation versus asset seeking: Implications for location choice of foreign direct investment. *Journal of International Business Studies*, 33(3): 403–421.

Meyer, K. E., & Nguyen, H.V. 2005. Foreign investment strategies and subnational institutions in emerging markets: Evidence from Vietnam. *Journal of Management Studies*, 42(1): 63–93.

Nachum, L. 2003. Liability of foreignness in global competition? Financial service affiliates in the city of London. *Strategic Management Journal*, 24: 1187–1208.

Rugman, A. M. 1981. *Inside the multinationals: The economics of internal markets*. New York: Columbia University Press.

Rugman, A. M. 2005. *The regional multinationals*. Cambridge: Cambridge University Press.

Rugman, A. M., & Verbeke, A. 2001. Subsidiary-specific advantages in multinational enterprises. *Strategic Management Journal*, 22(3): 237–250.

Rugman, A. M., & Verbeke, A. 2004. A perspective on regional and global strategies of multinational enterprises. *Journal of International Business Studies*, 35(1): 3–18.

Rugman, A. M., & Verbeke, A. 2007. Liabilities of regional foreignness and the use of firm-level versus country-level data: A response to Dunning et al. (2007). *Journal of International Business Studies*, 38(1): 200–205.

Rugman, A. M., & Verbeke, A. 2008a. A new perspective on the regional and global strategies of multinational services firms. *Management International Review*, 48(4): 397–411.

Rugman, A. M., & Verbeke, A. 2008b. The theory and practice of regional strategy: A response to Osegowitsch and Sammartino. *Journal of International Business Studies*, 39(2): 326–332.

Rugman, A. M., Verbeke, A., & Greidanus, N. 2005. Multinational enterprises and governments: An analysis of new trends. In M. J. Epstein & K. Hanson (Eds.), *The accountable corporation*: 145–169. Westport, CT: Praeger.

Sethi, D., Judge, W. Q., & Sun, Q. 2011. FDI distribution within China: An integrative conceptual framework for analyzing intra-country FDI variations. *Asia Pacific Journal of Management*, 28: 325–352.

Tung, R. L. 2008. The cross-cultural research imperative: The need to balance cross-national and intra-national diversity. *Journal of International Business Studies*, 39(1): 41–46.

Wang, C., Clegg, J., & Kafouros, M. 2009. Country-of-origin effects of foreign direct investment. *Management International Review*, 49(2): 179–198.

# 6

# EXPORTING TO KOREA

*Justin Paul and Hyunji Lee*

## Introduction

Exporting is one of the most commonly used and less risky entry modes when a firm is entering a foreign market, as it involves the least amount of internationalization. Exporting is considered a popular entry mode in comparison to M&As, international joint ventures and strategic alliances. According to the UNCTAD 2017 world investment report (UNCTAD, 2017), Seoul, Korea's metropolitan capital, is ranked fifth among 133 cities in terms of ease of doing business. With limited natural resources, Korea is highly dependent on international trade with a ratio of 80% of its GDP (Samil PWC, 2017). Korea exports a substantial portion of its manufactured goods and imports a variety of products. Chapter 2, on the economic environment, provides further information about the involvement of Korea in international trade. Recent FTAs with more than 15 countries and regions further increase the attractiveness of Korea as an export market for foreign companies. Hence, Korea offers global firms a promising atmosphere. You might then wonder: How can one ensure success in international business in Korea and what should one be careful of? To answer these questions, this chapter focuses on exporting to Korea and mainly discusses different dimensions of exporting to Korea. We begin with exporting as an entry mode and discuss the general aspects of export, then the opportunities for entering Korea through export and the risks that could follow. Next, the chapter gives some practical examples of how firms from different industries can utilize the specific local circumstances and enter the Korean market successfully.

## Exports in general

It is important to acknowledge that we are living in the era of globalization and as part of this globalization process, there is a need to trade products and services internationally in order to survive and leverage global opportunities. Therefore, studies have shown that, today, it is easier, in contrast to the past, for firms and companies, regardless of size, to sell goods and services across the globe (Paul et al., 2017). Exporting is a particularly attractive foreign entry mode for SMEs because of its low risk and little cost (Paul et al., 2017). Thus, the volume and number of exports from small and medium-sized companies have increased substantially in recent years. In the following, we define *exporting*.

Exports are the goods and services produced in one country and purchased by people in another country. In other words, it is worth noting that exports are the exchange of goods or services between two countries, where one of them is the producer. Exports have a substantial effect on the economy (Amadeo, 2019). Also, if the product or service is manufactured domestically and sold to other buyers from foreign countries, it is defined as an export. Exports are considered one of the oldest forms of international business that occur between nations. Technological developments have facilitated various exporting methods for products, goods, and information, including air shipping, mail, hand delivery, shipping by vessel, uploading and downloading from an internet site and so on. The export of services includes the distribution of information sent as an email, an email attachment or a fax.

Governments all over the world, in general, support and encourage exportation (Paul & Aserkar, 2013). Export helps in creating jobs, higher wages and brings improvement in the living standards of citizens. As their exports increase, in tandem countries' competitive advantages increase. The success of Japan and Korea between the 1960s and 1980s and in the 1990s, respectively, are attributed to their success in exports. Thus, they have carved a niche for themselves are now among the best providers of products in for example technology (Investopia, 2019). Economic growth is another effect of exporting. A government's diplomacy and foreign policy must facilitate economic trade in such a way that all trading parties obtain benefits. Exports then become a crucial component of a country's economy. Exportation facilitates employment generation and, in turn, stimulates domestic economic activities by creating employment, enhancing production and increasing revenues.

## Importance and characteristics of exports

Every country in the world is involved in some form of exporting of products or services. The growth of an economy is directly related to its exports. For example, Korean companies have succeeded in exporting cars and electronics while Arab companies export oil and petroleum products. It is important for a country to export, as they can generate revenue in terms of foreign exchange. Excess of imports over exports can adversely affect the process of economic growth. Ultimately, a lower export rate can mean a lower level of foreign exchange reserves. Similarly, in the international market a nation with lower foreign exchange reserves is perceived to have a low level of purchasing capacity. This was also one of the reasons why Korea and other Asian countries were so heavily affected by the Asian crisis, as described in Chapters 2 and 3 of this book.

Exporting has two distinct benefits: the first one being a low-cost foreign market entry mode, by which a firm can avoid the cost of establishing manufacturing operations in a foreign country, and second, exporting may help a company achieve experience curve effects and location economies (Hill, 2015). On the other hand, exporting does present some disadvantages. First, if a location for low-cost manufacturing exists outside the firm's home country, it may not be appropriate to export from an expensive home country to a low-cost country (Hill, 2015). Therefore, the location that creates more favorable conditions for value creation is the preferable place. Second, transportation cost is a determinant factor, as high transport costs can make exporting expensive or uneconomical, particularly for bulk products. Also, small firms commonly selling goods and services to foreign markets can find it more difficult to manufacture in a foreign country, but they might find it easier to export. However, it should be kept in mind that exporting is more challenging than serving the domestic market (Paul et al., 2017). The inexperience with some trade regulations, cultural distinctions, different languages and foreign-exchange situations are a possible reason for that (Daniels et al., 2007). Also, there are other elements that put a strain on resources and staff, which act as obstacles for exporting.

Exports have certain characteristics that arise from their own nature when they are constituted (Fu et al., 2009). In other words, export behavior depends mainly on the industry characteristics that it belongs to (Cavusgil & Zou, 1994). Among these characteristics are, trade barriers or government laws, regulations, policy, or practices that protect domestic products from foreign competition. Also, they include industry concentration (Zhao & Zou, 2002), industry export intensity (Naidu & Prasad, 1994), industry export orientation (Campa & Goldberg, 1997), industry import protection (Rojec et al., 2004), industry instability (Sakakibara & Porter, 2001), and industry technological intensity (Filatotchev et al., 2008). We can also consider as part of these characteristics, as we mentioned before, the several methods of exporting a product or good, which include mail, hand delivery, air shipping, shipping by vessel, uploading to an internet site or downloading from an internet site.

## Direct exports

Direct exporting can be defined as the process where a producer or supplier directly sells its product to an international market, either through intermediaries – such as sales representatives, distributors, or foreign retailers – or directly selling the product to the end user (Whetzel, 2018). In another definition, direct exporting involves an organization selling goods directly to a customer in an international market (Roy, 2017). Organizations can sell to a wide range of customers, some of whom act as intermediaries in the target market. Even if an intermediary is involved, the export is still direct because the intermediary is a customer based in the target market. Among the most important customers for direct-exporting organizations are importers, wholesalers, distributors, retailers, government procurement departments and consumers themselves. An example of direct export could be selling computer parts to a computer manufacturing plant outside of your country. It is very important to note that direct exporting requires some affirmative action like market research to locate markets for the product, international product distribution, creating a link to the consumers and collections.

There are some advantages for direct exporting to foreign countries including Korea. First, let us look at how direct exports will eliminate middlemen (export companies and most intermediaries), which will lead to greater profits and direct marketing. In direct exporting, sales calls to end-market retailers and resellers, even to companies with a direct need for the product can be handled by the supplier or domestic manufacturer's employees. Another advantage of direct exporting is the fact that all manufacturing is done at local facilities, which eliminates certain risks like those associated with production abroad and political factors in foreign countries. Other benefits to direct exports are: greater control over marketing, faster feedback from foreign markets and better protection of intellectual property rights.

Direct exports are not limited to the previous benefits but also include some disadvantages. The major disadvantages are the incursion of costs in order to create an exporting department, teaching employees about new documentation regarding exports, establishing new export protocols and procedures and attaining the ability to make and receive international payments (Whetzel, 2018). Certain developments in foreign markets such as exchange rate fluctuations and unpredictable orders also contribute to its disadvantages. There are other disadvantageous factors to be considered such as products that are not suitable for exporting like milk or other perishables and the need to invest in market research and the preparation of new marketing strategies. Also, major losses can be incurred due to a lack of exporting skills and experience. Then, there are those difficulties that all exporting firms have to face like breaking into target markets in trade blocs (intergovernmental agreement), difficulties that arise when breaking into markets whose currency is weaker than the company's domestic currency, and the unreliability of intermediaries who represent other organizations and will not always operate with the best interests of the exporting organization in mind. Thus, due to these increased costs, most small and medium-sized companies decide not to use direct exporting to Korea but indirect exporting, which is described next.

## Indirect exporting

Indirect exporting involves an organization that sells to an intermediary in its home country, who in turn sells the said product in the international market, assuming all the responsibility of preparing the paperwork and licenses needed for the shipping and marketing process. Those in charge of indirect exports are responsible for selling to the following intermediary customers: export/trading houses or export merchants, confirmation houses and those foreign organizations based on the organization's home country buying offices. There are two methods of indirect exporting: (1) selling to an export house or merchant exporter and (2) selling to either visiting or resident buyers.

Indirect exporting could be characterized as a fast-growing practice in foreign market entry because it projects less financial outlay for the manufacturer. The firm is not obligated to create or shape an overseas marketing infrastructure. This will result in its financial resources being committed to the lowest level which could create big benefits for indirect exporting (Roy, 2018). Firms with smaller means are unable to develop their own global marketing structure on account of a lack of enough capital to invest. Furthermore, export merchants will pay manufacturers against the purchase of their goods on order, so that their capital is not tied up.

From the firm's point of view, indirect exporting is the easiest way to create an entry strategy to gain access to a foreign market. This means that to some extent this process can be flexible and exporting activities can cease immediately if necessary. One of the most important advantages is that intermediary organizations are the ones in charge of all the exporting activities. This process also means that previous exporting experience is not mandatory. Therefore, all risks associated with shipping and payments to the international markets are assumed by the intermediary.

One of the greatest disadvantages is that the organization loses all control over overseas activities as they are transferred to the intermediary (Roy, 2018). By using indirect exporting, the firms that expand into their target markets are unable to gain any information on how that market operates. This has an adverse impact on the quality of services and/or value-adding activities and, in turn, the company's reputation in foreign markets may suffer. Using the indirect exporting method will also reduce part of the business' margin, not to mention that it will diminish the company's capacity to develop direct relationships or grow any new businesses with customers in foreign markets.

## Exporting to the Korean market

Despite its small geographical size, Korea has gained importance in the international market mainly due to three reasons. First, Korea is a sizeable and growing market. Second, its geographic location in Asia. As Korea is situated in the center of Northeast Asia, it has become a gateway to large markets such as Japan, China, and Southeast Asia. Third, it operates as a global test market due to its tech-savvy, demanding and trendsetting consumers. The Samsonite luggage from Samsonite and Toyota Lexus ES350 from Lexus are both prime examples of having used Korea as a test bed market. In this section, we discuss the characteristics of the Korean market that must be taken into consideration when a firm is exporting to the Korean market.

### Import market in Korea

Land in Korea is limited and does not provide sufficient raw materials and agricultural products. Thus, Korea is heavily dependent on imports for its energy, food and raw materials. The share of import in consumer goods has also been significantly increasing. Korea's top trading partners for imports were China (20.5%),

EU 28 (12.2%), Japan (11.5%), and the US (10.5%) in 2017 (Eurostat, 2018). Germany is the largest exporter to Korea among the EU nations. For the EU, manufactured goods are the most important goods in terms of export to Korea (Eurostat, 2018). The US's exports to Korea have been increasing, especially for basic, intermediate and consumer-oriented products.

## Opportunities in exporting to the market

Overseas companies that are planning to venture into the Korean market should pay attention to the key features of the market in order to get better gains. Active e-commerce, expansion of the premium market, consumer behavior and FTAs are the key features of the Korean market that must be utilized by the company for successful export.

### Active e-commerce

The South Korean infrastructure is highly digitalized (Karippacheril et al., 2016). The country has one of the fastest internet connections in the world. The penetration rate of smartphones in Korea is impressive with a rate of 100% for Koreans aged between 18 and 34 years (Statista, 2018). Accordingly, Koreans are familiar with e-commerce and make great use of mobile phones for commercial purposes. The online shopping transaction volume in Korea has been steadily growing (Statista, 2019a), reaching more than KRW90 trillion in 2017 (approximately 71 billion euro). The leading online platforms in Korea are Coupang, Gmarket, Auction, WeMakePrice, 11 Street and Yes24. These platforms are well known in Korea and highly frequented (Statista, 2019b).

A good example for active online commerce in Korea is Kakaotalk, a popular free mobile instant messenger application with 49 million active users and about 97% usage among smart device users (Kakaotalk, 2018). Kakaotalk began its service merely as a communication app in 2010 and expanded its market to various services. Kakaotalk offers services like 'Kakao Mart' which enables users to do grocery shopping online. The service includes home delivery of groceries at a preferred time. It also offers a 'Gifticon' service that Koreans commonly use to send presents to each other online, such as an imported good as a fancy present.

These platforms provide foreign companies an excellent opportunity to sell their products online in Korea, bypassing the multitiered distribution channel as we described earlier. While foreign companies could manage this process themselves and engage in direct exporting, SMEs could hire intermediaries to manage the whole exporting process and product placements in these online channels.

### 1. Jikgu – overseas direct purchase

The development of internet-enabled motivated Koreans to purchase foreign goods online. Around 2014, Korean consumers created a term *Jikgu* – an abbreviation of

*Haewoe Jikjeopgumae* (해외직접구매), meaning overseas direct purchase. This phenomenon was led by two key drivers – an enthusiasm towards rare imported goods and price sensitivity. Consumers who enjoy a *jikgu* purchase often seek unique and niche products that are unavailable in Korea. Korean consumers are known for their extensive price comparisons to choose the best option to import the goods themselves. Cross-border online shopping in Korea outran US$800 million in 2012 and the value rose to US$1.6 billion in 2014 (Iyer & Bennur, 2017). *Jikgu* was mainly practiced using large foreign online retail stores such as Amazon, eBay and iHerb. Furthermore, companies entering or planning to enter Korea should bear in mind that the products exported to Korea through *Jikgu* do not require local language labels, certification or safety tests. This development is of great significance for potential exporters to Korea because *Jikgu* products have already been directly purchased by Koreans and thus have a high chance of succeeding in the Korean market. If foreign companies would like to sell via this channel, they need to sell their products via major international platforms or Korean platforms. While such exporting can be a first step, sales volume would be limited.

### Shift in consumer behavior

Consumers in Asia-Pacific purchase premium products for self-esteem and status much more than compared to those in Europe and North America. Korean consumers' preference for premium and luxury goods grew despite political instability and economic downturns (Deloitte, 2017). The market share of imported luxury passenger cars has steadily increased (Kaida, 2019). The average cost of a bottle of red wine in Korea is more than KRW40,000 (35 euros), which is about 80% higher than the import price. Despite the high price, the increase in wine and automobile sales reflect that high cost does not seem to be an obstacle for Korean consumers. It is apparent that Korean consumers are trend sensitive as well as keen to purchase premium products.

With the rise of middle-class and young consumers, a new term, *Gachi Sobi* (가치소비), meaning 'value consumption', has become the latest consumption trend. Young Korean adults comprise the consumer group leading the value consumption trend in the country. As these young adults have had living and traveling experiences around the world through travel or exchange semesters, they not only demand the products that they had experienced overseas but are also willing to purchase them at a higher price. Overall, Korean consumers' taste has moved from focusing mostly on cost to a demand for diversity, value and quality factors.

### Free trade agreements (and support programs)

The Korean government has been keen on implementing various steps for its economic development and well-being. For rapid economic development, the Korean government has been continuing economic deregulation and liberalization. The government has been encouraging imports of technology and raw materials through international trade agreements such as FTAs with different regions. This shows that the government could play a more significant role in the economic and business sector of Korea.

Korea has signed multiple FTAs from countries all over the globe. As of 2017, Korea has 15 effectuated FTAs with 52 countries including the ASEAN, the EU (28), the US and China. Korea is currently under negotiation with 24 countries for eight further FTAs. The biggest share of Korea's import lies in raw materials followed by consumer goods and capital goods. In agriculture, forest and marine products the US is leading the market. Japan, China, the US and Germany are leading exports to Korea in chemical and industry manufacturers (KOIMA, 2018).

These FTA agreements have paved the way for substantial benefits to current and future exporters to Korea. The US and EU had a substantial increase in exports to Korea based on the FTAs (KOIMA, 2018). As a result of the Korea–Canada FTA, more than 97% of the agricultural export duties were eliminated. The Korea–US FTA (KORUS) enabled duty-free market entry of more than 90% of US goods.

Since Korea is heavily dependent on foreign trade and well integrated into the developed global value chain, there are programs that encourage penetration and investment in the Korean market. The EU gateway program is one such example of promoting EU firms to enter the Korean market. The program supports firms in entering difficult markets with high entry barriers such as regulations and culture. The main service of the EU gateway is assistance with business matchmaking (EUGateway, 2019). The small and middle enterprises of the EU can make use of such programs to enter the Korean market. When the FTAs and export subsidies like EU gateway are utilized with Korea's strong shipping and cargo infrastructure, export to Korea may indeed become a gateway to other Asian-Pacific markets. For instance, Laboratoire Soniam, a small French company that produces plant extracts used in the cosmetic industry, took advantage of the FTA. As part of the FTA, a number of barriers were lifted. Soniam utilized its 'made in France' image and its Ecocert certification for organic produce that made it such a success in the Korean market. As a result, the company witnessed an increase in its exports by 20% in 2016. Furthermore, the growing presence of Soniam in Korea enabled market entry opportunities for other neighboring countries such as Thailand, China and Vietnam (European Commission, 2016).

## Challenges in exporting to the Korean market

Every country has regulations and rules in place to govern trade and related practices, and Korea is no exception. The Korean market with all its unique characteristics has its own set of challenges for those interested in exporting. Several European companies have expressed difficulties in doing business in Korea (European Chamber of Commerce in Korea, 2017). In the following, we discuss the typical main challenges exporters to Korea face.

## Different business culture – change in contracts

In the last six decades Korea witnessed unprecedented economic growth. One of the key reasons for this was the *bbali-bbali* (빨리빨리) mind-set meaning demanding things to be done quickly. Hence, Koreans are highly flexible and adaptive to make changes and to meet the needs of customers. Therefore, companies entering the Korean market must be aware of this unique characteristic that sets the Korean market apart from others. This has positive implications when flexibility is requested from the exporter's side. However, this same characteristic may end up surprising some exporters when it concerns contracts.

In Korea, a contract is not sealed even after the official closing of the deal with the Korean counterparts or partners (Kohls, 2001). A contract is considered merely as the beginning of a long and fruitful business relationship. Therefore, a Korean business partner or customer could request a renegotiation for amending the already sealed contract regarding the quantity, product price and delivery terms. These are requested for no further payment. Therefore, if the exporter to Korea is not ready for this degree of flexibility, the business will not be successful due to misunderstanding from both sides.

## Different business culture – hierarchy Gapeul relationship

Korea is a very hierarchical society. Accordingly, every contract has a clear *Gapeul* relationship in Korea. *Gap* is the party that possesses a superior position while *Eul* is the subordinate position. Usually, the customer company or the larger company is the *Gap* and the service provider is the *Eul*. In indirect exporting, it is more likely that the agency is the *Eul*, especially when the agency firm is small. However, when a foreign firm is directly exporting to Korea and is working with the conglomerates, the Korean conglomerate will clearly be the *Gap* in such cases. Due to this strong hierarchy, it is pivotal to have the appropriate business attitudes based on your role during the discussions with partners and customers. However, the *Gapeul* relationship is less applied to foreign firms. The act of fairness toward importers helps build a good relationship and is recommended as many Koreans firms seek to build a good relationship with non-Korean firms (Choi, 2016). Although a *Gapeul* relationship is not strongly applied to foreign partners, it is still an important feature to understand and to be acquainted with in order to be well versed with the business dynamics in Korea.

## Chaebol in distribution channels

The Korean economy is strongly dependent on the conglomerate firms. The conglomerate firms like Lotte, Hyundai and Samsung play a significant role in distribution channels as well. Accordingly, store-based channels are concentrated to the big players, for example, Hyundai, Lotte and Shinsegae department stores, along with E-Mart, Lotte Mart and Home Plus discount stores. Hypermarkets have been recently developing in the Korean market. America's Costco, a wholesale retailer, is having success in Korea contrary to the failure of Carrefour and Walmart. E-Mart Traders, a hypermarket brand from Shinsegae is also developing its business. Another popular retailer form is TV home shopping, and the major players are also conglomerates such as CJ and Lotte. The conglomerates are not only dominating the distribution channels but also the logistics. Therefore, penetrating the Korean market with conglomerates as potential customers and/or rivals can be challenging for exporters to Korea, especially for the SMEs. It is difficult to penetrate the Korean market without the support of Korean conglomerates.

## Entering the Korean market

To enter the Korean market through export, it is vital to take time and consider the options carefully. The regulations are different for every entry mode of export. At the beginning foreign companies should engage in extensive market research to better understand the market environment, regulations and customers.

### *Market and regulation research*

Prior to entering the Korean market, a company should execute thorough preliminary market research. Korea has many unique regulations which can complicate business for foreign companies. Therefore, good market research should include not only the identification of possible competitors and extensive analysis on market entry but also an understanding of the complex Korean regulations surrounding the business environment (Shin, 2018). Moreover, it is vital to stay up to date on any FTA updates as it could save export cost.

For most home countries and regions, there are government representatives and consultations offering information for potential exporters to Korea. The US Department of Commerce's International Trade Administration offers Export.gov for general information on export to Korea and the US Department of Agriculture's Foreign Agriculture Service offers the latest updates on exporting agricultural goods. The UK Trade and Investment department established the Department for International Trade which also operates in the British Embassy in Seoul to support companies of British origin to export to the Korean market. Moreover, KOTRA offers the consultation service 'Invest Korea' for future exporters to the Korean market. A fee-based service may be considered for market analysis, as well as market analysis from KOIMA, Korean Importers' Association.

Firms should be aware that Korea could have different regulations on packaging and labeling compared to their home country. For instance, it is prohibited to use a photo of fruits when the actual fruit is not used for the product. In such cases only a fruit drawing can be used for the products label and package. According to the Korean Ministry of Food and Drug Safety, the food and beverage products that make its flavor only by using a combined congener may only use the word *scent* and are banned from using the word *flavor*. Such regulations must be studied carefully to adapt the product's labeling and packaging according to Korea's law.

## Follow-up to the customers

Korean consumer behavior is not only focused on cost, brand name, and quality such as health attributes but also on the well-established after-sales service. In the Korean business world, there is a saying that 'customers are kings' (Phrase: 고객이 왕이다). Consequently, Korean consumers are used to a high standard of customer support. A lack of proper customer support in the after-sales phase can substantially damage the company image since the reviews on social media such as Instagram, Facebook and blogs are powerful. Thus, exporting firms should not consider sales of the products as an end but should continue its after sales service to maintain customers.

## Entering the Korean market with direct export

Generally, intensive research on the market is pivotal prior to an investment. Then, the firm should decide how it should proceed with export based on the business form and product. In the case of direct export there are two options: e-commerce or setting up a direct sales branch or a subsidiary in Korea.

For smaller businesses, adding shipping options to Korea to an already existing online shop is the least cost demanding and the least risky method. Global logistics firms like UPS and DHL are used for shipping the packages. The biggest disadvantage of this export is that customers must be active in searching for the product abroad. Therefore, the export should focus merely on *Jikgu* buyers as they are usually highly motivated to search for overseas products online.

## Using existing platforms

For selling business-to-consumer products, one may set-up its own website with a purchase function. However, for better penetration the main e-commerce platforms should be utilized. By using one of the major existing platforms the risk of technical failures in the payment process is reduced.

The Korean e-commerce web platforms such as Gmarket, Auction and 11 Street can be used for exporting consumer goods without having a Korean corporate registration number. The non-Korean retailers can open a seller account, but the approval is not guaranteed from the platform side. Although e-commerce through these platforms may be the simplest export means, there are still several documents that must be submitted. These documents include a business registration certificate, a bank statement, a seller registration form and a confirmation letter (Gmarket, 2019). The fees differ across product categories. All documentation is usually in Korean. Thus, foreign companies might need the support of Korean speakers. For instance, Optimum Nutrition, a brand for health and dietary supplement protein powder, began direct exporting through e-commerce sites like iHerb and wholesale companies such as Costco. Platforms such as iHerb, offer Korean consumers the option to directly purchase (*jikgu*) their products. However, as Optimum Nutrition understood the sales potential of the Korean market, it has defined an official distributor in Korea to control their sales and other activities in the Korean market (Optimum, 2019). Currently, the labels and the packaging of products are in the Korean language. CJ&Y Global Korea, the partner distributor of Optimum Nutrition, manages the distribution of the products sold at Gmarket.

## 2. Setting up a direct sales branch/subsidiary in Korea

Establishing a sales branch or a direct subsidiary is an export option that can be especially beneficial to increase market presence and ease business with locals. A sales branch or a subsidiary are often strategically established in Seoul or the greater capital area including Bundang and Songdo. The capital area has become the hub for sales branches and subsidiaries as it enables easier contact with consumers and clients. Establishing a subsidiary may be a good option when the business has already grown with a strong market presence. In order to enter the Korean market through the export route, it is not mandatory to have a local agent under Korean law. However, foreign manufacturers often set up small sales branches with local staff to penetrate the market or establish a subsidiary when the export business is considered vital.

A foreign firm may practice sales activities with sales branches and subsidiaries in Korea. The sales branches are mainly guided by the foreign exchange transaction law. The major governing laws for subsidiaries are foreign investment promotion law and commercial code. A sales branch is free from third-party audits in Korea since its net income is included in the headquarters balance sheet. A subsidiary office is more suitable for a stronger relationship with the Korean business world. Since a subsidiary is founded as a local company, the firm can receive corporate income tax intensives that are not applicable to a branch sales office. To establish a subsidiary, a minimum of KRW100 million is required (Pinansky et al., 2015). In comparison, a sales branch can be established without any capital requirements. On average, two weeks and five weeks are required to set up a sales branch and a subsidiary, respectively.

## Entering the Korean market with indirect export

Small and medium-sized companies often engage in indirect exporting via an agent. In this case, finding the right and good partner presents a crucial task. The advantages of indirect exports in the Korean market are a reduction of risks due to language barriers and cultural differences as well as participating in a higher local network when local staffs are hired. The disadvantages are the risk of having an unreliable partner/agency, a lack of control and losing resources due to miscommunication with the agent for example while renegotiating a contract.

The importer (agent) must submit basic documents – an invoice, a bill of lading, a packing list and a certificate of origin for reporting import to the Korea Customs

Service. For the following categories, import customs clearance can be done by only submitting an import declaration form: Personal duty-free goods below the value of KRW150,000 and sample duty-free commercial samples with a value no more than US$250. The Korea Customs service offers a guide to the import clearance system in detail on its website (www.customs.go.kr/).

## Conclusion

Exporting is the least cost entry mode of internationalization to any foreign market, including Korea. When you are not sure about committing in a foreign market, exporting helps you to test the water to see if you can be successful. Most companies start with sporadic exports initially and then move onto regular exports and consider other entry modes later if they have confidence in the market based on their past experience of exporting. Korea is not an exception to this general trend. There are some frameworks such as the 7-P framework for international marketing (Paul & Mas, 2019) which can help companies to carry out feasibility analyses based on potential, path (growth), process, pace, pattern, problems and estimate likely performance in a new market such as Korea. It would be prudent to carry out such a potential-performance analysis in a specific industry, before switching entry modes.

In this chapter, we have provided an overview of the different types of exporting, distinguishing between direct and indirect exporting. Then, we have provided an overview of opportunities and challenges for foreign firms interested in exporting to Korea. On one hand, widespread adoption of e-commerce, overseas direct purchases, shift in consumer behaviors and numerous FTAs present attractive opportunities for foreign exporters. On the other hand, flexible contracts, hierarchical relationships in buyer–supplier relationships and tightly controlled distribution channels by chaebols pose challenges for any new, foreign entrant. We have provided specific recommendations for how foreign companies can export to Korea. Exporting, particularly, indirect exporting is easy for even small and medium enterprises and can be the first step when contemplating doing business in Korea.

### Case study: Xiaomi – from overseas direct purchase to sales branches

Xiaomi, a Chinese electronics manufacturer, has gained popularity among Korean consumers due to its reasonable price and good quality. The portable battery for mobile phones has become a must-have item in Korea. Xiaomi's air filter device and digital scale became best sellers on Gmarket. Recently, Xiaomi products that resemble popular expensive products of Dyson have become the new best sellers.

According to the Korea Customs Service, the *jikgu* purchases of Chinese products increased 226% in 2017 compared to 2015. Electronics have a 22% share of the *jikgu* purchase from China. For direct purchase from China, an increasing number of consumers are using Ali Express operated by Alibaba. Alibaba offers translation into Korean of its Ali Express service. Taobao, an e-commerce platform targeted for Chinese consumers does not offer any translation but offers products at lower prices. The price sensitive Korean consumers call these websites 'ant hell' (개미지옥) referring to the difficulty that one faces in trying to come out of these websites due to their attractive prices.

The criticism of *Jikgu* sales is the low-quality after-sales service. To expand sales and manage the Korean market more efficiently, Xiaomi Ltd. concluded a trademark exclusive license contract in 2017. The partnership had certain goals in place that became the foundation of this relationship. The goals were to increase sales and to offer a better after-sales service to Korean customers. Furthermore, Youmi is responsible for the translation of all Xiaomi products and its application Mijia and ultimately for building a Korean version of the smart-home ecosystem. As the exclusive distributor, Youmi manages 14 Xiaomi official stores throughout Korea, an online store Youmimall and the after-sales service.

## Sources

http://news.joins.com/article/22626496 Accessed 30 March 2019.
www.hankookilbo.com/v/fe4ff87d9173420fa233cb444ed3fe11 Accessed 30 March 2019.
http://news.joins.com/article/22626496 Accessed 30 March 2019.
http://news.mk.co.kr/newsRead.php?year=2017&no=560500 Accessed 30 March 2019.
www.youmi.kr/2018 Accessed 30 March 2019.

## Bibliography

### Key reference

Paul, J., & Aserkar, R. 2013. *Export import management*. Oxford University Press.

### Online sources

EUGateway. 2019. www.eu-gateway.eu/. Accessed 30 March 2019.
Korea Customs Service. 2019. www.customs.go.kr/ Accessed 30 March 2019.

Korea Importers Database. 2019. http://koima.net/koima_db/index.do Accessed 30 March 2019.
KOTRA. (Korea Trade-Investment Promotion Agency). 2019. www.kotra.or.kr Accessed 30 March 2019.
Statista. 2019. *E-commerce in South Korea – Statistics & facts* www.statista.com/topics/2529/e-commerce-in-south-korea/ Accessed 30 March 2019.

# References

Amadeo, K. 2019. *Exports and Their Effect on the Economy* www.thebalance.com/exports-definition-examples-effect-on-economy-3305838. Accessed 30 March 2019.
Campa, J. M., & Goldberg, L. S. 1997. The Evolving External Orientation of Manufacturing: A Profile of Four Countries. *Federal Reserve Bank New York Economic Policy Review*, 3(July): 53–81.
Cavusgil, S. T., & Zou, S. 1994. Marketing strategy-performance relationship: An investigation of the empirical link in export market. *The Journal of Marketing*, 58: 1–21.
Choi, C. B. 2016. Overseas exporter fairness and Korean importer's commitment. *Journal of Korea Trade*, 20(2): 186–198.
Daniels, J., Radebaugh, L., & Sullivan, D. 2007. *International business: Environment and operations* (11th Edition).
Deloitte. 2017. *Global powers of luxury goods*. https://www2.deloitte.com/content/dam/Deloitte/global/Documents/consumer-industrial-products/gx-cip-global-powers-luxury-2017.pdf. Accessed 30 November 2018.
European Chamber of Commerce in Korea. 2017. *European Business in Korea Business Confidence Survey 2017*. https://ecck.eu/wp-content/uploads/2015/10/BUSINESS-CONFIDENCE-SURVEY-2017_ENG.pdf. Accessed 30 November 2018.
European Commission. 2016. *Organic cosmetics producer finds success in South Korea EU-South Korea trade agreement has enabled French SME to boost international exports*. http://trade.ec.europa.eu/doclib/docs/2016/september/tradoc_154953.pdf. Accessed 30 November 2018.
Eurostat. 2018. *South Korea – trade in goods*. http://ec.europa.eu/eurostat/statistics-explained/index.php/South_Korea-EU_-_trade_in_goods. Accessed 30 November 2018.
Filatotchev, I., Stephan, J., & Jindra, B. 2008. Ownership structure, strategic controls and export intensity of foreign invested firms in emerging economies. *Journal of International Business Studies*, 39(7): 1133–1148.
Fu, D., Wu, Y., & Tang. 2009. The effects of ownership structure and industry characteristics on export performance. *The University of Western Australia Discussion Paper*, 10(9): 1–29.
Gmarket. 2019. *Registered overseas business operators*. http://member2.gmarket.co.kr//CustomerCenter/FaqSearch?IsAutoComplete=Y&SeqNo=3492&searchText=%ED%95%B4%EC%99%B8%20%ED%8C%90%EB%A7%A4. Accessed 30 March 2019.
Hill, C. W. L. 2015. *International business: Competing in the global marketplace* (15th ed.): 454. New York: McGraw Hill.
Investopia. 2019. *Export definition*. www.investopedia.com/terms/e/export.asp. Accessed 30 March 2019.
Iyer, J. H., & Bennur, S. 2017. *Retailing in emerging markets*. New York: Bloomsbury Publishing.
Kaida. 2019. *Imported car share*. www.kaida.co.kr/ko/statistics/kaidaShareList.do. Accessed 30 March 2019.

Kakaotalk. 2018. *4th quarter 2017 results* https://t1.kakaocdn.net/kakaocorp/operating/ir/results-announcement/3219.pdf. Accessed 30 November 2018.

Karippacheril, T. G., Kim, S., Beschel, R. P., & Choi, C. 2016. Bringing Government into the 21st Century: The Korean Digital Governance Experience. Washington, DC: World Bank Group.

Kohls, L. R. 2001. Learning to Think Korean. Boston, MA: Intercultural Press.

KOIMA (Korea importers association). 2018. *Korea's import*. http://koima.net/koima_net/importMarket/koreaImport.do. Accessed 30 November 2018.

Shin, J. H. 2018. *Too many 'pure' Korean regulations here: ECCK president*. Korea Herald, www.koreaherald.com/view.php?ud=20180425000770. Accessed 30 November 2018.

Naidu, G. M., & Prasad, V. K. 1994. Predictors of export strategy and performance of small-sized and medium-sized firms. *Journal of Business Research*, 321(1–2): 107–115.

Optimum. 2019. International distributors. www.optimumnutrition.com/en-us/international-distributors#LJskg6pxEHXbmtQ3.97. Accessed 30 November 2018.

Paul, J., & Aserkar, R. 2013. *Export import management*. Oxford University Press.

Paul, J., & Mas, E. 2019. Toward a 7-P framework for international marketing. *Journal of Strategic Marketing*, 1–21.

Paul, J., Parthasarathy, S., & Gupta, P. 2017. Exporting challenges of SMEs: A review and future research agenda. *Journal of World Business*, 52(3): 327–342.

Pinansky, T., Park, K. T., & Lee, E. 2015. *Establishing a business in South Korea: Thomson Reuters practical law* https://uk.practicallaw.thomsonreuters.com/0-575-2387?transitionType=Default&contextData=(sc.Default)&firstPage=true&bhcp=1#co_anchor_a640258. Accessed 30 November 2018.

Rojec, M., Damijan, J. P., & Majcen, B. 2004. Export propensity of Estonian and Slovenian manufacturing firms. Does foreign ownership matter? *Eastern European Economics*, 42: 33–54.

Roy, E. 2018. *Direct or indirect exporting: Which is the best fit for your business?* www.tradeready.ca/2017/topics/market-entry-strategies/direct-indirect-exporting-best-fit-business/. Accessed 30 November 2018.

Sakakibara, M., & Porter, M. E. 2001. Competing at home to win abroad: Evidence from Japanese industry. *The Review of Economics and Statistics*, 83(2): 310–322.

Samil PwC. 2017. *Doing business in Korea*. www.pwc.de/de/internationale-maerkte/assets/doing-business-and-investing-in-korea.pdf. Accessed 30 November 2018.

Statista. 2018. *Is your cellphone a smartphone, such as an iPhone, a blackberry or the like?* www.statista.com/statistics/539409/smartphone-ownership-by-age-in-selected-countries/. Accessed 30 November 2018.

Statista. 2019a. *Online shopping transaction volume in South Korea from 2008 to 2017.* www.statista.com/statistics/280922/b2c-e-commerce-sales-in-south-korea/. Accessed 31 March 2019.

Statista. 2019b. *Leading online retailers in South Korea in 2017, ranked by net e-commerce sales.* www.statista.com/statistics/297917/leading-e-retailers-in-south-korea-ranked-by-annual-web-e-commerce-sales/. Accessed 30 November 2018.

UNCTAD. 2017. *World investment report 2017.* http://unctad.org/en/PublicationsLibrary/wir2017_en.pdf. Accessed 30 November 2018.

Whetzel, J. 2018. *What are direct exports? by Joan Whetzel.* https://bizfluent.com/info-8478132-direct-exports.html. Accessed 30 March 2019.

Zhao, H., & Zou, S. 2002. The impact of industry concentration and firm location on export propensity and intensity: An empirical analysis of Chinese manufacturing firms. *Journal of International Marketing*, 10, 52–71.

# 7

# CROSS-BORDER M&As IN SOUTH KOREA

*Yi Yang and Yong Suhk Pak*

## Introduction

Cross-border M&As have been a preferred form of FDI in recent decades. The total value of outbound cross-border M&As in the world reached USD887 billion in 2016, a value higher than the total value of outbound greenfield projects in the world (UNCTD, 2018). This figure continues to increase.

Cross-border M&As are considered beneficial for both home and host countries. From the host country's perspective, cross-border M&As increase the international income of the host country, helping the host country to achieve a current account surplus (Hill & Hut, 2019). Also, cross-border M&A may benefit the host countries due to the spillover effect (Crespo & Contours, 2007; Spencer, 2008) and learning effect (Johanson & Vahlne, 2009; Zhang et al., 2010). Cross-border M&As bring essential resources, such as capital, technology, and management know-how, which may improve the employment rate, increase both learning opportunities and competition for domestic incumbents, and foster innovation and development of relevant industries (Hill & Hult, 2019).

One of the first studies on inward investment in Korea focused on the human side of M&As (Froese et al., 2008). Since the 2008 world financial crisis, more and more foreigners have invested in Korean firms (Froese, 2010). There are many reasons why foreign investors favor Korean companies. South Korea's steady economic growth, including an average GDP growth rate of around 3% per year, combined with its advanced infrastructure environment, supportive government policies, guidance for FDI, and relatively low prices have attracted foreign investors interested in cross-border M&As. Moreover, the highly educated and proficient Korean workforce also attracts investors in Korea. Korea has been recognized as poor in natural resources, but rich in human capital (Bae & Lawler, 2000; Froese et al., 2008; Kim & Slocum, 2008).

Korean firms have other merits as well, including their innovative capabilities (Lee et al., 2011) and the strategic location advantage for global firms who want to enter the Asian market (Kang et al., 2014). South Korea has been ranked number one on the Bloomberg Global Innovation Index, and its patent activity level is the top of the list. Korean firms have pioneered innovation in some industries, such as the semiconductor, gaming, and beauty industries. Korean firms are growing fast and playing more and more important roles in the global economy through active global expansion. Moreover, with geographical, cultural, and commercial linkages with other Asian countries, such as China, Japan, and Southeast Asian countries, foreign investors may attain a strategic locational advantage by investing in Korea. Korean subsidiaries may act as hubs with which global firms may connect, network, and enter into other Asian markets.

This chapter introduces both inbound and outbound cross-border M&As of Korean firms, discussing their value, location, and industry distribution in addition to providing a case study. We review the main regulations and foreign investment guidelines, describing the procedures by which foreign entities acquire Korean firms. Given the cultural uniqueness and relatively high language barrier in Korea, we provide insights into and list the business implications of post-merger integration in the Korean market.

## Inbound and outbound M&As in Korea

### Inbound M&As in Korea

Inbound M&As have been generally welcomed by the Korean government. Based on data from the Merger Market database, a professional research database of global M&A activities considered reliable by researchers, 455 deals worth 69.89 billion USD were recorded in the 10 years between 2008 and 2018. During this time, the number of inbound M&A cases generally showed an upward trend. M&As peaked in 2015 with a total of 52 deals, but activity has declined slightly from 2015 to the present (Figure 7.1). The year 2015 was considered as a landmark year for M&As globally.

Although the Terminal High Altitude Area Defense (THAAD) issue and the threat of a nuclear missile attack were big news in South Korea in 2016–2017, foreign investors actively sought to merge with and acquire South Korean companies during this time. According to the World Investment Report (UNCTD, 2018), the transaction value of cross-border M&As in 2017 decreased by 22% (USD694 billion) compared to 2016 (USD887 billion) for the world; however, a slight increase in Korea was recorded from 2016 to 2017, as shown in Figure 7.2.

During the last ten years, some well-known international acquisitions of Korean companies have occurred. For example, a global leading private equity fund company, Kohlberg Kravis Roberts & Co., spent USD935.5 million to acquire shares in LS Automotive and the copper foil and flexible copper clad laminate business division of LS Mtron Ltd., a subsidiary of the LS Group (Business Korea, 2017b: 0628).

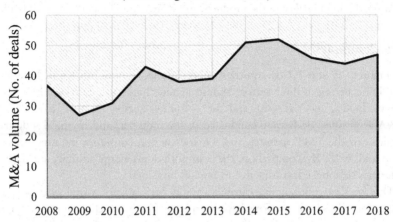

**FIGURE 7.1**  Inbound M&As in South Korea (by volume)

*Source:* White & Case, mergers.whitecase.com.

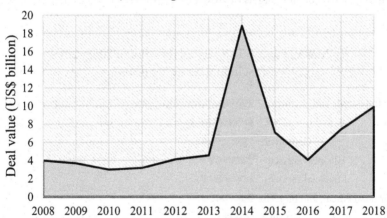

**FIGURE 7.2**  Inbound M&As in South Korea (by value)

*Source:* White & Case, mergers.whitecase.com

In addition, Affinity Equity Partners, an Asia-focused private equity firm based in Hong Kong, acquired Lock & Lock Co., a leading food container maker in South Korea, at a price of USD560.52 million (Business Korea, 2018: 0831).

Although economists examining the domestic investment banking industry comment that it will still take some time for foreign companies to invest in South Korean companies in earnest, Korean manufacturing companies have frequently attracted capital from cross-border M&As due to the maturity of the Korean manufacturing industry, the high quality of the products, and Korea's good reputation worldwide.

## Industry analysis

As Figures 7.3 and 7.4 demonstrate, inbound M&As in South Korea have been mainly occurring in three sectors: industrial and chemical industries, TMT (technology, media, and telecom), and the consumer sector. In total, 137 inbound M&A acquisition deals were conducted in the industrial and chemical industries, 97 deals in the TMT industry, and 49 deals in the consumer industry between 2008 and 2018. By comparison, the transportation, energy, mining, and utilities industries have been less attractive to foreign investors.

Due to their outstanding capabilities and performance worldwide in recent years, Korean technology firms have been particularly attractive targets to foreign investors. For example, S-Printing Solution, a division of the US-based HP, bought the printing division of Samsung Electronics for USD1.05 billion; this was the largest inbound acquisition deal in Korea for that year (Mail Business News Korea, 2018: 1216).

However, the Korean beauty industry has recently emerged as one of the most competitive industries in the country's economy. As a result, Korean cosmetics companies have become targets of cross-border M&As. Local cosmetics companies

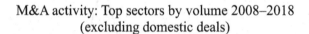

M&A activity: Top sectors by volume 2008–2018
(excluding domestic deals)

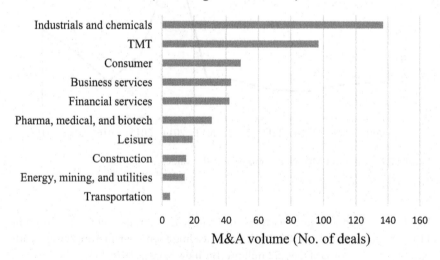

**FIGURE 7.3** Top sectors of inbound M&As in South Korea (by volume)

*Source:* White & Case, mergers.whitecase.com.

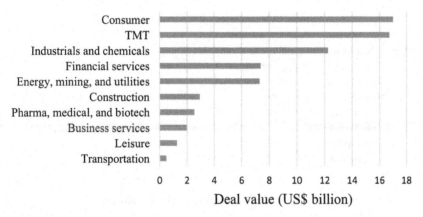

M&A activity: Top sectors by value 2008–2018
(excluding domestic deals)

Deal value (US$ billion)

**FIGURE 7.4**   Top sectors of inbound M&As in South Korea (by value)

*Source:* White & Case, mergers.whitecase.com.

are strong players in the domestic market, while multinational companies account for 35% of the market. Acquiring a local brand with a strong reputation seems to be a better strategy compared to entering the Korean market with a foreign brand. For example, L'Oréal has been operating in Korea since 1993 and its market share in Korea was only about 5% in 2018. L'Oréal announced the acquisition of 100% of the shares of Style Nanda, a Korean lifestyle makeup and fashion company, in May 2018, at a price of around USD40 million (L'Oréal, 2018a: 0502). As another example, the global consumer goods giant Unilever made a huge inbound deal in 2017. The company acquired a 95.39% share of Carver Korea, the maker of AHC cosmetics, at a price of USD2.7 billion (3.05 trillion won). The deal accounted for 32.6% of all domestic inbound deals made in 2017.

Additionally, insurance companies and banks have been in the spotlight since 2015. The sale price of ING Life Insurance stands at 2.5 trillion won (USD2.24 billion); this high pricing is expected to occur with other life insurance companies like KDB Life and PCA Life as well. Chinese insurance companies and financial holding companies will actively pursue acquisitions of Korean insurance companies by means of asset management and products, according to an analysis by the Korea Insurance Research Institute. Anbang's acquisition of Tong Yang Life Insurance was an example of this trend. In addition, the Korea Development Bank (KDB) also recently announced that it would sell off its stakes in 91 nonfinancial companies by 2018.

## Bidder countries

In addition to the US, as demonstrated in Figure 7.5, companies from Japan and Europe (e.g., the UK, Belgium, the Netherlands) have also been acquiring Korean

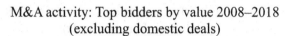

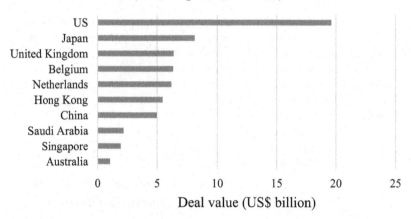

**FIGURE 7.5** Top bidders of inbound M&As in South Korea (by value)

*Source:* White & Case, mergers.whitecase.com.

companies. In addition, Chinese companies have emerged as important buyers, spending USD4.99 billion in total in the same 10 years. Chinese firms spent USD1.48 billion on acquiring Korean firms in 2018, which exceeded the inbound M&A value of USD1.34 billion by the United States. According to KOTRA (the government-operated Korea Trade-Investment Promotion Agency), China's acquisition trend is expected to accelerate further because of the enormous interest in the Korean technology, health care, and beauty industries (http://blog.investkorea.org/ wordpress/?p=7372).

According to the Merger Market database, the top bidder among inbound M&As in Korea during the last 10 years has been the US. For military and economic reasons, South Korea's relationship with the United States has been very close, which has encouraged US companies to invest in South Korea, especially through M&As. As shown in Figures 7.6 and 7.7, from 2008 to 2018, 121 M&A deals were made by US companies, accounting for 26.6% of the total number of deals in that decade. The total value of these 121 deals was USD19.63 billion, which accounted for more than 28% of the total value of inbound M&A transactions in Korea. According to the database, the most attractive Korean sectors to US firms have been the TMT, chemicals, and pharma industries.

## Outbound M&As in Korea

### Value

More and more Korean companies are taking advantage of cross-border M&As to gain a competitive advantage globally, expand their worldwide networks, and

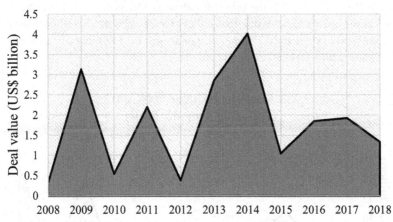

**FIGURE 7.6**   Inbound M&As from the US to South Korea (by value)

*Source:* White & Case, mergers.whitecase.com.

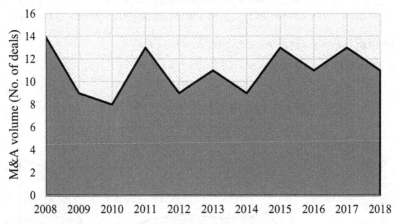

**FIGURE 7.7**   Inbound M&As from the US to South Korea (by volume)

*Source:* White & Case, mergers.whitecase.com.

achieve synergistic benefits. Although cross–border M&As are still a difficult challenge for many Korean companies, others are actively seeking investment opportunities outside of their home country.

Various environmental uncertainties have negatively impacted M&A activities in recent years across the world. Nevertheless, the emergence of buyers from the Asia-Pacific region, in particular from China, Japan, and South Korea, has increased acquisition activity in the region. South Korea can be seen as a bellwether of the emerging trend and a leader of outbound M&A activity throughout the region.

According to Figure 7.8, the value of outbound M&As in South Korea has fluctuated in the last 10 years, with a total value of about USD88.88 billion. However, in Figure 7.9, we see that the number of transactions has been increasing for the last ten years, in which 604 cases were recorded.

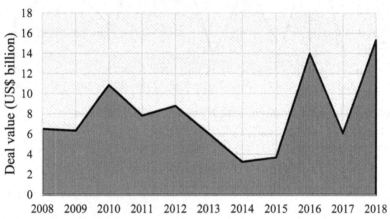

**FIGURE 7.8** Outbound M&As in South Korea (by value)

*Source:* White & Case, mergers.whitecase.com.

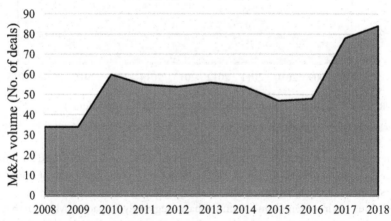

**FIGURE 7.9** Outbound M&As in South Korea (by volume)

*Source:* White & Case, mergers.whitecase.com.

Active government support of the expansion of outbound M&As has occurred since 2014. Figures 7.8 and 7.9 show us that South Korea's outbound M&As hit a new record of USD15.33 billion with 84 deals in 2018, which is higher than the previous record of USD13.99 billion with 48 deals in 2016. Korean Chaebols lead this trend. For instance, Samsung Electronics acquired Harman International Industries at a price of USD8.6 billion in November 2016, which has been recorded as South Korea's largest outbound deal so far (Samsung Newsroom, 2016: 1114). Food giant CJ CheilJedang closed its largest acquisition deal in 2018, acquiring US food distributor Schwan's Company for USD1.84 billion (Reuters, 2018: 1115). Moreover, small and middle-sized firms are also actively expanding their internationalization through market- and strategic-asset-seeking acquisitions (Lee et al., 2013).

## Outbound M&As by industry

Cross-border M&As, economic globalization, and integration into the global production system combined to help Korean firms make full use of domestic and international resources to seek development. South Korean firms interested in cross-border M&As have generally focused on natural resources such as energy, mining, utilities, industrial activities, and chemicals (Figure 7.10).

However, in recent years, the accumulative number one industry – energy, mining, and utilities – has fallen; instead, the manufacturing industries account for more than half of the total. In recent years, from 2015 to 2018, as shown in Figure 7.11, the top three sectors have been the industrial and chemical, consumer, and TMT industries. The energy, mining, and utilities industries ranked fourth. Moreover, the

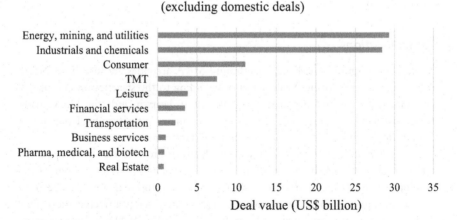

M&A activity: Top sectors by value 2008–2018
(excluding domestic deals)

**FIGURE 7.10**  Top sectors of outbound M&As in South Korea (by value)

*Source:* White & Case, mergers.whitecase.com.

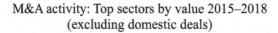

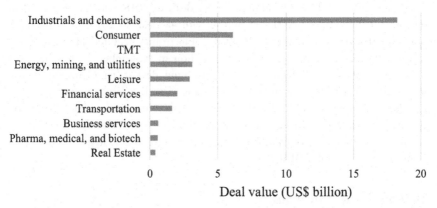

**FIGURE 7.11** Top sectors of outbound M&As in South Korea from 2015 to 2018

*Source:* White & Case, mergers.whitecase.com.

service industry, including leisure, financial services, and business services, increased sharply in recent years. Due to the intangible characteristics of the service industry and its institutional protection by the local government, carrying out international M&As has been difficult in those industries compared to the manufacturing industries. For many Korean companies, growth has been difficult. By contrast, domestic service companies such as Naver and NCsoft have increased their involvement in international M&As in other industries. Despite these difficulties, the major players in the internationalization of Korean companies are beginning to focus on service companies. Clearly, government and institutional support will be needed to maintain this trend.

## Target locations

As shown in Figure 7.12, Korea's outbound M&A activities are mainly in North America and neighboring Asian regions. According to the statistics on cumulative deal values, the top five destinations in the last 10 years include the US, Canada, Australia, China, and Japan. The US has been the main destination for Korean outbound M&As for the last decade and the trend continues.

As a newly industrialized country, South Korea is growing fast and playing the catch-up game. Under these conditions, acquisitions of advanced technologies from developed economies, such as the US and Japan, are indispensable. As the most targeted destination for Korean investors, the United States attracted more than USD9 billion in investment in 2017 and 2018. In 2017, 19 M&A deals targeting US firms worth a total of USD1.6 billion were made, and 28 M&A deals with a value of USD7.59 billion were made in 2018. Deal volume therefore increased

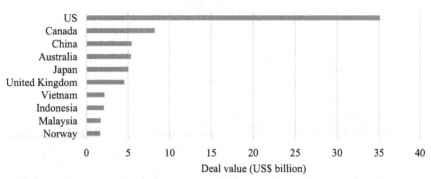

M&A activity: Top targets by value 2008–2018
(excluding domestic deals)

**FIGURE 7.12** Top targets of outbound M&As in South Korea (by value)

*Source:* White & Case, mergers.whitecase.com.

in 2018. At the time of writing, it was reported that South Korean chemical and silicone producer KCC Corp., the quartz and ceramics supplier Wonik QnC, and the private equity firm SJL Partners would jointly purchase the US silicone company Momentive Performance Materials at a price of USD3.1 billion (Merger and Acquisitions, 2018: 0914).

Several Japanese firms were also acquired in the same two years. For example, as reported by *Korean Economic Daily*, Lantern Advisory & Investments acquired seven solar power plants in Japan at a price of USD665 million in total. In addition, MBK Partners spent USD360 million acquiring Tasaki and USD355 million to acquire a 68.31% stake in Kuroda Electric in 2017 (The Investor, 2018: 0124).

In order to expand their production bases in countries specializing in cheap labor to hedge high domestic labor costs and seize market opportunities in emerging countries, Korean firms have conducted some M&As in Southeast Asian countries, such as Vietnam, Indonesia, and Malaysia. Vietnamese involvement in the global value chain, manufacturing labor proficiency, and industry infrastructure have made Vietnam a destination country for Korean manufacturing firms. As a result, the value of outbound M&A transactions from Korea to Vietnam ranked number three ahead of China in 2017–2018, as shown in Figure 7.13.

## M&A procedures in Korea

### FDI legal regulations

In order to complete M&As in South Korea effectively, foreign companies must conduct M&A transactions in accordance with the relevant Korean laws. For FDI in South Korea, all investors must comply with legal regulations, including the FIPL and the FETL. The FIPL was enacted by the South Korean government in order

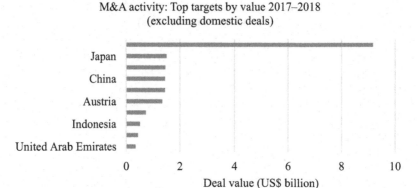

FIGURE 7.13  Top targets of outbound M&As in South Korea (by value), 2017–2018

*Source:* White & Case, mergers.whitecase.com.

to promote investment in Korean companies by foreign investors. The MOCIE is the main government agency that deals with matters related to foreign investment according to the FIPL. The MOCIE has focused a large portion of its energies on foreign exchange banks and KOTRA, which has international trade offices, subsidiaries, and branch offices.

According to the FIPL, foreign investment is defined as the ownership of shares or equity in a Korean company accompanied by participation in the management of the company and other involvement. Specifically, in order to qualify as foreign investment under the FIPL, the amount invested must be at least 100 million Korean won, and the foreign entity must own at least 10% of the voting shares of equity in the Korean company after the acquisition (KOTRA, 2018). However, according to the FIPL, there are some exceptions that may also be considered as foreign investment even if the foreign acquirer does not own 10% of the voting shares or equity in the Korean company. The scope of exceptions may be slightly adjusted every year, which need to consult with KOTRA for more details (www. investkorea.org).

## Foreign investment notification

If a foreigner invests more than 100 million Korean won or acquires more than 10% equity in the investment, the investment is regarded as a foreign investment. As a foreign investor, it is necessary to notify the Korean government about the specific information of investment transactions in advance (report to foreign exchange bank or KOTRA), including the amount of investment fund, the relevant information (name, address, industry, business content, registered capital, etc.) of the investing and target companies, and so on. This notification is important because only after this notification in advance can the Korean target company get the investment fund from the bank, and the remittance of the investors can be formally regarded as the investment fund as the proof of equity acquirement. Investors need to report to the government again after all the equity transactions have been completed in order to be officially recognized as foreign investment by the government.

### Equivalent status of foreign investors

In general, foreign investors and foreign-invested companies are treated the same as Korean citizens and Korean companies with respect to their business activities. In addition, the provisions on tax benefits under Korean tax laws applicable to Korean citizens and companies are equally applicable to foreign investors and foreign-invested companies.

### FDI incentives

In order to encourage more foreign companies to invest in Korea through M&As, the Korean government offers various FDI incentives to foreign investors in the form of tax support, cash grants, and land support, depending on the focal industry (high-tech or not), location (e.g., special tax discount zones), value of the FDI, and other qualifications. The Korean government reserves the right to adjust these qualifications and incentives as circumstances change. Interested investors are recommended to consult with KOTRA in advance for more detailed incentives for FDI (www.investkorea.org).

### M&As through share purchasing

Acquisition of a business entity can be achieved in two ways: (1) purchase of new shares issued at the time of an increase in capital and (2) purchase of existing shares held by a shareholder or shareholders. Normally, issuance of new shares is determined by the company's board of directors, which has the right to determine the class and number of shares to be issued, issuing price per share, and payment date. Acquisition of new shares is achieved through processes known as subscription and allocation. The share subscription application form must be delivered to the existing shareholders, who have preemptive rights. The company name, total number of new shares to be issued, par value per share, issuing price, payment date, and the bank to which payment should be made must be included on the application. The subscriber must pay the price by the payment date; all subscribers that complete this process become new shareholders on the day following the payment date.

Second, a foreign entity may acquire existing shares. An agreement between the seller and purchaser is required in the transfer of shares. For a valid transfer, delivery of share certificates is also required. For registered share certificates, shares may be transferred simply by delivering the share certificates; no endorsement is necessary. However, no delivery of share certificates is required for transfer of shares of KSE-listed or KOSDAQ-registered companies whose equity is held by the Korea Securities Depository.

If a purchaser of shares intends to exercise his or her rights as a shareholder, that purchaser must be listed in the shareholders' registry. Therefore, when a foreign investor acquires registered shares from an existing shareholder, the investor must receive the share certificates from the existing shareholder, present them to the company, and ask the company to amend the shareholders' registry. However, a purchaser who acquires share certificates in a bearer form is not required to request amendment of the shareholders' registry; he or she must deposit the share certificates in the company in order to exercise his or her rights.

## Foreign investment procedures

The Korean government's investment policies specify a series of processes for FDI in Korea. For newly founded companies, the process is outlined in Figure 7.14. However, for the acquisition of existing Korean firms, the registration of incorporation

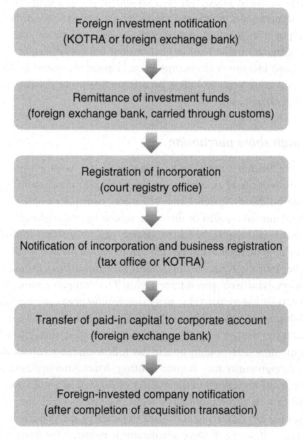

**FIGURE 7.14**  Foreign investment procedures in Korea

*Source:* investkorea.org.

and notification of incorporation and business registration processes may be omitted. However, a foreign investment notification (either to KOTRA or a foreign exchange bank) must still be issued before sending the investment funds to the bank.

## Follow-up management

If a foreign investor acquires existing shares from a Korean company, the foreign investor will be required to file a report with the Reporting Agency within 30 days after the date of acquisition. For Korean companies that have become the target of foreign investment, the investment must be registered with a foreign exchange bank or KOTRA within 30 days after payment of the contribution or share purchase price.

All changes in the shareholdings or company name after registration of a foreign-invested company must be registered. When necessary, registration shall be canceled by the authority of MOITE or the head of the entrusted organization.

## Post-M&A integration in Korea

Management after acquisition has always been a problem. To change or not to change; that is the question. After an M&A is completed, the acquirer may enter into the acquired firm and participate in or take over its management. In order to achieve the goals of the acquisition, on one hand, the acquirer must ensure the stability of the acquired firm. On the other hand, in order to pursue synergy effects, some changes or adjustments may be necessary to allocate resources better and leverage competencies in this post-M&A integration stage.

Organizational changes brought about by cross-border M&As may influence employees' psychological states, increase their uncertainty and anxiety, and decrease job security and satisfaction (Froese et al., 2008; Reichers et al., 1997). In some cases, employees' negative emotions may increase their turnover intention. Due to organizational restructuring and changes in management, employees may face new challenges, such as learning new skills and getting used to new operational procedures, which may cause frustration and disappointment (Barnett & Carroll, 1995). Moreover, M&As often increase complexity and conflict due to changes in the power structure of the board of directors. All these factors may cause difficulties in the post-M&A integration stage and increase employees' negative attitudes toward the organization (Dahl, 2011).

In the Korean context, there are three remedies to mitigate the difficulties and negative influences of cross-border M&A:

1   Leveraging of cultural factors and implementing organizational restructuring at an appropriate level;
2   Increasing communication and interaction with employees; and
3   Increasing employees' participation in organizational decision-making.

### Remedy 1: implementing organizational restructuring at an appropriate level

Korean culture is based on historical Confucianism. Collectivism, seniority, patriarchy, high power distance, and high risk avoidance are the important characteristics of Korean culture (Hofstede, 1983). Because of these typical cultural features, Korean corporate culture is also group-oriented. In accordance with collectivism and Confucianism, Korean employees tend to look at their supervisors in a certain way (*Nunchi*) and seldom express their opinions and suggestions to their supervisors. Because of high power distance, employees have very little autonomy in decision-making. However, this does not mean that they always want to stick to the rules. In fact, Korean employees may be curious and expectant about the new corporate culture, especially when Western companies are involved in the M&A (Ahn & Park, 2004). They may wish to experience an egalitarian organizational culture, which would make it possible to use first names, express their opinions openly, experience freedom from a hierarchical relationship based on seniority, eliminate gender differences, and have more open competition.

As a foreign investor, in order to achieve good results at the integration stage, it is necessary to understand and consider the optimistic expectations of Korean employees, leveraging the benefits of cultural differences and choosing the right timing to make appropriate adjustments. The relevant research shows an inverted U-shaped relationship between organizational restructuring and employees' job satisfaction (Pak et al., 2015). Korean employees' job satisfaction increases as organizational restructuring increases up to a certain level or peak. Implementing excessive restructuring over and above expected changes causes Korean employees to feel stressed and diminishes satisfaction.

### Remedy 2: increasing communication and interaction with employees

Differences in national and corporate cultures may cause difficulties in communication and integration between the acquirer and the employees of the acquired company. Communication will always play an important role in enhancing the sharing of knowledge and reducing context-related misunderstandings between foreign expatriates from the acquiring firm and employees of the acquired firm (Nahapiet & Ghoshal, 1998; Pak et al., 2018). Communication fosters mutual affection and trust and natural formation of social capital. Through this process, cognitive gaps and affective distances between the two parties can be diminished, thus reducing the differences and contradictions between the foreign acquirers and local employees and promoting integration to a new stage.

In Korea, the language barrier is high. English is not an official language, and it is hard to communicate in English. Adding this to the collectivistic organization culture, foreign expatriates may find it hard to communicate with Korean employees. These difficulties may extend the social distance and result in misunderstandings, confusion, and conflict. Therefore, it is important for foreign acquirers to learn Korean and understand Korean organizational culture, a gesture that Korean employees appreciate and that helps reduce the tension caused by differences.

## Remedy 3: increasing employees' participation

In the post-merger integration period, employees may feel nervous and anxious about upcoming changes. During the M&A process, increasing their participation may effectively improve employee job satisfaction. Participation allows Korean employees to understand clearly the upcoming changes resulting from the acquisition, thereby reducing tension and anxiety. They may have the opportunity to express their opinions and make suggestions for integration and development. Participation is also a new experience for acquired Korean enterprises. In line with Remedy 1, a new corporate culture may have long been awaited by Korean employees. Participation increases employee confidence, improves self-esteem, fosters commitment to the organization, and boosts job satisfaction.

## Conclusion

With its neighboring countries China and Japan in Northeast Asia, South Korea plays an important role in world FDI. In order to attract inward FDI and promote the internationalization of Korean firms, the Korean government has endeavored to provide both advanced "hardware" infrastructure and convenient "software" institutional support. As Korean firms build more and more connections and networks with other global firms and global markets, they have accumulated relevant knowledge and experienced internationalization processes. Active learning between Korean firms and foreign MNEs may further promote communication and cooperation across borders. Moreover, as *Hallyu* (Korean popular music, drama, and other cultural content) becomes popular worldwide, Korean firms have become better known by people around the world. Despite efforts by the Korean government to provide a supportive environment, target Korean firms are likely to have unique cultural features that make post-M&A integration a challenge. When both foreign investors and Korean employees work together, important synergies may result. As Korea plays a larger role in the global economy, cross-border M&As remain an interesting research topic.

## Case study: L'Oréal's acquisition of Style Nanda

As the largest cosmetics supplier in the world, L'Oréal, with a history of over 100 years of cosmetics manufacturing and distribution with 34 international brands and more than 80,000 employees worldwide, announced on May 2, 2018, that it would acquire 100% of Style Nanda, an emerging popular Korean beauty brand (L'Oréal, 2018). Earlier, the media had reported that L'Oréal would buy 70% of Style Nanda's shares for 400 billion Korean won, but the acquisition turned out to be a take-over of Style Nanda (Edaily, 2018). The transaction was finalized on June 20, 2018, though the purchase price was not announced (L'Oréal, 2018). The acquisition was L'Oréal's first acquisition of a Korean cosmetics brand; this business deal has had a far-reaching impact on the Korean cosmetics industry.

As one of the most promising industries in South Korea, the cosmetics industry has been designated for deregulation by the Korean government to promote its further development. In 2015, the Korean government adopted several successive policies to abolish the need for submission of a mental health certificate for cosmetics businesses applying for licenses, shorten the licensing review time, and expand the scope of the functional cosmetics category (KOTRA, 2017). Government deregulation of the Korean cosmetics industry has improved efficiency in terms of production and operations. Korea's total cosmetics production revenue exceeded 10 trillion Won for the first time in 2015, reaching 10,732.8 billion won, an increase of nearly 20% over the previous year (Cosmetic Mania News, 2017). Cosmetics production continued to grow by 21.6% in 2016, reaching 13,051.4 billion Won. Despite the influence of the turmoil caused by the Terminal High Altitude Area Defense (THAAD), there was still a slight increase of 3.6% in 2017 to 13,515.5 billion won. There were 829 companies that produced and distributed cosmetics in 2012; however, the number of registered companies in the Korean Food and Drug Administration (KFDA) reached 11,834 in 2017, with an average annual growth rate of 265.5%. The rapid growth of the Korean cosmetics industry could not have been achieved without the active innovation of firms in the industry. From 2016 to 2017, the number of categories of cosmetics production increased to 125,766, meaning that 6,715 categories had been added within a year (Cosmetic Mania News, 2017).

Style Nanda started operations in 2004 focusing on online distribution of apparel. Then, with the rapid growth of the cosmetics industry, the firm entered into the cosmetics market by launching its 3CE makeup brand in 2009. Answering to the needs of "millennials" (the new generation of consumers who are active on social media and pursue personal improvement through product acquisition), 3CE concentrated on uniqueness of products and pursued creative and cutting-edge designs by taking advantage of Style Nanda's multichannel international distribution network (including its iconic flagship companies in Korea and Japan). In a very short time, the sales revenue of 3CE brand products constituted more than 70% of Style Nanda's total revenue, which was about 127 million euros in 2017. Also, 3CE was named the favorite brand of Chinese travelers in 2017 (Korea Joongang Daily, 2018).

The takeover has been expected to bring synergy effects that are beneficial for both L'Oréal and Style Nanda. L'Oréal believes that they can secure a better market position in the "millennials" segment of the Korean and Chinese markets and beyond. Style Nanda has gained global recognition by merging with a world-class brand. As So Hee Kim (CEO and founder of Style Nanda) said, "We strongly believe that this transaction will be a landmark breakthrough for Nanda. Grounded on L'Oréal's solid support and global platform, we envisage expansion of Style Nanda's international footprint, becoming a world-renowned brand to lead global trends in beauty" (L'Oréal, 2018).

## Sources

Cosmetic Mania News. 2017. *Cosmetics production performance surpassed 13 trillion Korean Won.* www.cmn.co.kr/mobile/sub_view.asp?news_idx=23535. Accessed 28 June 2017.

Edaily. 2018. *L'Oréal embraces Korean Stylenanda by acquiring 100% stake.* www.edaily.co.kr/news/read?newsId=01895846619205312&mediaCodeNo=257&OutLnkChk=Y. Accessed 5 May 2018.

L'Oreal. 2018a. *L'Oréal acquires Korean Stylenanda,* www.loreal-finance.com/eng/news-release/loreal-acquires-korean-stylenanda-1256.htm. Accessed 02 May 2018.

L'Oreal. 2018b. *L'Oréal finalizes the acquisition of Korean Stylenanda.* www.loreal-finance.com/eng/news-release/loreal-finalizes-the-acquisition-of-korean-stylenanda-1267.htm. Accessed 5 May 2018.

Korea Joongang Daily. 2018. *L'Oreal purchases 100% stake in Stylenanda,* http://koreajoongangdaily.joins.com/news/article/article.aspx?aid=3047694. Accessed 5 May 2018.

KOTRA. 2017. *Doing Business in Korea,* www.investkorea.org/en/index.do

## Bibliography

### Key references

Froese, F. J. 2010. Success and failure in managing foreign acquisitions in South Korea and Japan: Lessons from Renault, General Motors and Daimler Chrysler. *Global Business and Organizational Excellence*, 30(1): 50–59.

Froese, F., Pak, Y. S., & Chong, L. 2008. Managing the human side of cross-border acquisitions in South Korea. *Journal of World Business*, 43: 97–108.

## Online sources

KOTRA. 2017. *Doing Business in Korea*, www.investkorea.org/en/index.do
KOTRA. 2018. *Doing Business in Korea*, www.investkorea.org/en/index.do
White & Case, mergers.whitecase.com

## References

Ahn & Park. 2004. A study on job stress and organizational commitment of Korean Labors after international M&A. *International Business Journal*, 15(3): 1–29.

Bae, J., & Lawler, J. J. 2000. Organizational and HRM strategies in Korea: Impact on firm performance in an emerging economy. *Academy of Management Journal*, 43(3): 502–517.

Bae, J., & Rowley, C. 2001. The impact of globalization on HRM: The case of South Korea. *Journal of World Business*, 36(4): 402–428.

Barnett, W. P., & Carroll, G. R. 1995. Modeling internal organizational change. *Annual Review of Sociology*, 21(1): 217–236.

Business Korea. 2017a. Foreign Investors Seek to Merge, Acquire S. Korean Companies. www.businesskorea.co.kr/news/articleView.html?idxno=19679. Accessed 28 June 2017.

Business Korea. 2017b. LS Group Signs Partnership Agreement with KKR. www.businesskorea.co.kr/news/articleView.html?idxno=18807. Accessed 28 June 2017.

Crespo, N., & Fontoura, M. P. 2007. Determinant factors of FDI spillovers – what do we really know? *World Development*, 35(3): 410–425.

Dahl, M. S. 2011. Organizational change and employee stress. *Management Science*, 57(2): 240–256.

Froese, F. J. 2010. Success and failure in managing foreign acquisitions in South Korea and Japan: Lessons from Renault, General Motors and Daimler Chrysler. *Global Business and Organizational Excellence*, 30(1): 50–59.

Froese, F., Pak, Y. S., & Chong, L. 2008. Managing the human side of cross-border acquisitions in South Korea. *Journal of World Business*, 43: 97–108.

Hill, C. W. L., & Hult, G. T. M. 2019. *International business: Competing in the global marketplace* (12th Edition.). New York: McGraw-Hill Education.

Hofstede, G. 1983. The cultural relativity of organizational practices and theories, *Journal of International Business Studies*, 14(2): 75–89.

Johanson, J., & Vahlne, J. E. 2009. The Uppsala internationalization process model revisited: From liability of foreignness to liability of outsidership. *Journal of International Business Studies*, 40(9): 1411–1431.

Kang, I., Han, S., & Shin, G. C. 2014. A process leading to strategic alliance outcome: The case of IT companies in China, Japan, and Korea. *International Business Review*, 23(6): 1127–1138.

Kim, K., & Slocum, J. W., Jr. 2008. Individual differences and expatriate assignment effectiveness: The case of US-based Korean expatriates. *Journal of World Business*, 43: 109–126.

KOTRA. 2017a. *Doing Business in Korea*, www.investkorea.org/en/index.do

KOTRA. 2017b. *Korea's leading industries 2017: Beauty & cosmetics*. www.investkorea.org/en/published/publications03.do Accessed 5 May 2018.

KOTRA. 2018. *Doing Business in Korea*, www.investkorea.org/en/index.do

Lee, H., Lee, K., & Kwak, J. 2013. Sequential internationalization of small-and medium-sized enterprises from newly industrializing economies: The Korean experience in China. *Asian Business & Management*, 12(1): 61–84.

Lee, P. Y., Lin, H. T., Chen, H. H., & Shyr, Y. H. 2011. Dynamic capabilities exploitation of market and hierarchy governance structure: An empirical comparison of Taiwan and South Korea. *Journal of World Business*, 46(3): 359–370.

Mail Business News Korea. 2018. Korea's four-year M&A tally reaches $38 billion, Samsung Elec tops list. https://pulsenews.co.kr/view.php?year=2018&no=783282. Accessed 30 December 2018.

Merger & Acquisitions. 2018. Korean firms ink deal to acquire momentive. https://cen.acs. org/business/mergers-acquisitions/Korean-firms-ink-deal-acquire/96/web/2018/09. Accessed 14 September 2018.

Nahapiet, J., & Ghoshal, S. 1998. Social capital, intellectual capital, and the organizational advantage. *Academy of Management Review*, 23(2): 242–266.

Pak, Y. S., Luo, H., & Yang, Y. 2015. Organizational change and employee satisfaction in the post cross-border M&A integration in Korea. *Korean Management Review*, 44(6): 1661–1684.

Pak, Y. S., Sun, Q., & Yang, Y. 2018. Influences of expatriate managerial styles on host-country nationals' turnover intention. *Asian Business & Management*, doi.org/10.1057/ s41291-018-0047-5.

Reichers, A. E., Wanous, J. P., & Austin, J. T. 1997. Understanding and managing cynicism about organizational change. *Academy of Management Perspectives*, 11(1): 48–59.

Reuters. 2018. South Korean food giant CJ buy U.S. frozen food company for $1.84 billion. www.reuters.com/article/us-schwan-s-company-m-a-cj-cheiljedang/south-korean-food-giant-cj-buy-u-s-frozen-food-company-for-1-84-billion-idUSKCN1NK0GI. Accessed 15 November 2018.

SAMSUNG Newsroom. 2016. Samsung Electronics to acquire HARMAN, accelerating growth in automotive and connected technologies. https://news.samsung.com/global/ samsung-electronics-to-acquire-harman-accelerating-growth-in-automotive-and-con nected-technologies. Accessed 05 May 2018.

Spencer, J. W. 2008. The impact of multinational enterprise strategy on indigenous enterprises: Horizontal spillovers and crowding out in developing countries. *Academy of Management Review*, 33(2): 341–361.

The Investor. 2018. Korea's M&A market slows for 2nd straight year in 2017. www.theinves tor.co.kr/view.php?ud=20180124000592. Accessed 05 May 2018.

United Nations Conference on Trade and Development. 2018. World Investment Report 2016: Investor Nationality: Policy Challenges. UN.

White & Case, mergers.whitecase.com

Zhang, Y., Li, H., Li, Y., & Zhou, L. A. 2010. FDI spillovers in an emerging market: The role of foreign firms' country origin diversity and domestic firms' absorptive capacity. *Strategic Management Journal*, 31(9): 969–989.

# 8

# LEARNING FROM KOREA

*Martin Hemmert*

## Introduction

Korea is well known for its comprehensive and effective learning from other countries. Throughout the last century, Koreans have relentlessly studied Western countries and Japan to learn how to establish well-functioning economic systems, design and manage governmental and corporate organizations, and manufacture low-cost and high-quality products. Foreign methods and products were imported, imitated and swiftly adapted to the Korean cultural and institutional context (Kim, 1997). Partially as a result of this pervasive learning process from abroad, Korea has become a rich and technologically advanced country. Some Korean companies are now regarded as global leaders in knowledge- and technology-intensive industries (Hemmert, 2018).

These rapid advancements of Korean firms suggest that it is time to change the perspective from a foreign viewpoint and, instead of regarding Korea merely as a diligent student of other countries, to also consider what foreign companies and managers can learn from their Korean counterparts. This is the theme of this chapter, which focuses on two aspects of learning from Korea: technological learning and managerial learning. With regard to technological learning, the acquisition of Korean firms' technologies and innovations by non-Korean firms will be analyzed. Furthermore, as Korean firms have developed specific and highly effective managerial systems and processes throughout the last decades, the potential for managerial learning from Korea will also be discussed. In each section, areas of Korean excellence are first identified, followed by a discussion on how non-Korean firms can effectively learn from their Korean counterparts. Finally, the findings and implications for non-Korean firms are summarized in the Conclusion.

# Technological learning from Korea

## What to learn?

On a general level, the technological competitiveness of Korean firms can be assessed by their global business performance in technology-intensive industries. Throughout the last decades, Korean firms have been rapidly gaining global market share across various knowledge-intensive manufacturing industries, including automobiles, semiconductors and mobile phones (Hemmert, 2018). This trend is continuing: in 2017, Samsung Electronics became the world's largest vendor of smartphones as well as the largest semiconductor manufacturer. The combined global market share of Samsung Electronics and SK Hynix surpassed 20% in the overall semiconductor industry and 60% in the memory chip market (Shaffer, 2017; Gartner Newsroom, 2018).

Science and technology statistics reveal that Korean companies are strongly investing in their technological capabilities and gaining high returns from these investments (Table 8.1). Korea's overall R&D intensity, defined as the ratio of a country's R&D expenses in relation to its GDP, exceeds 4% and is far higher than in other technologically leading countries such as the USA, Japan and Germany. Most of Korea's R&D is financed and conducted by the business sector, and the country's business-financed R&D intensity is the highest among all countries in the world (OECD, 2017). In 2016, 49.4% of all business R&D has been attributable to the electronics, computer and communication industries, showing that Korean companies' R&D investment is concentrated on the information and communications technology (ICT) sector (Ministry of Science and ICT, 2018). Furthermore, Korean firms also file a high number of patents following the Patent Cooperation Treaty (PCT) procedure, which offers the possibility to seek patent rights in a large number of countries through a single international application in one patent office (OECD, 2017). The number of such globally oriented patent applications per unit of GDP in high-tech sectors, such as ICT and biotechnology, is higher in Korea than in other leading countries (Table 8.1), indicating that Korean companies' strong R&D investment is paying off in terms of intellectual property production.

**TABLE 8.1** Science and technology indicators of selected countries, 2015

|  | Korea | USA | Japan | Germany |
|---|---|---|---|---|
| R&D intensity (%) | 4.23 | 2.79 | 3.29 | 2.93 |
| Business-financed R&D intensity (%) | 3.15 | 1.79 | 2.56 | 1.92 |
| ICT patent applications/billion US$ of GDP* | 3.12 | 0.91 | 1.95 | 0.61 |
| Biotechnology patent applications/billion US$ of GDP* | 0.39 | 0.28 | 0.25 | 0.16 |

*Source*: OECD (2017).

* Patent applications under the Patent Cooperation Treaty; GDP at current prices and purchasing power parities.

Further insights into the general development and particular areas of strength of Korea's technological competitiveness can be gained from an analysis of the country's technology trade, which includes cross-border trade of intellectual property rights such as patents and trademarks, and payments for technology services and R&D activities in other countries. Korea's technology exports increased more than 50-fold between 2000 and 2016, illustrating the steeply accelerating global importance of Korean technology (Table 8.2). Moreover, while technology imports are still larger than exports, reflecting the extensive usage of global technologies by Korean companies, the country's technology trade is now much more balanced than in the past due to the rapid increase in technology exports. Most of these technology exports are related to information and communication services and devices (Figure 8.1), confirming Korea's strength in the ICT sector as indicated by global patent statistics (Table 8.1).

**TABLE 8.2** Development of Korea's technology trade

| Year | Technology exports (million US$) | Technology imports (million US$) | Technology export/import ratio |
|------|----------------------------------|----------------------------------|--------------------------------|
| 2000 | 201 | 3,063 | 0.07 |
| 2005 | 1,625 | 4,525 | 0.36 |
| 2010 | 3,345 | 10,234 | 0.33 |
| 2016 | 10,687 | 14,842 | 0.72 |

*Source:* Ministry of Science and ICT (2018).

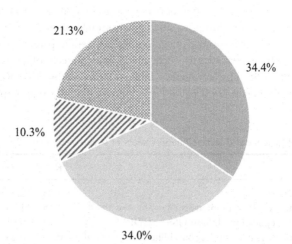

- Information and communication services
- Information and communication devices
- Automobiles
- Others

**FIGURE 8.1**  Korea's technology exports by industry, 2016

*Source:* Ministry of Science and ICT (2018).

Finally, Korea's technological strength can also be assessed through the lens of the lead market concept. Lead markets, understood as countries that, driven by local demand preferences and local environmental conditions, induce global innovations (Beise, 2004), may be viewed as an application of Porter's diamond framework of national competitive advantage (Porter, 1990) in the context of innovation leadership and technology diffusion. Price and cost, demand, transfer and export and market structure advantages have been identified as attributes of lead markets (Beise, 2004). In the case of Korea, companies such as Samsung Electronics have achieved global technological and market leadership in important semiconductor product lines such as memory chips since the early 1990s (Shin & Jang, 2005; Song & Lee, 2014). This leading position was subsequently extended to the mobile phone industry through the development of pioneering technologies in collaboration between large assembly firms, their suppliers, and equipment manufacturers (Choung et al., 2014). Korea's strong position in the ICT industries was further strengthened by government policies, which focused on the rapid formation of internet infrastructure and the fast adoption of related technology standards (Hovav et al., 2011). Additionally, Korean customers not only quickly adopted internet-based products and services but also turned out to be highly demanding in terms of product quality as well as speed and reliability of services, fueling competition among Korean firms and inducing them to become world-leading competitors in ICT products and services. As a result of all these factors, Korea may be regarded as a global lead market in major parts of the ICT sector.

In summary, Korean companies, supported by their strong R&D investment as well as by governmental policies and demand-side factors, have become leading global competitors in various technology- and knowledge-intensive industries. Korea is particularly strong in ICT products and services such as semiconductors, mobile phones, and mobile applications, suggesting that from a non-Korean perspective, there is much to learn from Korean firms in these industries.

## How to learn?

How can non-Korean companies acquire technological knowledge from their Korean counterparts, particularly in industries where Korea is technologically leading, such as the ICT sector? One potential means of learning are contractual arrangements with Korean firms, such as licensing in or buying intellectual property from them. As the international technology trade analysis in the previous section has revealed, such contract-based technology transfer from Korea to other countries is rapidly gaining in importance. However, there are also major limitations for cross-border technology acquisition by relying on the licensing or purchase of intellectual property only, for two reasons.

First, technologically leading companies, in Korea as elsewhere, will often be unwilling to share or even sell their most valuable intellectual property to other companies, as such technology sharing or selling may have negative implications for their future competitiveness. Subsequently, foreign companies could potentially leverage the technologies they have acquired from their Korean counterparts by developing more advanced products and services based on these technologies and thereby strengthen their competitive positions vis-à-vis Korean firms. The high uncertainty regarding the competitive implications of technology licensing has been identified as a major transaction cost which often dissuades firms from licensing out or selling their intellectual property (Teece, 1988), in particular when it is highly valuable (Arora & Ceccagnoli, 2006).

Second, there are limitations in the effectiveness of technology transfer when it is exclusively or predominantly based on formal legal titles and the sharing or transfer of written documents such as patents, utility models or blueprints. These limitations are due to the "stickiness" of technological knowledge (von Hippel, 1994), which is often deeply embedded in organizational routines of companies which possess this knowledge (Nelson & Winter, 1982). In other words, as much technological knowledge is tacit and not codified in written documents such as patents or blueprints, its transfer to other organizations is often ineffective unless the sharing of written documents is accompanied by intensive and sustained person-to-person interaction.

Therefore, in order to increase the effectiveness of technological learning, non-Korean companies should engage in major efforts to build strong relationships with technologically leading Korean firms that go beyond formal contractual knowledge transfer agreements and may include strategic alliances and joint ventures. Trust, tie strength and shared visions and systems between participating companies have all been found to greatly enhance interorganizational knowledge transfer (Van Wijk et al., 2008). Such strong relationships could be built within the context of supply-chain relationships where non-Korean firms are either the suppliers or the customers of their Korean partners.

Furthermore, a strong learning orientation with sufficient resource deployment and a fundamental willingness to learn from the partner is also crucial for effective technological knowledge acquisition from other companies (Simonin, 2004). A similar approach is recommended in order to gain cutting-edge technological knowledge from lead markets (Beise & Cleff, 2004). In order to address the need to build strong ties with technologically leading firms and to facilitate the interorganizational transfer of advanced technological knowledge, the setup of R&D units in close geographical proximity to partner firms is regarded as a highly effective organizational arrangement for multinational firms (Phene & Almeida, 2008).

Survey data on foreign companies' R&D activities in Korea show that the number of firms that are conducting R&D and the size of their R&D investments have steeply increased from a low base over the last two decades. The number of foreign firms with R&D activities increased from 60 in 1999 to 102 in 2002 (Kim, 2003), 259 in 2009 (KOITA, 2011), and 375 in 2014 (Ministry of Trade, Industry and Energy, 2016). Furthermore, their R&D expenses rose from KRW85 billion in 1999 to KRW2.12 trillion in 2014. The proportion of foreign companies' R&D expenses to all Korean business R&D increased from 0.8% to 6.2% during the same period (Kim, 2003; Ministry of Trade, Industry and Energy, 2016). This ratio, which indicates the relative weight of foreign companies' R&D spending in a country, has reached a level similar to Japan (6.6%) but is still considerably lower than in major

Western countries such as the USA (16.7%), France (21.0%), Germany (22.4%) and the UK (51.3%) (OECD, 2017). In summary, while the R&D activities of foreign companies in Korea still play a relatively minor role in Korea, they are rapidly expanding. This indicates that Korea is increasingly being viewed as an important location to acquire technological competencies by non-Korean firms.

An analysis of foreign companies' subsidiaries in Korea with R&D activities in 2012 (Figure 8.2) shows that most of these companies originate from advanced countries, specifically, the USA, Japan, and EU countries. Furthermore, most of them fall to technologically advanced manufacturing industries such as automobiles,

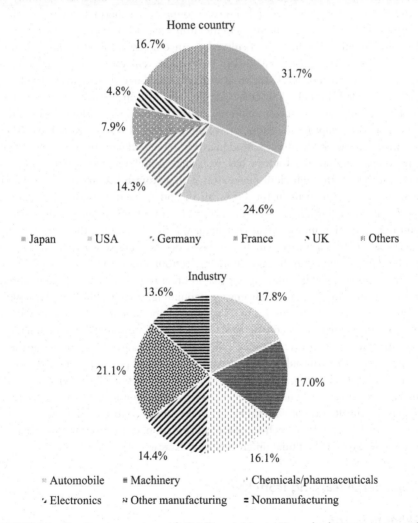

**FIGURE 8.2**    Foreign companies with R&D activities in Korea by home country and industry, 2012

*Source:* Lim (2012); Hemmert et al. (2015).

machinery, chemicals/pharmaceuticals, and electronics. The most frequently stated reason on why they considered conducting R&D in Korea as advantageous is close collaboration with proximate customers. Furthermore, the most frequent types of external collaboration partners are customers and suppliers, with whom 35% and 27% of all foreign subsidiaries collaborated, respectively (Lim, 2012). These data altogether suggest that most foreign firms which have set up R&D activities in Korea are technologically advanced and focus on close technological collaboration with Korean customers and suppliers.

A study on the antecedents of the growth of foreign-owned R&D labs in Korea has shown that the strongest growth-enabling factor is the managerial autonomy of R&D labs from headquarters in their home countries. Furthermore, their growth is supported by technology sourcing activities from external and firm-internal sources but diminished by the amount of cultural distance between the firms' home country and Korea (Hemmert et al., 2015). In a similar vein, case examples of foreign companies with major R&D activities in Korea reveal that these firms technologically succeeded through close collaboration with Korean partners and customers and by developing customized solutions for the Korean market, which sometimes can be used as templates for business development in Asia at large (KOTRA, 2017). An in-depth case study of a US-headquartered semiconductor firm has found that the company's Korean subsidiary has succeeded in building cutting-edge innovation capabilities through close interaction with a Korean lead user, on one hand, and its own parent firm in the USA, on the other hand. Subsidiary executives could effectively engage in such interaction due to a high amount of managerial autonomy. Another important success factor was the expertise of the Korean technical staff at the subsidiary which was based on their previous work experience with other companies in the Korean microelectronics industry (Lim et al., 2017).

In summary, these findings suggest that in order to learn effectively from Korea, non-Korean firms should actively engage in building strong technological ties with Korean firms. An effective means to do so is the establishment of R&D units within Korea and seeking close collaboration with Korean customers and suppliers in industries where Korea is technologically leading, such as the ICT sector. Furthermore, foreign firms' subsidiary managers in Korea should be given sufficient autonomy for local initiatives and technological interaction with local partners. Such managerial autonomy appears to be particularly important for effective knowledge acquisition in the case of Western firms, where strong control by the parent company could render local technological collaboration ineffective due to frictions caused by substantial cultural differences with Korea.

## Managerial learning from Korea

### What to learn?

In addition to technological competencies, Korean companies have also acquired managerial competencies that greatly enhance their global competitiveness. These managerial competencies have been built over decades when organizational practices in Korean firms were established based on various roots (Hemmert, 2018). Korean culture is essentially linked to Confucianism, which thereby constitutes an important foundation of Korean managerial practices. Additionally, Korean companies' management systems were also strongly influenced by Japan, the USA and the military-style industrialization that shaped the Korean manufacturing sector from the 1960s to the 1980s. Building on these various foundations, Korean companies have developed a distinct set of managerial practices which are particularly visible in the domains of strategy, leadership, and HRM (Hemmert, 2018). They enabled them to grow quickly and compete effectively in knowledge-intensive industries, such as electronics, microelectronics and automobiles, on a global level, with a particularly strong performance in China and other emerging markets.

In the strategy domain, Korean firms stand out for their highly aggressive, opportunity-centered strategic orientation. They seek growth by expanding their activities into new industries as well as into new geographical markets. The strong growth orientation of Korean firms and business groups manifests itself through their high degree of diversification (Chang, 2003) and their fast expansion into global business (Hemmert, 2018). Furthermore, as discussed in the previous section, Korean firms also strongly invest in the development of new products and services as another avenue for future growth. Such growth-centered strategies are fundamentally risky, as firms which apply these strategies are expanding into new types of businesses and business environments they have not been familiar with hitherto. However, Korean firms often managed to succeed with their growth-seeking strategies by implementing them quickly and flexibly. They have been breaking conventional wisdom in many industries on how long it takes to build a new facility and develop a new product or to enter a new market. This high speed has been enabled by various managerial tools, such as expedited decision-making processes (Song & Lee, 2014) and the setup of task forces (Shin & Jang, 2005). Furthermore, Korean firms are highly flexible on how a specific business project or goal may be achieved, both with regard to internal resource allocation and to external collaboration. Fundamentally, they show a strong pragmatism and swiftly change the way a plan is being implemented if they find that a different approach is more effective than what was initially planned. Overall, the combination of aggressive expansion and fast and flexible implementation frequently enables Korean companies to compete effectively on a global level (Hemmert, 2018).

In the leadership domain, Korean companies tend to rely on the charismatic leadership of top-level executives, such as the chairmen of business groups, who have strong capabilities to motivate and inspire employees (Dorfman et al., 1997). While charisma is a trait of individuals, it can be observed that charismatic business leaders are particularly effective in Korea and therefore are frequently elevated to top-level positions. Korean top-level executives rely on a range of leadership tools, including corporate values, goal setting and crisis creation. Whereas corporate values are formulated in many companies around the world, they are particularly important in Korea. Corporate values in Korean companies are linked to the personal values of business leaders and at the same time are emphasized in training programs and incorporated in operating guidelines for staff members' activities (Chung et al., 1997). As a result, a strong alignment between top-level leadership and organizational behavior is often achieved. Goals tend to be highly ambitious and highly specific (Cho & Yoon, 2001), and they are set not only for organizational units of companies but also for individual employees in order to motivate them strongly. Furthermore, Korean business leaders sometimes deliberately create crises within their companies by devising highly ambitious business plans which induce employees to make extraordinary efforts in order to achieve what is needed and to avert failure (Kim, 1998). The process of overcoming such crises often elevates companies to a much higher level of competitiveness, as employees search for new, innovative ways to be more effective. Overall, many Korean companies have achieved outstanding business performance through the strong leadership of their top-level executives.

Finally, in the human resource management (HRM) domain, Korean companies engage in strong and comprehensive efforts when recruiting new employees. They assess not only applicants' professional skills and capabilities, but also the fit of their personalities with the firm's organizational culture in order to secure highly effective personnel (Froese et al., 2018). Moreover, Korean companies are heavily investing in their employees' skill formation by regularly subjecting them to training programs. These training programs are mostly organized by corporate training centers and target all managerial levels, not only new employees. Furthermore, they are often highly tailored to specific types of tasks and positions in order to maximize participants' relevant professional skill formation (Hemmert, 2018). Lastly, since the 1990s, many Korean firms have transformed their employee compensation and promotion systems, which formerly were mostly seniority-oriented in line with Confucian traditions and Japanese practices. Companies now offer strong performance incentives to individual employees, including bonus payments, fast-track promotion opportunities and profit-sharing systems. These HRM tools are effective in enhancing the performance of Korean managers and employees, who tend to be highly ambitious and achievement-oriented (Bae & Lawler, 2000).

Overall, these managerial practices have greatly contributed to the strong competitiveness of Korean companies in recent decades. The practices have enabled companies to acquire dynamic capabilities, understood as a firm's ability to integrate, build and reconfigure internal and external competencies to address rapidly changing environments and thereby renew competencies that provide the firm with a competitive advantage (Teece et al., 1997). Specifically, Korean firms have gained competitive strength by acquiring the following capabilities (Hemmert, 2018):

- The capability to seize opportunities
- The capability to endure and overcome difficulties
- The capability to learn from past experiences, including both successes and failures

- The capability to learn from others
- The capability to act quickly
- The capability to change procedures flexibly

In summary, there are various managerial practices in the strategy, leadership and HRM domains, which greatly help many Korean firms with gaining and sustaining competitive advantage and which non-Korean firms could therefore study and adopt to strengthen their own competitiveness. However, depending on the industry and market environment and the cultural context a company is operating in, the attractiveness of these managerial tools and the ease of learning them is likely to differ (Figure 8.3).

With regard to the industry and market environment, Korean managerial practices appear to be particularly attractive for firms that are exposed to high volatility and rapid change, as the managerial practices are focused on finding rapid and effective responses in a changing business environment. In a market context, a high degree of volatility and change can be observed in emerging markets, which tend to grow strongly and exhibit high political and regulatory uncertainty and weak institutions. In an industry context, high-tech industries such as the ICT sector are particularly dynamic and often feature disruptive innovations, which render an established business model obsolete and replace it with a new one (Christensen, 1997). Therefore, learning and adopting Korean managerial practices will yield the highest returns for companies which operate in emerging markets and in industries that feature rapid technological change.

With regard to the cultural environment, various managerial practices of Korean companies, such as strong leadership by executive managers and effective teamwork by members of task forces and corporate units, have foundations in Korean cultural traditions. Therefore, some adjustment is needed for effectively transferring Korean managerial practices to different cultural environments, and the larger the cultural distance between Korea and the target location, the more challenging this

|  |  | Cultural similarity to Korea | |
|---|---|---|---|
|  |  | High | Low |
| Dynamism of industry and market environment | High | Easy to adopt, highly attractive | Challenging to adopt, highly attractive |
|  | Low | Easy to adopt, less attractive | Challenging to adopt, less attractive |

**FIGURE 8.3**   Ease of adoption and attractiveness of Korean management practices across business environments

*Source:* Hemmert (2018).

adjustment can be expected to be. Specifically, two Korean cultural features can be clearly linked to managerial practices of Korean firms: high power distance and collectivism (Hemmert, 2018). Consequently, Korean management practices may be transferred with relative ease to other countries with high power distance and collectivistic cultures, such as the East Asian countries and territories which have been grouped together with Korea into the "Confucian Asia" cluster in the GLOBE study (Gupta & Hanges, 2004): China, Japan, Taiwan, Hong Kong and Singapore. Conversely, the transfer to locations with low power distance and highly individualistic cultures, such as Northern European countries, can be expected to be more challenging, as more cultural adjustment will be required.

In summary, from the perspective of non-Korean firms, there is much to learn from the managerial practices of their Korean counterparts, which have developed a wide range of effective tools in the strategy, leadership and HRM domains. These tools are most effective in business environments with high dynamism and uncertainty, such as the ICT sector, and are easiest to transfer to locations which are culturally similar to Korea, such as other East Asian countries.

### How to learn?

Research on cross-border managerial knowledge transfer suggests that similarly to technological learning, a few fundamental conditions greatly enhance the effectiveness of such transfer processes (Gupta & Govindarajan, 2000): First, there needs to be a sufficient learning motivation and learning capacity at the receiving side. Second, the knowledge source needs to be willing to share the relevant information and expertise. Third, the knowledge transmission channels should be as broad and diverse as possible. These points indicate that in order to absorb Korean managerial knowledge effectively, non-Korean firms need to be aware of the managerial learning potential and should build and leverage strong relationships with Korean partners. Many non-Korean firms have already established such relationships with Korean firms, including supply-chain collaborations and strategic alliances.

However, there are also two major differences between technological and managerial knowledge transfer on the interorganizational level. First, in contrast to technological knowledge, managerial knowledge mainly consists of organizational practices and is therefore not protected by intellectual property rights, such as patents and utility models. Therefore, there is rarely a need for formal legal transfer arrangements (e.g., licensing contracts) with the companies which constitute the knowledge sources. Second, managerial knowledge is strongly embedded in organizational routines of companies and is therefore even more tacit than technological knowledge, which tends to be codified to a relatively higher extent in documents such as patents and blueprints.

These two differences have important implications for managerial learning from other companies. On one hand, when compared with technological knowledge acquisition, there are less legal and formal obstacles for acquiring managerial knowledge from other companies. In other words, once non-Korean companies have identified Korean managerial practices they would like to adopt, they may study and emulate them freely, without being obligated to enter formal transfer agreements with Korean firms. On the other hand, the strongly tacit nature of managerial knowledge implies that transferring such knowledge effectively across organizations is highly challenging. As was already discussed in the context of technological learning, tacit knowledge is highly "sticky" and therefore difficult to transfer across organizational and geographical boundaries. Furthermore, the adoption of new managerial systems or tools amounts to an organizational innovation from the perspective of the firm where it is introduced, and the successful implementation of organizational innovations is particularly demanding. In order to implement such innovations effectively, all members of an organization affected by its introduction should be actively involved in the adoption process in order to strengthen acceptance. Moreover, the presence of sponsors and champions who provide the necessary resources and create enthusiasm within the adopting organizations is highly important. Finally, organizational innovations should be tailored to the needs of the companies that introduce them (Leonard-Barton, 1988).

These considerations suggest that while managerial learning from Korean firms can be initiated and conducted freely, the effective implementation of Korean managerial tools in non-Korean firms is challenging and requires a high amount of commitment. In addition to the general difficulties of adopting new managerial tools and methods, the cultural distance between Korea and the location of the adopting company constitutes an additional challenge, as discussed in the previous section.

The adoption of Japanese managerial tools in Western countries illustrates the potential and the challenges of cross-border managerial learning. Managerial techniques which were initially developed in Japanese companies, such as the efficient organization of supply chains for just-in-time delivery or the institutionalization of continuous improvement (*kaizen*), have been introduced in non-Japanese firms since the 1990s under the overarching concept of 'lean production' and have helped many of these firms with gaining or regaining competitiveness (Marodin & Saurin, 2013). However, the effective absorption of the relevant managerial knowledge by non-Japanese firms has often been difficult and slow. For example, after establishing a joint manufacturing plant with Toyota, it took General Motors many years to fully understand the relevant Japanese managerial concepts and to transfer the knowledge to its other sites and factories (Inkpen, 2008).

In view of these observations, non-Korean firms need a strong commitment and a high amount of patience in order to effectively absorb managerial knowledge from their Korean peers. Senior executives should strongly communicate the potential benefits of learning from Korean firms, and managers and employees should become broadly involved in the adoption process in a participatory manner, facilitating the adaptation of Korean managerial tools to the context of the adopting company. While leveraging business relationships with Korean firms, learning transfer channels should be as strong and diverse as possible to ease and expedite the absorption of managerial knowledge. Similarly to technological learning, non-Korean firms may first absorb Korean managerial knowledge at their subsidiaries in Korea and subsequently transfer this knowledge to other geographical locations. Another potential way of enhancing managerial learning from Korea, which has been chosen by some Chinese and Indian firms, is the hiring of capable Korean managers for executive positions at their headquarter locations (Hemmert, 2018).

## Conclusion

The analysis in this chapter has shown that there is a strong potential for non-Korean firms to learn from their Korean peers, both technologically and managerially. With regard to technological knowledge, Korean firms have become world-leading in various knowledge-intensive industries, such as semiconductors and mobile communications. In managerial terms, they have developed effective managerial tools in the strategy, leadership and HRM domains which often give them a strong edge in global competition. Korean technological and managerial knowledge overall appears to be most valuable in dynamic and volatile business environments, suggesting that learning from Korea is particularly attractive for firms in high-tech, fast-moving industries and in emerging markets that tend to feature high dynamism and uncertainty.

However, learning from Korea is also challenging for non-Korean firms, for various reasons. The relevant technological and managerial knowledge is often strongly tacit and thereby difficult to absorb. Furthermore, due to cultural differences, the cross-border transfer of managerial knowledge is particularly challenging and time-consuming. Therefore, non-Korean firms need a strong commitment and a high amount of patience in order to learn effectively from their Korean peers. First of all, an awareness needs to be created that Korean companies possess technological and managerial knowledge that provides them with strong global competitiveness and that such knowledge should therefore be absorbed, whenever possible. Establishing such an awareness requires good communication of the fast progress and strong competencies of Korean firms, which were lagging behind their Western and Japanese counterparts in the past, by non-Korean firms' managers. Furthermore, non-Korean firms should establish strong relationships with Korean firms in order to learn from them effectively. In view of the many challenges and difficulties of cross-border knowledge transfer, technological and managerial learning often will initially be conducted most effectively by subsidiaries of non-Korean firms located in Korea, which may subsequently pass on the knowledge they have absorbed to their companies' sites in other countries.

## Case study:   Ericsson–LG

Ericsson–LG is a joint venture between Ericsson, a major global competitor in the telecommunication network industry from Sweden, and LG Electronics a leading Korean electronics and mobile phone producer. The joint venture of the two companies started in 2010 when Ericsson acquired Nortel's majority ownership stake of 75% in LG Nortel, a joint venture established in 2005.

Ericsson–LG focuses on the engineering and design of telecommunications equipment. The company has approximately 900 employees, and the majority among them work in its R&D center in Anyang, with 500 engineers. The company invests KRW100 billion (approximately equivalent to USD100 million) into R&D annually, which amount to about one third of its domestic sales in Korea.

Ericsson's high R&D investment in Korea is motivated by the country's position as a global lead market in mobile phone network technology. The pace of innovation in Korea, which has a smartphone penetration rate of over 90%, provides Ericsson–LG with an opportunity to be 12 to 18 months ahead of the rest of the world. This first mover advantage is supported through close long-term relationships with all three major mobile phone service providers in the country: Korea Telecom, LG U Plus, and SK Telecom. Ericsson–LG is also collaborating with Korean start-ups which develop relevant technologies.

As an outcome of these collaborations and its own R&D efforts, Ericsson–LG succeeded in various first-to-the-world technology introductions. Now, the company focuses its efforts on taking the lead in the development of the newest generation of "5G" network technologies. For example, in 2016 and 2017 it conducted a series of outdoor trials with SK Telecom and BMW Korea, establishing high-performance network connections with automobiles at a driving speed of 170 km/h. Leveraging Korea's strong R&D infrastructure and leading position in mobile network technologies, Ericsson–LG thereby sees itself at the forefront of the Fourth Industrial Revolution.

## Sources

Ericsson–LG 2017. *News. Ericsson, SK Telecom and BMW Group Korea reach new world record speed with 5G.* Feb 7, 2017. www.ericsson.com/en/news/2017/2/ericsson-sk-telecom-and-bmw-group-korea-reach-new-world-record-speed-with-5g. Accessed 23 November 2018.

Ericsson–LG 2018a. *Overview.* www.ericssonlg.com/site/ericssonlg/menu/131.do. Accessed 23 November 2018.

Ericsson LG 2018b. *R&D Overview.* www.ericssonlg.com/site/ericssonlg/menu/147.do. Accessed 23 November 2018.

KOTRA – Korea Trade-Investment Promotion Agency. 2017. Ericsson–LG. In KOTRA (Ed.), *KOTRA Success Cases of Foreign-Invested Companies*: 82–84. Seoul: KOTRA.

# Bibliography

## Key references

Hemmert, M. 2018. *The evolution of tiger management: Korean companies in global competition.* Oxon, New York: Routledge.

Kim, L. 1997. *Imitation to innovation: The dynamics of Korea's technological learning.* Boston: Harvard Business School Press.

Song, J., & Lee, K. 2014. *The Samsung way: Transformational management strategies from the world leader in innovation and design.* New York: McGraw-Hill.

## Online source

OECD – Organisation for Economic Co-operation and Development. 2019. *OECD. Stat, main science and technology indicators.* https://stats.oecd.org/Index.aspx?DataSet Code=MSTI_PUB.

# References

Arora, A., & Ceccagnoli, M. 2006. Patent protection, complementary assets, and firms' incentives for technology licensing. *Management Science,* 52(2): 293–308.

Bae, J., & Lawler, J. J. 2000. Organizational and HRM strategies in Korea: Impact on firm performance in an emerging economy. *Academy of Management Journal,* 43(3): 502–517.

Beise, M. 2004. Lead markets: Country-specific drivers of the global diffusion of innovations. *Research Policy,* 33(6/7): 997–1018.

Beise, M., & Cleff, T. 2004. Assessing the lead market potential of countries for innovation projects. *Journal of International Management,* 10(4): 453–477.

Chang, S. J. 2003. *Financial crisis and transformation of Korean business groups: The rise and fall of chaebols.* Cambridge: Cambridge University Press.

Cho, Y. H., & Yoon, J. 2001. The origin and function of dynamic collectivism: An analysis of Korean corporate culture. *Asia Pacific Business Review,* 7(4): 70–88.

Choung, J. Y., Hwang, H. R., & Song, W. 2014. Transitions of innovation activities in Latecomer Countries: An exploratory case study of South Korea. *World Development,* 54(1): 156–167.

Christensen, C. M. 1997. *The innovator's dilemma: When new technologies cause great firms to fail.* Boston: Harvard Business Review Press.

Chung, K. H., Lee, H. C., & Jung, J. H. 1997. *Korean management: Global strategy and cultural transformation.* Berlin: Walter de Gruyter.

Dorfman, P. W., Howell, J. P., Hibino, S., Lee, J. K., Tate, U., & Bautista, A. 1997. Leadership in Western and Asian Countries: Commonalities and differences in effective leadership processes across cultures. *Leadership Quarterly,* 8(3): 233–274.

Froese, F. J., Sekiguchi, T., & Maharjan, M. P. 2018. Human resource management in Japan and South Korea. In F. L. Cooke & S. Kim (Eds.), *Routledge handbook of human resource management in Asia:* 275–294. Abingdon: Routledge.

Gartner Newsroom. 2018. *Gartner says worldwide sales of smartphones recorded first ever decline during the fourth quarter of 2017.* www.gartner.com/newsroom/id/3859963.

Gupta, A. K., & Govindarajan, V. 2000. Knowledge flows within multinational corporations. *Strategic Management Journal,* 21(4): 473–496.

Gupta, V., & Hanges, P. J. 2004. Regional and climate clustering of societal cultures. In R. J. House, P. J. Hanges, M. Javidan, P. W. Dorfman, & V. Gupta (Eds.), *Culture, leadership, and organizations: The globe study of 62 societies:* 178–218. Thousand Oaks: Sage.

Hemmert, M., Lim, C., & Kim, S. 2015. What drives the R&D capacity growth of foreign subsidiaries? A study of MNE subsidiaries in Korea. *Asian Journal of Technology Innovation*, 23(2): 121–139.

Hovav, A., Hemmert, M., & Kim, Y. J. 2011. Determinants of internet standards adoption: The case of South Korea. *Research Policy*, 40(2): 253–262.

Inkpen, A. 2008. Knowledge transfer and international joint Ventures: The case of NUMMI and general motors. *Strategic Management Journal*, 29(4): 447–453.

Kim, L. 1998. Crisis construction and organizational learning: Capability building in catching-up at Hyundai Motor. *Organization Science*, 9(4): 506–521.

Kim, K. 2003. *Current status and challenges of foreign-owned companies' R&D activities. STEPI Policy Report 2003–15*. Seoul: Science & Technology Policy Institute. 김기국, 외국인투자기업의 R&D 현황 및 과제. 정책자료 2003–15, 과학기술영구원.

KOITA – Korea Industrial Technology Association. 2011. *Analysis of the development of R&D investments and employee size of foreign companies with research labs in Korea. KOITA R&D Statistics report 2011–1.* 한국산업기술진흥협회, 국내연구소 보유외국인투자기업의 R&D투자 및 인력 동향분석 KOITA R&D통계리포트 제2011–1호.

KOTRA – Korea Trade-Investment Promotion Agency. 2017. *2017 KOTRA success cases of foreign-invested companies.* Seoul, Korea, IK: KOTRA.

Leonard-Barton, D. 1988. Implementation characteristics of organizational innovations: Limits and opportunities for management strategies. *Communication Research*, 15(5): 603–631.

Lim, C. 2012. *Report on the foreign direct investment firms and the policy for promoting collaborative R&D among firms and universities and public R&D institutes*, Seoul, Korea, IK: Ministry of Knowledge Economy. 임채성, 외국인투자기업과 국내 산학연간 공동 R&D활성화 방안 연구 보고서. 서울: 지식경제부.

Lim, C., Hemmert, M., & Kim, S. 2017. MNE subsidiary evolution from sales to innovation: Looking inside the black box. *International Business Review*, 26(1): 145–155.

Marodin, G. A., & Saurin, T. A. 2013. Implementing lean production systems: Research areas and opportunities for future studies. *International Journal of Production Research*, 51(22): 6663–6680.

Ministry of Science and ICT. 2017. *Statistics report on the technology trade of Korea in accordance with OECD TBP Manual 2016*. Ministry of Science and ICT. 과학기술정보통신부, 2016 기술무역통계보고서.

Ministry of Science and ICT. 2018. *2016 Survey of Research and Development in Korea*. Ministry of Science and ICT. 과학기술정보통신부, 2016년도연구개발활동조사 보고서.

Ministry of Trade, Industry and Energy. 2016. *The foreigner investment enterprise management fact-finding survey: Management status of foreign-invested companies (2013–2015)*. Ministry of Trade, Industry and Energy. 산업통상자원부, 외국인 투자기업 경영실태조사: 외국인 투자기업 경영실태(2013~2015).

Nelson, R. R., & Winter, S. G. 1982. *An evolutionary theory of economic change*. Cambridge: Harvard University Press.

OECD – Organisation for Economic Co-operation and Development. 2017. *Main Science and Technology Indicators, Volume 2017, Issue 1*. Paris: OECD Publishing.

Porter, M. 1990. *The competitive advantage of nations*. New York: Free Press.

Phene, A., & Almeida, P. 2008. Innovation in multinational subsidiaries: The role of knowledge assimilation and subsidiary capabilities. *Journal of International Business Studies*, 39(5): 901–919.

Shaffer, B. 2017. *Semiconductor industry continues upward trend toward record year, IHS Markit says.* https://technology.ihs.com/598336/semiconductor-industry-continues-upward-trend-toward-record-year-ihs-markit-says.

Shin, J. S., & Jang, S. W. 2005. *Creating first-mover advantages: The case of Samsung electronics.* SCAPE Working Paper No. 2005/13, Department of Economics, National University of Singapore.

Simonin, B. L. 2004. An empirical investigation of the process of knowledge transfer in international strategic alliances. *Journal of International Business Studies*, 35(5): 407–427.

Teece, D. J. 1988. Technological change and the nature of the firm. In G. Dosi, C. Freeman, R. Nelson, G. Silverberg, & L. Soete (Eds.), *Technical change and economic theory*: 256–281. London, New York: Pinter.

Teece, D. J., Pisano, G., & Shuen, A. 1997. Dynamic capabilities and strategic management. *Strategic Management Journal*, 18(7): 509–533.

Van Wijk, R., Jansen, J. J. P., & Lyles, M. A. 2008. Inter- and intra-organizational knowledge transfer: A meta-analytic review and assessment of its antecedents and consequences. *Journal of Management Studies*, 45(4): 830–853.

Von Hippel, E. 1994. "Sticky Information" and the locus of problem solving: Implications for innovation. *Management Science*, 40(4): 429–439.

# PART III
# Marketing and managing in Korea

# 9

# MARKETING IN KOREA

*Fabian Jintae Froese and Sarah Reckelkamm*

## Introduction

South Korea (henceforth Korea) has been an attractive market for foreign companies due to its substantial size, economic growth, and affluent consumers. Currently, more than 51 million people live in Korea, and the GDP per capita stands at around US$38,000 (International Monetary Fund, 2018). Korea can be considered a medium-sized industrialized economy, roughly comparable to that of Italy or Spain. Unlike those countries, however, Korea does not belong to a major trading union like the European Union. To increase trade, Korea has developed FTAs with several countries and trading unions, including the European Union, Chile, New Zealand, and Peru. As a result, foreign companies have increasingly invested in and/or exported to Korea (also see Chapters 5 and 6).

In this chapter, we discuss the opportunities and challenges of marketing in Korea from the perspective of foreign companies, with a focus on marketing issues related to products/services, pricing, promotion, and distribution (place) (AMA, 2013; McCarthy, 1960), the so-called 4Ps. To be successful in a certain market, a company has to base its activities on the needs and wants of the customers in that specific market while also handling environmental restrictions such as laws, industry agreements, norms, and so on (Grönroos, 1989). According to Song et al. (1997), marketing plays a central role in effectively and efficiently translating market information into product concepts and then positioning the product offerings in the target market. Doyle (2003) identified two key features for marketing management: the selection of the target market and the design of the marketing mix. Any decisions concerning the marketing strategy have to involve these two features. While Korea presents an attractive market, the political, legal, economic, and cultural environments pose challenges for foreign companies, meaning those companies have to consider whether and how alterations in terms of product/services, price, promotion, and place are important for success in the Korean market.

In the following, we provide a brief overview of the Korean consumer market and marketing strategy, and then we discuss the 4Ps in more detail. The chapter ends with a summary of our conclusions.

## The Korean consumer market

In this section, we describe several special features of the Korean consumer market. Within a short period, Korea has catapulted itself from a poor, developing country to a rich, industrialized economy. This is important to consider, because values and consumer preferences can vary substantially between generations (Froese, 2009). Traditionally, marketing efforts target younger people. However, the Korean population has been rapidly rising and constantly aging. In 2008, the average age was 37 years, rising to 41 years in 2016 (The Korea Herald, 2017). With this rapidly aging population, senior consumers hold a growing importance in the so-called silver market. Companies must face this demographic change and adjust their products and marketing campaigns in order to meet the needs of a comparatively older customer base.

Korea used to have a traditional understanding of family and the role of mothers as homemakers. Even today, Korea is a gendered society with pronounced differences in preferences, stereotypes, and behaviors between men and women (Nam et al., 2011. The everyday shoppers in Korea are mostly women, who buy most of the goods for the whole family. Therefore, companies that offer their products should consider the persistent gender roles in society and adjust their marketing accordingly. The fertility rate and corresponding family size have shrunk substantially in recent years. Until recent years, most adult children have lived with their parents until getting married, but in recent years Korea has seen a steady rise of single-person households. As a consequence, there is a higher importance of convenient, efficient, and smaller-sized product solutions.

Korea is also a tech-savvy nation. It has the highest average internet connection speed in the world, and about 90% of the population has internet access (Statista, 2018). This excellent infrastructure provides the basis for the rapidly increasing importance of e-commerce. Almost anything can be purchased online and usually at a much cheaper cost than in the stationary retail stores. The market share of e-commerce has risen to 18% and is continuing to rise further (Santander Trade Portal, 2019a).

Another important feature of the Korean consumer market is a strong brand consciousness. Korean consumers link certain brands to superior quality and attribute high status and prestige to them. Large, well-known Korean companies such as Hyundai or Samsung enjoy this brand premium. While Koreans used to show xenophobic attitudes and avoided foreign brand names, many Koreans nowadays associate foreign goods with premium images, for example, wine from France or luxury apparel from Italy. Therefore, local branding and possible country-of-origin effects should be considered. Nevertheless, Korean consumers have low customer loyalty, not hesitating to switch brands if they perceive a better quality and/or status.

In its campaign to attract more tourists, Korea has been branded as 'dynamic Korea'. Indeed, the Korean market can be characterized as highly dynamic with new trends emerging and diffusing quickly. Once a trend has been established, other customers and competitors quickly follow suit. There are some trends that have conquered Korea by storm and remain strong. For instance, coffee shops played no major role in Korea, but once Starbucks entered the market, other foreign coffee companies followed, and soon Korean companies created their own coffee shops. The Korean company Caffe Bene overtook Starbucks within two years (Global Coffee Report, 2013). However, there still remain many trends that spread rapidly and disappear just as quickly. Foreign companies can fight legal battles against copycats – and will win – but the enforcement of rights can be expensive and take a long time.

## The marketing strategy in an international context

Facing an 'ever changing, ever challenging market' (Borden, 1984: 11), companies have to define an overall marketing strategy that helps to achieve the desired behavior of trade and consumers by combining certain practices and procedures. Borden (1942) recognized 'innumerable combinations of marketing methods and policies' (Borden, 1984: 8) and therefore identified the marketing strategy (based on Culliton, 1948) as a mixture of elements useful in pursuing a certain market response. The marketing mix consequently refers to 'a set of controllable tactical marketing tools that the firm blends to produce the response it wants in the target market' (Kotler et al., 2005: 34). In the international context, companies have to incorporate the international dimension by considering multiple markets, deciding on how to coordinate them, and how the marketing strategy fits each market the best.

One major question when internationalizing is to which degree products, practices, distribution channels, and prices can be standardized. According to Kotler et al. (2005), companies decide between a standardized marketing mix (using the same product/service, promotion, and distribution channels in all markets internationally) and the adapted marketing mix, where the marketing mix elements are adjusted to each international target market. This requires a good understanding of the market conditions and cultural characteristics of customers in the respective market. As customers in different countries have wide-ranging cultural backgrounds, needs, preferences, demands, purchasing power, and shopping patterns, companies often adjust their marketing strategy to the target market, although essential additional costs may arise (Kotler et al., 2005). Since companies try to maximize their benefits, they often choose the 'glocal' approach, which is where parts of the marketing strategy are standardized (or globalized) and others are localized. While products tend to be standardized to generate substantial savings in manufacturing costs, and often well-known distribution channels are used so that companies can build on their experience and expertise related to these channels, prices are often localized because of differences concerning price levels, cost, taxes, and competition. Also, the promotion of products and services tend to be localized to overcome cultural and language differences, to use media that is popular in that country, and to meet customers' needs and tastes in order to generate a larger market share and return (Kotler et al., 2005; Walker et al., 1992).

To be successful in a specific market, companies must be well-aware of situational factors, including the competition, technology, economic conditions; the political factors like legal and regulatory environments; and specific consumer needs (Mooradian et al., 2013). Those factors might all be tremendously different from what a company is used to in their home market, and therefore, they may affect how a certain product or service can be sold in the new market. In the following, we discuss each of the 4Ps in detail and provide recommendations on whether and how foreign companies should adapt their marketing.

## Product

The first element of the marketing mix is product/service – basically anything (mainly physical objects and services) that can be offered by a company to a target market for attention, acquisition, use, or consumption (Kotler et al., 2005). When a certain product or service is introduced to a new market, it might be necessary to make alterations due to legal, cultural, or economic reasons. Before bringing a product or service into the market, it is inevitable to analyze whether and which alterations have to be made. According to Walker et al. (1992), there are three major options concerning the standardization or adaptation of a product, depending on the extent to which a product will be modified:

- Standardization
  In this case, the company decides to market the same product in all countries. This decision is made for products that are not culture-sensitive (e.g. jet aircraft engines, basic steel, chemicals) based on the assumption that customer needs are similar in every market. Only minimal modifications regarding the labeling and language of the product manual will be implemented. The advantage of this approach is lower cost due to economies of scale, but products may still fail to meet customers' demands. Examples of the standardized approach are Coca-Cola, Heineken beer, and Philips shavers (Kotler et al., 2005).
- Adaptation to local conditions
  If there are different regulations and/or minor differences in customer taste in the target market, firms can largely keep the product as is and only make some minor modifications, such as changes in voltage, packaging, and color. This might be the case for products like computers, cars, or calculators.
- Development of a new product
  If there are major regulatory restraints and/or major differences in consumer demand, then it might be necessary to make substantial modifications or develop a completely new product in order to enter a certain market. This affects a substantial part of the costs of the product. Examples include packaged food or personal-care items (Kotler et al., 2005).

Due to the medium size of the Korean economy, most foreign firms should use a standardized approach or the minor adaptation approach when selling in Korea. It would be expensive to develop a new product only for the Korean market. Given the vast differences in consumer preferences due to cultural differences, some Western companies have developed new or largely modified products for China or Japan and then offer those products in neighboring Asian countries, such as Korea. For instance, L'Oreal's R&D center in Shanghai develops cosmetics products for the general Asian region.

While Korea is an attractive market, the regulatory environment sometimes puts in barriers for foreign companies. If foreign companies plan to enter the Korean market, they need to comply with the Korean regulations. Chambers of commerce and business associations can provide some initial guidance on local regulations.

The economic environment and corresponding consumer preferences have evolved rapidly in the last few decades. While South Korea used to be a developing country with limited capital producing rather low- to medium-quality goods in the past, it has evolved into a country producing products and services of increasing quality and the latest technology. Examples are the Hyundai Genesis 2016, which constantly ranks among the top luxury cars, or the Samsung mobile phones that are the most-sold mobile phones in the world (Gartner, 2018; U.S. News, 2019). As the quality and popularity of Korean products increase, the level of Korean consumers' sophistication and demand for quality increase. Although the Korean market still shows a relatively low degree of product diversity, and foreign companies' products have not been popular in the past due to xenophobia, the demand for foreign products rises. As we discuss further in the section on price, it is difficult to compete with Korean companies on cost; instead, most foreign companies distinguish themselves by providing high-quality products.

Foreign companies that want to enter this promising market have to understand the Koreans consumers in order to meet their needs. To adjust to the dynamism of the Korean market, they have to permanently analyze the market and preempt market trends with new features or products. Foreign companies can leverage perceptions of foreign products' superiority by premium product positioning and offering high quality as well as good service. One company that has perfected high-quality service is the Korean start-up Coupang. Coupang offers expedited delivery service and exceptional politeness.

## Price

When offering a specific product or service to a market, companies have to decide on the price. Pricing is a powerful instrument for leveraging profits and stimulating demand. In contrast to domestic business, international business can add substantial costs, possibly resulting in an escalation of product cost. While cost is not the only determinant of the price, companies need to consider costs. If firms export products to another country, they may face additional costs for transportation, tariffs, importer margins, wholesaler margins, and retailer margin (Daniels et al., 2015).

MNEs may charge different prices in different countries and regions to optimize their profitability. At the same time, they need to consider that an increased transparency concerning prices, for example, due to the use of the internet, increases the pressure regarding pricing levels. Thus, MNEs might not be able to pass on all additionally occurring costs to the customers. This means that product profitability, given the same final price, can vary substantially across countries. Based on the list price, companies often negotiate and offer discounts, trade-in allowances, and credit terms to adjust the price to the customers' perceptions in a given competitive situation (Kotler et al., 2005).

It is often difficult to adopt a standardized pricing strategy across countries, as there are several differences between countries that have to be considered, for instance, differences concerning the fluctuation of exchange rates, costs (e.g., for raw materials, labor, transportation), competition, local and global demand, distribution channels, taxes, regulative restrictions, or governmental interventions, as well as the strategic positioning of the company in the specific market (Walker et al., 1992).

The Korean won (KRW) is a freely floating currency with substantial fluctuation against major currencies. Figure 9.1 shows a historical overview of currency fluctuation between the euro and Korean won. While 1 euro was worth almost KRW2,000 in March 2009, it dropped below KRW1,200 in April 2015. Fluctuations in the range of 10% can easily occur within one month. This complicates pricing for specific products. Setting the price too high would damage competitiveness,

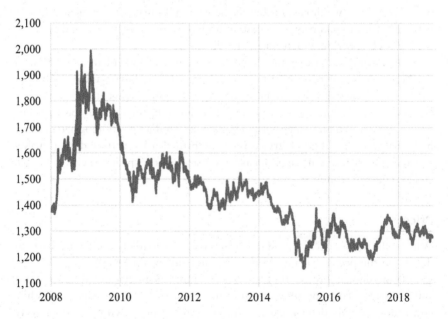

**FIGURE 9.1** Currency exchange rates

*Source:* European Central Bank (2019).

while a low price would erode profits. It is difficult to fluctuate prices and fully pass on those changes in prices due to currency fluctuations to customers. For instance, because of the soaring KRW in 2009, European companies were not able to export any French cheese or Italian ham to Korea. Thus, foreign companies needed to find a middle ground.

When a company enters the Korean market, it has to make a decision between different pricing strategies. Here, we distinguish between two extreme pricing strategies: skimming and penetration (Daniels et al., 2015). Skimming means that companies charge a relatively high price to profit from the attractiveness and newness of a product. Foreign products in Korea can often demand a price premium, as they are associated with higher brand value. Foreign products are often sold at a higher price compared to their home markets, particularly in product segments where they a enjoy competitive advantage. For instance, French wine, Italian fashion, and German premium cars can demand a price premium in Korea. However, due to global price transparency, foreign companies need to be careful not to set the price too high.

A second strategy is 'penetration', where companies try to maximize the volume of sold products by setting a relatively low price. When a product is established in the market, the price competition increases (Mooradian et al., 2013). Due to the increased price consciousness of Korean consumers, the importance of moderate prices and discount stores has increased in recent years (Lee & Trim, 2008). Therefore, it is also difficult for foreign companies to compete with large Korean companies in terms of price.

## Place

The third P, place, deals with 'activities that make the product available to target customers', the so-called distribution system or distribution channels (Kotler et al., 2005: 34). Each country has its own national distribution system that is historically intertwined with its cultural, economic, and legal environments (Walker et al., 1992). The establishment and maintenance of an effective and efficient distribution network in a foreign country are two of the biggest challenges when entering a foreign market (Walker et al., 1992).

To achieve effective market access, it is crucial to acquire knowledge about the foreign market's channel features and determine a strategy for how to enter these complex distribution systems (Kotler et al., 2005). Therefore, a company has to make decisions concerning selecting, motivating, and controlling channel members and possible cooperation (Kotler et al., 2005; Mooradian et al., 2013). In order to decide and design a distributional system, it is necessary to define where, how, and when the product or service will be bought; if there is any customer support (service, information and training, maintenance, etc.) required; if there are special demands on quality and safety of the distribution; and if different means of distribution might conflict (Mooradian et al., 2013). Distribution channels across markets are often difficult to standardize. Factors that influence the distribution of consumer products within a country include the cost of retail workers, legislation (e.g., operating hours), the ability of retailers to carry large inventories, and the potential lack of retail space (Daniels et al., 2015). In Korea, labor cost is relatively low, legislation lenient, and the cost of retail space varies; for example, in downtown Seoul it is very high but is relatively low elsewhere.

Walker et al. (1992) identified several problems that occur when choosing a distribution channel in the international context: First, the level of economic development (e.g., weak infrastructure, lack of refrigeration) and the role of state-controlled middlemen may limit the possibilities of distribution channels so that the channel that would fit the best might not be available. This is not a problem in Korea anymore. Second, existing middlemen might be already in a cooperation or have exclusive contracts with other (mostly local) manufacturers. This is a serious channel in Korea, as we discuss later. Third, once a distribution channel has been chosen, it may be difficult to change due to barriers to the termination of a relationship, for example, in the form of contractual arrangements. A premature termination can have a negative impact on future cooperation, including with other potential partners, or it can even lead to being barred from the marketplace. This could be challenging but possible in Korea. Fourth, international marketers use various distribution channels that are difficult to control.

The Korean distributional system is characterized by strong horizontal and vertical fragmentation. There often exist multitiered wholesale systems with powerful middlemen and retailers and multiple intermediaries between producers and consumers. This sequential retail system can lead to higher-than-normal retail prices due to extra handling costs (Lee & Trim, 2008). Many distributional channels are controlled by or at least in cooperation with a chaebol. Therefore, it might be especially difficult to install effective and efficient distributional structures without a Korean partner. Additionally, the comparatively strong interventionist policy of the Korean government can pose further challenges for foreign companies (Lee & Trim, 2008).

Studies have shown that many companies use multichannel retailing to provide a unique shopping experience for their customers, as these often use different channels during their selection–decision–buying process (Stone et al., 2002). 'Mom-and-pop stores' still have a large role, although their importance in the Korean market diminishes. Another relic of the time when Korea was a developing country is traditional markets, the so-called *sijang*, for example, the Gwangjang *sijang* in downtown Seoul, where almost anything, mostly local products, can be bought at a very low price. These traditional markets still coexist with modern distribution channels. These distribution channels usually play no major role for foreign companies. Within the offline distribution channels, hypermarkets, retail stores, and convenience stores play a major role (Santander Trade Portal, 2019a). Moreover, high-priced foreign products are usually offered in department stores. When using one of these traditional channels, a good shelf position and merchandising are essential in order to succeed. Therefore, a sales representative can enhance a company's success (Raymond & Lim, 1996).

The Korean market is characterized by the rapid emergence of e-commerce, especially due to a high affinity and openness of Korean consumers regarding the Internet and new technologies as well as a very good IT infrastructure. About 18% of sales are completed online, and even 81% of Korean consumers use the internet for product research first (Google & Kantar TNS, 2015; Santander Trade Portal, 2019a). Korea is the third-biggest e-commerce market in Asia (Santander Trade Portal, 2019a). The most successful online shopping properties are gmarket.co.kr, 11st.co.kr, auction.co.kr, wemakeprice.com, and coupang.com (Nielsen Korea Digital Headquarters, 2018). One measure to combine the online and offline approaches is the so-called click-and-collect, where consumers can order online and pick up their order at a pick-up station in the outlets (Santander Trade Portal, 2019a). The technological advancement and openness of Korean consumers toward online activities become additionally evident when facing some special kinds of stores in Korea. One example is the Homeplus virtual store, while another is the Kyobo virtual bookstore in subway stations, where customers can choose groceries or a book by scanning the matching QR code at major subway station screens (Ascential Information Services Limited, 2011; Bloter & Media Inc., 2011).

When foreign companies decide to build distributional channels, they have several options. First, they can build relationships with domestic channel partners. In Korea, usually large companies and chaebols own strong distributional channels. If there is a possibility of cooperation, foreign companies can enter these channels via a strategic partnership or rely on Korean agents and distributors. Additionally, there exist specialized channel partners with extensive experience with Korean partners and distributional networks. If it is affordable, foreign companies can also create their own distribution network, but this is only feasible in exceptional cases. Foreign companies can also rely on e-commerce. When setting up e-commerce it is recommended to hire or cooperate with Korean IT experts and web designers who have experiences with successful Korean websites. As some customers have certain concerns regarding the security of online trade as well as regarding the quality of the product due to a lack of physical contact and the anonymity of the retailer, companies should rely on a multichannel strategy (Keng Kau et al., 2003).

## Promotion

Promotion refers to the presentation of messages intended to encourage the sale of a product. This includes activities that communicate the qualities of the offered product or service in order to convince customers to buy it (Kotler et al., 2005). The particular combination of elements in a promotion strategy is called the promotion mix. A company can determine the usage of one or several promotional activities to be personal selling, advertising, sales promotion activities, and publicity/public relations activities (Daniels et al., 2015). Additionally, there are several branding options. The company has to decide whether to use its brand, in general, to use a manufacturer's brand or private brand, to use one brand or multiple brands, and to use worldwide brands or local brands (Daniels et al., 2015). In the past, Korean companies have used multiple brands and frequently created new brands when introducing a new product (Yoo & Winsor, 2009). While this helped them to gain some new customers and sales, this approach resulted in poor brand equity and customer loyalty. In consequence, major Korean companies have decided to focus on and develop their brands while avoiding multiple brand strategies.

When introducing a product to a new market, companies often make alterations regarding promotion and advertising to fit the new social, economic, and political environments (Walker et al., 1992). Differences in product knowledge, benefit expectations, buying motives, and language make the standardization of promotion very difficult. If a standardized approached is used despite these differences, the advertising may fail (Raymond & Lim, 1996). Also, additional factors such as culture (e.g., different perceptions of humor or different meanings of certain colors), competitive conditions, execution (e.g., poor color reproduction in print ads), and different levels of media usage (e.g., through use and availability of media or regulations and limitations regarding allowed frequency and amount of time for advertising) can hinder the promotion from achieving its desired outcome (Kotler et al., 2005; Walker et al., 1992). Even if only one of these factors does not fit, a whole promotion campaign can miss its goal. One well-known example of adjusting according to cultural and language difficulties is Cola-Cola. When Cola-Cola expanded to the Chinese market, they looked for a group of Chinese characters that resembled the sound of the American 'Cola-Cola'. But those characters actually meant 'bite the wax tadpole'. Coca-Cola ended up changing its name into a Chinese term that sounded similar but that meant 'happiness in the mouth' (Solberg, 2018). Similarly, companies have to pay attention to the language and translations in Korea.

A wide range of advertising mediums are used throughout Korea (see Figure 9.2). The mediums with the highest spending are TV advertising (US$3,072 million)

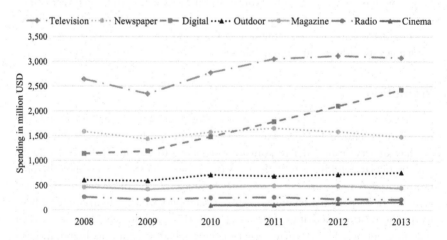

**FIGURE 9.2** Advertising expenditure in South Korea (by medium)

*Source:* Statista (2014).

and digital advertising (US$2,425 million). Despite the constant rise of online advertising importance, television advertising remains the media with the biggest impact on consumers (Santander, 2019b). Television advertising may pose an extra challenge to foreign companies, as many companies are locked out during prime time due to high costs or because local chaebols have already bought those time slots (Raymond & Lim, 1996). Nevertheless, traditional forms of marketing, such as advertisements in the newspaper, in a magazine, or on the radio, are of great importance to reaching different customer segments. While companies can reach many people through advertisements in free newspapers like *Metro*, specific target groups can be reached through advertising in magazines (Santander Trade Portal, 2019b). The use of demonstrations and free samples is also very common and can convince potential customers to purchase by demonstrating the product's high quality.

There are some additional unique features to consider when advertising in Korea. In comparison to Western countries, the Korean promotion system uses sales promotions extensively. Companies use a push strategy to convince their customers to buy their products. For advertising in Korea, celebrity promotion is very common and an important factor in success in the Korean market. Foreign companies may use well-known Korean or famous Western celebrities to promote their products. While in Western countries celebrities promote products like apparel, perfume, cosmetics, or luxury groceries, in Korea celebrities are used for campaigns in any product category. Additionally, the importance of groups in Korea becomes apparent, as situations involving groups are utilized more in commercials in Korea in comparison to more individualistic countries (Alden et al., 1993). Furthermore, Korea is a high-context culture, and therefore, parts of the message of an advertisement may not be directly stated but, rather, communicated implicitly and indirectly (Cho et al., 1999). There are also several regulations for advertising certain types of products, for example, alcohol, cigarettes, pharmaceuticals, and other products, and therefore the use of a Korean advertising agency may reduce the risk of non-compliance to these regulations and Korean particularities in advertising campaigns (Raymond & Lim, 1996; Santander Trade Portal, 2019b).

## Conclusion

Due to its economic size and growth, Korea is an attractive market for foreign companies to sell their products and services. At the same time, the Korean market is very competitive and, in many segments, dominated by a few large Korean chaebols. The legal and cultural environment differs substantially from most other markets and complicates marketing in Korea. Foreign companies are recommended to carefully analyze the Korean market and carefully weigh whether and how to modify their products/services.

This chapter provided an overview of consumer trends and an analysis of the 4Ps (product, price, place, promotion) of marketing. The Korean consumer trends have some unique features. The changing demographics, particularly the rapidly aging population and the change in family structure, pose new opportunities and challenges for both Korean and foreign companies. Korea embraces e-commerce, and so should foreign companies. Koreans, like other Asians, are very brand conscious, although not necessarily very loyal to their brands. This is an opportunity for foreign companies to enter the market. The highly dynamic nature of the Korean market offers opportunity and major challenges for foreign companies because it is difficult for foreign companies to respond swiftly to changing customer demands.

In line with economic progression, Korean consumers have become more demanding. Due to the fierce competition, it would be difficult for foreign companies to compete on price. Rather, for foreign companies to succeed, they need to provide high quality and innovative products that distinguish themselves from their Korean competitors, which would then allow the company to command a price premium. Vertical and closed distribution channels often controlled by chaebol companies pose barriers for foreign companies to enter the market. Collaboration with local partners and taking advantage of e-commerce are potential strategies for foreign companies. If foreign companies intend to make major inroads into Korea, they should launch aggressive promotion campaigns, including using well-known celebrities. In summary, Korea is an attractive market if companies put into practice the insights into Korean marketing and specific managerial recommendations included in this chapter.

## Case study:  Nike, Inc. in South Korea

Nike Inc., an American MNE, was founded in 1964. Today, it is one of the largest suppliers of sports apparel and equipment, with approximately 74,000 employees and revenues of US$35,285 billion worldwide. Nike has seven distribution centers, located in Belgium, Canada, China, Japan, South Korea, and the United States (Nike News, 2011). From there, several wholesalers and retailers are supplied with Nike products. Nearly 15% of the revenue stems from Nike's sales in Asia-Pacific and Latin America. In South Korea, Nike operates eight factories for shoes and equipment, a distribution center in Incheon, and several stores, mostly in the areas of Seoul and Daegu. Additionally, Nike operates an online shop where customers can order the products to be sent directly to their homes.

Nike offers only a limited range of products in Korea in comparison to their home market. Examples are a number of shoes (Korea: 607, US: 846), jackets and vests (Korea: 94, US: 151), or bags (Korea: 88, US: 131) for men in the Korean and American online shop. Additionally, the prices of products vary between markets served. Table 9.1 shows the prices of selected products in the Korean, American, and German Nike

**TABLE 9.1** Prices for selected products of Nike in Korea, the United States, and Germany

| Product | Price Korea | Price US | Price Germany |
|---|---|---|---|
| Women's Shoes: Nike Air Force 1 '07 | KRW129,000 (USD114.59) | USD90 | EUR100 (USD113.72) |
| Backpack: Nike Brasilia | KRW49,000 (USD43.52) | USD50 | EUR35 (USD39.80) |
| Men's Jacket: Nike Air | KRW119,000 (USD105.70) | USD100 | EUR80 (USD90.98) |
| Women's Golf Polo: Nike Dri-FIT | KRW83,300 (USD73.99) | USD55 | EUR70 (USD79.61) |

online shops; the only product that was less expensive in Korea than in the United States was the backpack.

Nike engages in several kinds of sponsorships and events as part of their promotion strategy. For instance, Nike designed the Korean team's uniform for the 2013 World Baseball Classic and, as the official sponsor of the Korea Football Association, the uniform for the national team for the 2014 FIFA World Cup in Brazil. In 2014, Nike opened its largest sports brand store in the Gangnam shopping district in Seoul. In the 19,375-square-foot space, Nike offers not only a wide range of its products but also special services and programming, such as a weekly Nike+ Training Club session. For the store's opening, Nike hosted a week of festivities with famous Korean athletes (e.g., soccer legend Ji-Sung Park), musicians (e.g., Gaeko), and celebrities (Nike News, 2014). Nike also organizes huge events, such as flash mobs, football freestylers, martial arts performers, an obstacle challenge, and an 'Art of Mercurial IX' installation to promote its new Mercurial Vapor IX boots. They also hold sports events like 'We Run Seoul', a race with about 30,000 participants. Mostly, events include additional offers as special training, mobile gaming apps that encourage Koreans to do certain challenges in order to earn points and trophies, and entertainment zones with elements of dancing, music, and product presentations. Another marketing coup of Nike was the 'Run It' song and music video, showing top Korean artists and athletes. Within this campaign, Nike also released print and digital advertising as well as consumer activations, for example, a fan-made lyric video version, where fans could send videos via Kakao, a Korean mobile instant messaging application. The involvement of fans and customers is one main characteristic of the marketing campaigns in Korea. Besides the previously given examples, Nike started its Korea Unlimited campaign in 2016. Nike unveiled daily missions on the campaign site and encouraged fans and customers to engage by making posters and offering T-shirts as well as customized gifts. More than 30,000 user contents have been created.

## Sources

Campaign Asia-Pacific. 2013. *Nike creates original song to reach Korea's 'senegis'*. www.campaignasia.com/video/nike-creates-original-song-to-reach-koreas-senegis/442458. Accessed 15 January 2019.

Freshness Creative Corp. 2013. *Nike Mercurial Vapor IX – "Gangnam Style" Launch Event*. www.freshnessmag.com/2013/02/19/nike-mercurial-vapor-ix-gangnam-style-launch-event/. Accessed 15 January 2019.

Nike Homepages: www.nike.com/kr, www.nike.com/us/, www.nike.com/de Accessed 15 January 2019.

Postvisual. 2016. *2016 Nike unlimited Korea*. www.postvisual.com/?p=4987. Accessed 15 January 2019.

United States Securities and Exchange Commission. 2018. FORM 10-K: Annual Report Pursuant to Section 1 or 15(d) of the Securities Exchange act of 1934 for the fiscal Year ended May 1, 2017 or Transition Report Pursuant to Section 1 or 15(d) of the Securities Exchange Act of 1934 for the Transition Period from to. Commission File No. 1–10635: NIKE, Inc. www.sec.gov/Archives/edgar/data/320187/000032018717000090/nke-5312017x10k.htm. Accessed 15 January 2019.

## Bibliography

### Key references

Kotler, P., Armstrong, G., Harris, L., & Piercy, N. 2005. *Principles of marketing*. Harlow: Pearson Education Limited.

Yoo, C., & Winsor, R. D. 2009. The changing face of Korean marketing management. In C. Rowley & Y. Paik (Eds.), *The changing face of Korean management*. London: Routledge.

### Online sources

KITA Org. 2019. *Korea international trade association*. www.kita.org/global/tradeKorea.do. Accessed 4 January 2019.

Santander Trade Portal. 2019a. *South Korea: Distributing a product*. https://en.portal.santander-trade.com/analyse-markets/south-korea/distributing-a-product?&actualiser_id_banque=oui&id_banque=54&memoriser_choix=memoriser. Accessed 10 January 2019.

Santander Trade Portal. 2019b. *South Korea: Reaching the consumer.* https://en.portal.san tandertrade.com/analyse-markets/south-korea/reaching-the-consumers. Accessed 10 January 2019

Statistics Korea. 2019. *Statistics Korea.* http://kostat.go.kr/portal/eng/index.action. Accessed 4 January 2019.

# References

Alden, D. L., Hoyer, W. D., & Lee, C. 1993. Identifying global and culture-specific dimensions of humor in advertising: A multinational analysis. *The Journal of Marketing,* 57(2): 64–75.

American Marketing Association. 1985. AMA board approves new marketing definition. *Marketing News,* 1(1).

American Marketing Association. 2013. *Definition of marketing.* www.ama.org/ AboutAMA/ Pages/Definition-of-Marketing.aspx. Accessed 11 January 2019.

Ascential Information Services Limited. 2011. *Tesco opens virtual store in South Korea.* www. retail-week.com/technology/tesco-opens-virtual-store-in-south-korea-/5028571. article?authent=1. Accessed 18 January 2019.

Bloter & Media Inc. 2011. *"지하철 기다리며 책 사자"교보문고 가상서점.* www.bloter. net/archives/86210. Accessed 18 January 2019.

Borden, N. H. 1942. *The economic effects of advertising.* Chicago: Richard D. Irwin.

Borden, N. H. 1984. The concept of the marketing mix. *Journal of Advertising Research,* 4(2): 7–12.

Central Intelligence Agency. 2017. *Import-partners.* www.cia.gov/library/publications/the-world-factbook/fields/403.html#AF. Accessed 9 January 2019.

Cho, B., Kwon, U., Gentry, J. W., Jun, S., & Kropp, F. 1999. Cultural values reflected in theme and execution: A comparative study of US and Korean television commercials. *Journal of Advertising,* 28(4): 59–73.

Culliton, J. W. 1948. *The management of marketing costs.* Boston: Division of Research, Graduate School of Business Administration, Harvard University.

Daniels, J. D., Radebaugh, L. H., & Sullivan, D. P. 2015. *International business: Environments and operations.* Pearson: Essex.

Doyle, P. 2003. Managing the marketing mix. In M. J. Baker (Ed.), *The marketing book*: 287–313. London, New York: Routledge.

European Central Bank. 2019. *Ecb Euro reference exchange rate: South Korean Won* (KRW). www.ecb.europa.eu/stats/policy_and_exchange_rates/euro_reference_exchange_rates/ html/eurofxref-graph-krw.en.html. Accessed 18 January 2019.

Froese, F. J. 2009. *Convergence of work values in Tokyo, Seoul, and Shanghai? Cross-country and intergenerational comparisons,* unpublished doctoral dissertation: Waseda University.

Gartner, Inc. 2018. *Gartner says worldwide sales of smartphones recorded first ever decline during the fourth quarter of 2017.* www.gartner.com/en/newsroom/press-releases/2018-02-22-gartner-says-worldwide-sales-of-smartphones-recorded-first-ever-decline-during-the-fourth-quarter-of-2017. Accessed 17 January 2019.

Global Coffee Report. 2013. http://gcrmag.com/market-reports/view/coffee-gangnam-style. Accessed 18 March 2019.

Google & Kantar TNS. 2015. *The consumer barometer survey 2014/15.* www.consumerba rometer.com/en/graph-builder/?question=S14&filter=country:korea. Accessed 18 January 2019.

Grönroos, C. 1989. Defining marketing: A market-oriented approach. *European Journal of Marketing,* 23(1): 52–60.

International Monetary Fund. 2018. *World economic outlook database*. www.imf.org/external/pubs/ft/weo/2017/02/weodata/index.aspx. Accessed 18 March 2019.

Keng Kau, A., Tang, Y. E., & Ghose, S. 2003. Typology of online shoppers. *Journal of Consumer Marketing*, 20(2): 139–156.

Kotler, P., Wong, V., Saunders, J., & Armstrong, G. 2005. *Principles of marketing*. Essex: Pearson Education Limited.

Lee, Y. I., & Trim, P. R. 2008. Entering the South Korean market: A marketing-planning process model for marketers based in overseas companies. *Business Strategy Series*, 9(5): 272–278.

McCarthy, J. E. 1960. *Basic marketing: A managerial approach*. Illinois: R. D. Irwin.

Mooradian, T., Matzler, K., & Ring, L. 2013. *Strategic marketing*. Pearson Higher Ed.

Nam, K., Lee, G., Hwang, J. S. 2011. Gender stereotypes depicted by Western and Korean advertising models in Korean adolescent girls' magazines. *Sex Roles*, 64: 223–237.

Nielsen Korea Digital Headquarters. 2018. PC 주요 서비스별 웹사이트 순위. www.koreanclick.com/top10/pc_service_ranking.html?cate=C. Accessed 18 January 2019.

Raymond, M. A., & Lim, J. W. 1996. Promotion and trade mix considerations for entering and competing in the Korean market. *Journal of Marketing Theory and Practice*, 4(1): 44–55.

Santander Trade Portal. 2019a. *South Korea: Distributing a product*. https://en.portal.santandertrade.com/analyse-markets/south-korea/distributing-a-product?&actualiser_id_banque=oui&id_banque=54&memoriser_choix=memoriser. Accessed 10 January 2019.

Santander Trade Portal. 2019b. *South Korea: Reaching the consumer*. https://en.portal.santandertrade.com/analyse-markets/south-korea/reaching-the-consumers. Accessed 10 January 2019.

Solberg, C. A. 2018. *International marketing: Strategy development and implementation*. London, New York: Routledge.

Song, X. M., Montoya-Weiss, M. M., & Schmidt, J. B. 1997. The role of marketing in developing successful new products in South Korea and Taiwan. *Journal of International Marketing*, 5(3): 47–69.

Statista. 2014. *Advertising expenditure in South Korea from 2008 to 2015, by medium* (in million U.S. dollars). www.statista.com/statistics/386471/advertising-expenditures-by-medium-south-korea/. Accessed 18 January 2019.

Statista. 2018. *Internet usage in South Korea*. www.statista.com/topics/2230/internet-usage-in-south-korea/. Accessed 18 March 2019.

Stone, M., Hobbs, M., & Khaleeli, M. 2002. Multichannel customer management: The benefits and challenges. *Journal of Database Marketing & Customer Strategy Management*, 10(1): 39–52.

The Korea Herald. 2017. *Average age in Korea rises to 41.2*. www.koreaherald.com/view.php?ud=20170420000725. Accessed 18 January 2019.

U. S. News. 2019. *Best Luxury Midsize Cars*. https://cars.usnews.com/cars-trucks/rankings/upscale-midsize-cars. Accessed 17 January 2019.

Van Waterschoot, W., & Van den Bulte, C. 1992. The 4 P classification of the marketing mix revisited. *The Journal of Marketing*, 56(4): 83–93.

Walker, O. C., Boyd, H. W., & Larreche, J. C. 1992. *Marketing strategy: Planning and implementation*. Boston: McGraw-Hill/Irwin.

World Trade Organization. 2019. *Total merchandise trade*. http://stat.wto.org/StatisticalProgram/WSDBViewData.aspx?Language=E. Accessed 18 January 2019.

Yoo, C., & Winsor, R. D. 2009. The changing face of Korean marketing management. In C. Rowley & Y. Paik (Eds.), *The changing face of Korean management*. London: Routledge.

# 10

# HUMAN RESOURCE MANAGEMENT IN KOREA

*Jinxi Michelle Li and Fabian Jintae Froese*

## Introduction

Korea possesses a highly educated labor force, as evidenced by the highest rate of college graduates in the world with 70% among 25- to 34-year-olds (OECD, 2017) and third rank in the world human capital rankings (World Bank, 2018). This is astonishing considering Korea used to be a poor, developing country, not long ago. Thus, nowadays, Korea offers a large pool of highly qualified talent for multinational enterprises.

This chapter provides an overview of the HRM system in Korea. The HRM system in Korea has undergone substantial change during the last decades in line with social and economic changes. As discussed in Chapter 2, Korea used to be a poor, developing country until the 1960s. Until then, no systematic HRM system existed, at least not in the sense of modern HRM. As Korean companies, including chaebols, grew in size, they had to develop HRM systems to manage their people. At the beginning, Korean HRM was greatly influenced by Confucianism and Japanese HRM (Froese et al., 2017; Tung et al., 2013). Under the influence of Confucianism, traditional HRM in Korea was characterized by mass, annual recruitment of new graduates, lifetime employment and seniority-based rewards. Although such HRM policies were a useful growth strategy in the past, they were not effective in times of rapidly changing business environments. A trigger for major change was the Asian financial crisis in 1997, when the International Monetary Fund (IMF) imposed changes in the regulatory system and liberalized the market. This resulted in major changes in Korean HRM policies which have transformed into an ability- and performance-based appraisal and pay system, involving appraisal feedback and 360-degree appraisal (Froese et al., 2017; Jun & Rowley, 2014; Tung et al., 2013).

While the Korean labor force is highly educated, declining fertility rates and a rapidly aging population have resulted in a shrinking labor force. This presents a major challenge for HRM in the years to come. Another HRM challenge is the reformed labor market structure in response to the Asian financial crisis towards a higher degree of flexibility and contingent workers. Considering such recent changes, this chapter also discusses corresponding major HR challenges. In the next section, we provide an overview of recent historical developments in HRM.

## HRM systems in Korea

Korean HRM can be summarized into the following periods: pre-1987, 1987 to 1997 and post-1997 (Tung et al., 2013). The Declaration of Democratization in 1987 and the Asian financial crisis in 1997 are the most far-reaching events in the history of Korean HRM.

The pre-1987 HRM system is characterized by a seniority-paternalistic system and Korean firms hired loyal, hardworking employees to promote the growth of their business. During this period, Korea adapted the state-sponsored, export-oriented and labor-intensive growth model of industrialization (Amsden, 1987). During the period from 1987 to 1997, Korean firms aimed to increase performance through a new HRM system which could enhance employee competencies and promote teamwork. As such, a competency-based HRM system was adopted alongside the previous seniority-based system. The HRM system in the post-1997 period is characterized by performance-based, 'top talent'-focused and flexibility-oriented paradigm. Many Korean firms became global players through strategies of restructuring, downsizing and benchmarking. (Tung et al., 2013).

Table 10.1 summarizes HRM systems in Korea across the three periods. Our overview is organized into six major components of HRM systems including organizational culture, recruitment and retention, training and development, performance management, compensation and rewards and labor unions. Interestingly, major changes were implemented in all components of the HRM system over time, except for organizational culture, which has been somewhat resistant to change (Froese et al., 2008).

## Organizational culture

Under the influence of Confucian work ethics, which emphasize paternalism, loyalty and respect for elders and seniors, the organizational culture of Korean companies can be summarized as top-down decision-making, favoring seniority and paternalistic leadership (Hemmert, 2017). As such, decision-making power and authority are concentrated in the higher levels of organizational hierarchies (Hildisch et al., 2015), and performance evaluations are mostly conducted by seniors in the organizations (Park, 2001; Jun & Rowley, 2014).

In addition, group orientation is a typical trait of Korean organizations (Jöns et al., 2007). Teamwork and socialization within teams and companies are important to build trust and loyalty. Thus, training, company trips (e.g., trips to Cheju Island), and outings (e.g., sports activities) are an integral part of their work

**TABLE 10.1** Summary of HRM in Korea

| | Pre-1987 (seniority-based) | 1987–1997 (seniority and competency-based) | Post-1997 (performance-based) |
|---|---|---|---|
| Organizational culture | Top-down decision-making, favoring seniority, paternalistic leadership and harmony-oriented under the influence of Confucianism, an emotional support mechanism such as *yongo* is also important | | |
| Recruitment and retention | Regular mass recruitment of new graduates | More rational process (e.g., irregular recruitment on demand, promotion by selection) | Active recruitment from external market, more flexible labor market |
| Training and development | Extensive training for all, further education for high-potentials | Career development programs and fast-tracking promotions for high potentials | Extensive training for regular and higher performing employees only |
| Performance management | Seniority-based system | Competency-based grade system, more systematic evaluations (e.g., multiraters) | Performance-based appraisals, more systematic evaluations (e.g., annual pay, management by objectives) |
| Compensation and rewards | Seniority-based, complex compensations system | Seniority and competency-based due to consideration for competence in hiring and promotions | Performance-based, increasing use of group-level and profit-sharing compensations |
| Labor unions | Does not play a major role | More active labor movements and development of blue-collar internal labor market since 1987, only half companies have effective labor-mgt. committees | |

*Source*: Own summary based on literature review.

(Froese et al., 2017; Kraeh et al., 2015). Colleagues usually have lunch, coffee and dinner together. Socialization even extends beyond the organizational boundaries and colleagues go out for after work drinks, so-called *hoesik* (Bader et al., 2018; Kraeh et al., 2015). Furthermore, it is common for colleagues to attend each other's family gathering (e.g., weddings, funerals). Korean organizations are also known for long work hours. Koreans not only work longer hours each day than their European counterparts, but they also take fewer holidays (Froese et al., 2017).

Group orientation and belonging to the in-group are important. Family, hometown and alumni have huge impacts on interpersonal relationships within the organization. These relationships are critically important to understand the HRM of Korean organizations. For instance, many Korean firms prefer to recruit employees based on commonly shared ties along these three dimensions. For some companies, most key managers have the same hometown (*jiyon*), school (*hakyon*), and/or blood (*hyulyon*) (Park, 2001; Horak, 2017). The *jiyon*, *hakyon* and *hyulyon* are all included in the domain of *Yongo*, which means Korean informal social networks or Korean forms of social capital. *Yongo* can jeopardize fairness and lead to corruption if misused. But those with influential *Yongo* have more chances to improve their lives and make a career. *Yongo* and related practices are prevalent on the upper management level in Korean companies (Horak, 2017).

The influence of seniority is still strong in Korean HRM (Horak & Yang, 2019) despite the prevalent performance-based system nowadays. Although the performance-based system is consistent with best practices worldwide, this system could bring some challenges in the Korean context. For instance, overemphasis on short-term results could lead some employees to sacrifice long-term objectives, and thereby corporate innovation may suffer (Tung et al., 2013). Horak & Yang (2019) insisted that seniority will continue to influence the Korean HRM system because culture is difficult to change, and seniority is an important cultural element in Korea. Therefore, Korean firms need to build on the positive aspects of seniority as it is an "integral feature of the cultural context" (Horak & Yang, 2019: 22). In addition, more indigenous HRM systems suitable for the Korean context should be created to overcome the side effects of Western best practices. For example, an emotional support mechanism such as *jul*, *yongo*, or *jeong* need to be understood to enable HRM systems to work more effectively in Korea.

## Recruitment and retention

In the pre-1987 period, Korean firms tended to recruit university graduates for entry-level positions and these new graduates mostly gradually advanced to upper level positions in the organization. Firms also preferred generalists to specialists because generalists are easier to be indoctrinated into the company's culture through intensive training and socialization programs (Tung et al., 2013).

During the early 1990s, Korean firms began adopting various new practices in the HRM system. Recruitment processes were more rationalized and systematic. For instance, competence became a very important factor in hiring and promotion decisions. Unlike the regular mass recruitment of new graduates in the pre-1987 period, firms began to adopt new practices such as irregular recruitment on demand and/or promotion by selection during the 1987–1997 period. Aside from the employment security provided in the pre-1987 period, a new perspective known as 'lifetime career' was introduced since 1987. This new perspective contributed to a gradual decline in the practice of employment security (Tung et al., 2013).

Since the Asian financial crisis in 1997, Korean firms have adopted a market-based and performance-oriented HRM system. Korean firms have expanded their recruiting sources and actively seek talent at all levels from the external labor market. For instance, among Samsung's domestic workforce of 110,000, 36% were recruited from other organizations (Froese et al., 2017). Member firms within large corporations also adopted different recruiting approaches. For example, SK Telecom hired experienced people for its internet business, while it employed new graduates for its mobile network operator business. (Tung et al., 2013).

Since the Asian financial crisis of 1997, the Korean labor market has become much more flexible. Consequently, researchers have lamented the associated risks of reduced job security and reduced morale among Korean employees (Bae et al., 2011; Froese et al., 2017). In response, firms need to find ways to better retain their employees in Korea. For instance, IBM Korea adopted a telecommuting system in June 2005. At that time, it was an innovative and groundbreaking initiative. Employees could apply for a telecommuting option, and the location of work was not important for performance appraisal. As such, some female employees used the telecommuting system to work overseas while staying with family members who expatriated to foreign countries. However, most Korean companies have not implemented telecommuting because of the organizational culture emphasizing socialization and face time (Kim et al., 2015).

For foreign companies, it can be difficult to recruit and retain Korean employees. In general, Korean job applicants prefer to work for Korean companies (Froese & Kishi, 2013). In a survey of more than 2,000 job applicants in Asia, Froese and Kishi (2013) found that 62.5% of Korean applicants preferred to work for Korean companies. They prefer to work for large Korean companies such as Samsung. While 35.6% preferred Western companies, only 1.9% wanted to work for Japanese companies. Korean applicants are concerned about the image of a company and its country (Froese & Kishi, 2013). Well-known companies such as Google from the US can easily attract employees (Universum, 2018). Thus, foreign companies should pay attention to their employer and country image to attract and retain employees. If all fails, they can offer an attractive compensation package, which is particularly effective in Korea compared to other Asian countries (Froese, 2013).

## Training and development

The lifetime employment in the pre-1987 period enabled Korean companies to invest in extensive training to develop their employees. Extensive training about job skills, language skills, corporate culture and policies were provided to all employees at different career stages. Also, many companies provided their high-potential employees with opportunities to further their education at home or abroad (Tung et al., 2013).

During the 1987–1997 period, many Korean companies began to adopt career development programs and fast-tracking promotions for their high-potential employees alongside the extensive training in the previous years. For example, Samsung established the Regional Specialist Program in 1990 to help younger employees obtain language skills and learn the local culture (Tung et al., 2013).

After the Asian financial crisis in 1997, extensive training and development were provided to regular and high performing employees, while irregular workers and

TABLE 10.2 Employee involvement activities in Korean companies

|  | Job rotation (%) | Multi-skilling programs (%) | Small group activities (%) | Proposal systems (%) |
|---|---|---|---|---|
| 2005 | 40.4 | 35.5 | 55.7 | 68.6 |
| 2007 | 38.9 | 37.3 | 44.5 | 63.1 |
| 2009 | 30.0 | 20.9 | 40.2 | 48.5 |
| 2011 | 40.2 | 33.2 | 48.0 | 46.8 |
| 2013 | 34.7 | 31.6 | 46.7 | 49.5 |
| 2015 | 30.1 | 35.1 | 48.0 | 51.0 |

*Source:* Kim and Oh (2018).

low performers had little chance to receive proper training. In addition, firms tried to enhance employee creativity and absorptive capacity for new knowledge and technology as well as the development of problem-solving skills (Tung et al., 2013).

According to Kim and Oh (2018), 30% to 40% of Korean companies conduct regular job rotation, but the percentage has been declining in recent years. While the multi-skilling programs tailored to core occupations tend to remain consistent, small group activities and proposal systems tend to decrease (see Table 10.2). This means employee involvement activities are inclined to reduce recently and this phenomenon is consistent with the current reports indicating the ongoing decline of the 'workplace innovation index'. Small-group activities and proposal systems, as well as HRD, are all integral parts of the 'workplace innovation index'. Along with the decrease in employee involvement, worker engagement and internal development, as well as long-term development, have also consistently declined in the past decade. This means Korean companies no longer adopt Japanese employment systems which emphasize internal and long-term development of HR through long-term employment (Kim & Oh, 2018).

Even though many Korean companies are cutting costs by reducing training, we recommend foreign companies to offer training to key personnel, including overseas trips to and international assignments in the global or regional headquarters. Korean employees can learn the corporate culture, increase their network, learn best practices in headquarters, and transfer these skills back to the Korean subsidiary (Froese et al., 2016). In addition, given the Confucian culture emphasizing learning, such training can motivate employees. At the same time, if companies make substantial investments in training, they could tie in employees with retention contracts, which would stipulate repayment of training cost if the employee leaves the company within a certain period, for example, two years.

## Performance management

Along with the seniority-based performance system in the pre-1987 period, a competency-based grade system was also implemented around the early 1990s.

In order to motivate high performers, Korean companies began to adopt more systematic performance evaluations such as the use of multiple raters during the 1987–1997 period (Tung et al., 2013).

The Asian financial crisis of 1997 triggered a dramatic change in organizational structures and thereby team systems became much more prevalent among Korean companies. The popularity of the team system has greatly influenced promotion systems in Korea. Unlike seniority-based appraisal systems in the pre-1997 period, since 1997, performance-based appraisal systems, which require fair evaluation as a prerequisite, became prevalent. As such, more systematic evaluation systems including an annual pay system, management by objective and multiple evaluation systems (especially evaluation of subordinates for supervisors) were commonly used in Korean companies (Kim & Bae, 2004).

According to 2015 statistics by Kim and Oh (2018), 25% of Korean employees are promoted to a certain position based on their seniority (e.g., years of service), and 30% to 40% of Korean employees are promoted only when there is a job opening. Also, 35% of Korean companies implemented merit pay systems, and 70% of them used the cumulative method in which the amount of upgrade is accumulated.

The American company 3M successfully implemented job- and performance-based HRM systems in 2005. 3M Korea searched for a new HRM system that fit with the new business environment such as globalization, fierce competition, restructuring and performance-orientation. The company presented the change patterns in HR trends based on a benchmarking of 3M Japan to solve problems such as multilevel job structures, seniority-based promotions (ignorance of performance) and an unfair compensation system. The company eventually changed the HRM systems into an American style job- and performance-based system. The major changes were in the areas of promotion process, job-based pay, job evaluation and the dual-ladder career system (Ahn, 2008).

## Compensation and rewards

The compensation and reward system in Korea was based on seniority in the pre-1987 period. According to this system, all employees who joined the company at the same time received the same pay, and that pay was increased automatically every year regardless of performance. The compensation system was complex, and it consisted of basic salary, bonuses and various allowances (Tung et al., 2013).

In the 1987–1997 period, the Korean compensation system was based on a combination of competence and seniority. This was due to the high consideration for competence in hiring and promotion decisions at that time. The Doosan group, a major heavy-industry business group in Korea, first adopted an annual pay system in 1994. However, the incentive system could not enhance employee performance, and there were no major differences in pay between low and high performers (Tung et al., 2013).

Korean compensation after the financial crisis in 1997 was primarily based on performance. The percentage of firms that adopted a performance-based compensation system increased dramatically from 20% in 2000 to 66.7% in 2012. Under this system, there were huge pay differences even among employees at a similar job level. Performance-based compensation is more widespread among larger companies and more often applied to white-collar employees in higher positions. However, performance-based compensation systems vary substantially across industries and organizations in Korea and many Korean companies still use a combination of Western-style performance-based compensation and seniority. In addition to individual-level performance-based compensation, Korean companies increasingly consider group-level performance-based compensation as well as profit-sharing agreements, based on financial criteria (Froese et al., 2017; Tung et al., 2013).

According to Kim and Oh (2018), an annual salary system has increased steadily since 2005, and gain/profit sharing has fluctuated in the last decades. However, gain/profit sharing with formulae have been consistent at the level of 35%, and employee stock ownership plans have declined. Furthermore, the peak wage system, a system that gradually reduces pay for senior workers several years before retirement, has increased dramatically over the last decades and 41.7 % of large firms have adopted it (see Table 10.3).

## Labor unions

The political events of democratization in 1987 had a profound impact on the Korean labor movement. Labor union members were nearly 2 million in 1989 and 3,200 strikes occurred between July and September 1987. Most of these movements aimed to increase wages and obtain the freedom to establish the union of a worker's choice (Park, 2001).

Labor unions have taken some major initiatives in HR changes since 1987. The demands for equality made by labor unions have triggered the abolishment of discriminatory wage differentials between white- and blue-collar workers, the decline or abolition of pay differentials based on performance, as well as an accelerated increase in wages and improvement of benefits. As a result, the blue-collar internal

**TABLE 10.3** Compensation systems in Korean companies

|  | Annual salary system (%) | Gain/profit sharing (%) | Gain/profit sharing with formula (%) | Employee stock ownership plan (%) | Wage peak system (%) |
|---|---|---|---|---|---|
| 2005 | 62.7 | 52.6 | 35.2 | 10.7 | 2.9 |
| 2007 | 63.4 | 46.5 | 32.7 | 11.6 | 5.4 |
| 2009 | 64.0 | 38.5 | 27.6 | 5.4 | 5.9 |
| 2011 | 68.0 | 52.7 | 34.8 | 8.4 | 12.9 |
| 2013 | 72.1 | 48.8 | 34.9 | 7.8 | 15.9 |
| 2015 | n. a. | 33.8 | n. a. | 7.0 | 27.0 |

*Source:* Kim and Oh (2018).

*Note:* n.a. = not applicable.

**TABLE 10.4** Labor-management committees and industrial relations in Korea

|      | Establishment of labor-management committees (%) | Effective labor-management committees (%) | Labor relations (%) |
|------|--------------------------------------------------|-------------------------------------------|---------------------|
| 2005 | 82.4                                             | n. a.                                     | 75.0                |
| 2007 | 91.2                                             | n. a.                                     | 73.6                |
| 2009 | 88.4                                             | 47.6                                      | 74.0                |
| 2011 | 94.0                                             | 53.0                                      | 65.5                |
| 2013 | 95.6                                             | 52.1                                      | 64.2                |
| 2015 | 93.8                                             | 51.0                                      | n. a.               |

Source: Kim and Oh (2018).

Note: % in the column of labor relations indicates the % of firms that evaluated their labor relations positively. n.a. = not applicable.

labor market has been developed in large corporations and firms with unions. To decrease labor costs derived from such movement, Korean companies have implemented various techniques for workplace innovation such as multi-skilling, job integration, relocation and automation (Kim & Oh, 2018).

According to Kim and Oh (2018), companies with effective labor-management committees (or the labor-management committees that function properly) only comprised 50% of all Korean companies, although most Korean companies established the committees. In addition, labor relations were evaluated more negatively as time went by during the last decades (see Table 10.4).

Overall, labor unions can exert a strong influence on corporate management. Foreign managers should be aware of the role of labor unions and manage the relations carefully. An empirical study by Park (2004) found that foreign companies had more and longer labor disputes than domestic firms. Thus, foreign firms in Korea could experience more conflicts in labor relations than domestic companies because of the cultural and institutional differences, remoteness of decision-making, withdrawal threat and employment insecurity. Particularly foreign firms from countries not used to managing labor relations may consider professional consultation and support to manage those relations. On top of labor unions, which pose significant challenges, especially for foreign firms, there are further challenges inherent within the Korean labor market, which we next review and discuss.

## Challenge 1: aging workforce

According to the Korean National Statistical Office, 38.2% of the Korean population will be 65 years or older by 2050, making it the 'most aged society' among OECD countries. With the increasing elderly population, Korea needs to find a sufficient supply of human resources to replace its retirees (Tung et al., 2013).

As Korean society ages, more and more companies have adopted a peak wage system (see Figure 10.1). Up to 2013, the drastic increase in the peak wage system

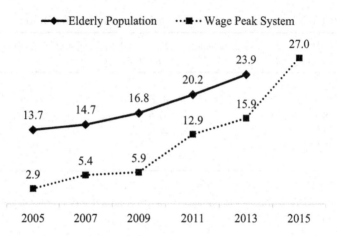

**FIGURE 10.1** Elderly population and wage peak system

*Source:* Kim and Oh (2018).

*Note:* Unit of measurement: %.

could be explained by Korea's elderly population alone, but following 2013, the new increase in retirement age (from 56 to 60) influenced further change in the peak wage system (Kim & Oh, 2018).

Utilizing the current aging workforce could be a solution for the shortage of workforce caused by an increasingly elderly population. Since the new policy on retirement age in 2016, most Korean companies have extended the retirement age and adopted a peak wage system. Some companies have also extended the employment contract with retired workers who can contribute to company performance. As for a gradual retirement program, Korean companies could benchmark the German labor law for elderly employees in which elderly workers reduce working hours from a certain point in time and the employer compensates for the wage disadvantages caused by the shortening of working hours. Korean elderly workers prefer a long-term career plan or employment, as well as group-based appraisal and compensation. They also like to work in the field of coaching or feedback where they can utilize their expertise and experience. As such, Korean companies need to consider these preferences to motivate elderly workers. As for the start-ups unrelated to the previous job experience of elderly workers, the Korean government should provide a networking system or training programs to ensure their business is successful (Kim et al., 2017). Foreign firms could play a leading role in integrating older workers and even actively recruit older workers from Korean competitors.

Utilizing foreign and North Korean workforce could also help overcome the shortage of workers caused by the aging population in South Korea. North Korea has a higher rate of fertility and population growth than South Korea. In addition,

North Korea has human resources with great learning capabilities, as well as lower salary expectations (Lee et al., 2012).

The Kaesong Industrial Complex (or a joint North–South Korea industrial complex) has attracted great attention of South Korean companies since the 2019 New Year speech by Kim Jong-un in which he addressed the possible reopening of the complex. The complex was established in 2002 and had brought many benefits to both North and South Korea until 2016 when the South Korean government closed the complex due to the frequent rocket launches of North Korea. The complex has been a good model to utilize the North's low salary, excellent human resources alongside the South's advanced technology.

## Challenge 2: managing foreign workers

With the increasing number of foreign workers, Korean HRM has faced a challenge in managing diversity. According to the Immigration Information Division in South Korea Ministry of Justice, the number of foreigners staying in Korea was over 2.3 million in October of 2018. The continuous economic growth since the 1988 Seoul Olympic Games has accelerated the increase in foreign workers because domestic workers tend to avoid 3D (dirty, dangerous and demeaning) jobs, and thus, foreign workers are needed to replace the vacancies of 3D jobs.

Foreign workers in Korea have mostly worked for SMEs and suffered from poor working conditions (e.g., low wages, long working hours, dangerous work environment), delayed payment of wages and violation of employment contract, as well as cultural misunderstanding. The working conditions and treatment of foreign workers have greatly improved since the Act on Foreign Workers' Employment in 2003, which aims to protect foreign workers from abuse by errant or dishonest employers. The Korean government has also supported some religious organizations such as churches to assist foreign workers' adjustment in Korea. Religious organizations have provided foreign workers with food, living space and free medical services, as well as legal counseling and job search assistance services.

In addition to proper regulations and living support for foreign workers, social network systems such as mentoring programs between senior and new foreign workers as well as cyber communities among foreigners could help them accelerate adjustment. Therefore, social network systems could be a solution to the challenges of managing foreign workers (Li et al., 2016).

Foreign workers have also suffered from cultural misunderstandings because of the unique culture of Korean corporations such as high hierarchy between new and old employees, face-saving and lip services. CCT (cross-cultural training) programs could promote the cultural adjustment of foreign workers in Korea and thereby could be a solution for the challenges of managing them. In order to promote foreign workers' adjustment in Korean workplaces, the Human Resource Development Service of Korea has managed and conducted employment training since 2007. This training is a mandatory education program for all foreign workers with a certain visa and has provided information on labor and immigration laws, safety in various occupations, and Korean culture. Training for Korean employers and employees who work with foreigners should also be included in employment training because Koreans also need to understand foreign workers and their culture. The training for Koreans could be conducted simultaneously with the programs for foreign workers. The employment training should deal with controversial or problematic issues in the workplace and Koreans and foreigners need to discuss these issues to promote understanding each other (Li & Kim, 2014). Chapter 10 provides more background information and recommendations for managing highly skilled expatriates. Foreign companies can play a role model in managing a multicultural workforce by integrating both highly and lowly skilled foreigners into their company.

## Challenges 3: managing contingent workers

Numbers of contingent workers in Korea increased dramatically following the Asian financial crisis in 1997. This is because many companies outsourced all business functions except core functions. The tendency to avoid hiring regular workers due to the economic crisis has also accelerated the increasing recruitment of contingent workers (Kim & Oh, 2018).

The challenges in managing contingent workers include negative work attitudes, relatively low performance and discriminatory treatment. It has been found that contingent workers lack job skills and teamwork and have low work engagement and performance. Moreover, there are no systematic HR practices for contingent workers, and they have little chance of regular promotion and retirement guarantees. Contingent workers also have lower pay than regular workers (Kim, 2008).

Korean companies need more proactive strategic HR practices to overcome the low morale and performance of contingent workers. In order to prohibit the discriminatory treatment of contingent workers, the non-regular workers (protection) law was enacted or amended on December 21, 2006, and has been in force since July 1, 2007. Although this law prohibits any discrimination in benefits, most Korean companies neglect it because temporary agencies are responsible for pay and benefits of contingent workers. As such, companies could motivate contingent workers by providing incentives to them. Over time, companies are advised to converge pay differentials, even at the expense of stagnating pay of regular workers. For instance, health care labor unions in Korea have used 30% of regular workers' pay increase for the regularization of contingent workers and improvement in their treatment. In order to motivate contingent workers, it is necessary to provide them with more intrinsic rewards such as more chances for growth and development as well as to become regular workers. A fair performance appraisal and compensation system are mandatory for this (Kim, 2008).

## Conclusion

In line with socioeconomic developments, Korean HRM has undergone major changes. In the past, the development can be categorized into three periods: pre-1987, 1987 to 1997, and post-1997. The Declaration of Democratization in 1987 and the Asian financial crisis in 1997 are two milestones that greatly influenced Korean HRM. The Korean HRM before 1987, which emphasized seniority and lifetime employment, was largely influenced by Confucianism and Japanese HRM. During the period between 1987 and 1997, a competency-based HRM system was adopted in combination with the previous seniority-based system. The events of political democratization movement also triggered the development of labor unions that helped improve working conditions. In response to the Asian financial crises and external pressures, the Korean HRM system adopted a US-style performance-based HRM system. The accompanying flexible labor market resulted in lower employee morale and a flexible labor force (Bae et al., 2011). Despite all these major changes in HRM, the corporate culture of Korean companies has remained largely the same, as Korean culture is rather rigid and does not change fast (Froese et al., 2008; Horak & Yang, 2019).

Current socioeconomic development put pressure on Korean HRM. In this chapter, we elaborated on three challenges: an aging workforce, an increasing foreign workforce and a contingent workforce. Better utilizing the current aging workforce, foreign and North Korean workforce could solve the problems of labor shortage in Korea. To overcome the challenges of managing foreign workers due to cultural misunderstandings and poor working conditions, social network systems such as mentoring programs and online community, stricter enforcement of regulations, and training are advisable. As for the challenges of managing contingent workers associated with negative work attitudes and poor performance, Korean companies should provide them with more incentives and intrinsic rewards as well as equal treatment with regular workers.

It is important for foreign managers to understand the prevalent Korean HRM system to be able to decide whether to maintain the global HRM system and/or localize some of their practices (Froese et al., 2008). Foreign companies can be more proactive in the implementation of various HRM practices than domestic firms. For instance, foreign companies have recruited more female workers, used more multirater systems, and invested more in the development of a core workforce. With a higher pay level than domestic firms, foreign companies have also adopted more performance-based compensation with annual pay systems (Park, 2004). Future research could explore the differences and effectiveness of HRM practices between domestic and foreign companies. The cases of DHL Korea, IBM Korea and 3M Korea in this chapter could bring some insights to the HRM practices at foreign companies in Korea. We hope that this chapter has provided a good overview of HRM in Korea and inspired more researchers, policy makers, and managers to tackle the HRM challenges in the current era of globalization.

## Case study: DHL Korea – successful adoption of a job-based system

As a world leading logistics company, DHL has over 360,000 employees in over 220 countries and territories. DHL Korea was established in 2001 and has the highest market share in logistics in Korea. Its major competitors are FEDEX and UPS and they compete for price, speed and service.

The talent management and culture highlight *speed*, *right first time*, *can do spirit* and *passion*. DHL provides all employees with the Certified International Specialist (CIS) program, which is a world-class comprehensive training on the fundamentals of international shipping and company strategy. The CIS program is the same throughout the world and it consists of various specialized modules based on different divisions, individuals, jobs and positions. All courses provide a unique experience using discussions and role-plays. Those who finish the training courses are given a Success Passport which could be used for their promotions.

Unlike other domestic logistic companies, DHL Korea has no temporary or contract workers since the company considers customer contacts as the core of the value chain. The company's average length of service per employee is 11 years, and their turnover rate is lower than 5%. The company has a Hiring Manager system in which all department managers determine the required present manpower and select their own subordinates. Departments with a shortage of labor should apply and get approval from the HR department before the interview and selection process. The company uses internal job postings for recruitment for job vacancies.

As for benefits, the company has Appreciation Week during which employees are provided with free movies and food. Moreover, there is a regular Town Hall Meeting to promote communication between executives and employees. As a childrearing support program, the company provides female employees with mentoring time with senior workers. The company also has DHL Got Talent (singing and dancing competition) and CEO Dinner with CIS Award (excellent employee award) to motivate employees.

DHL Korea has decided to adopt a job-based system and since 2003 has hosted many presentations to explain the system because of the many problems of the previous seniority-based system such as difficulties in improving employee competencies and performance. The company-wide system for job-based pay has been adopted since 2006 and this means employee pay is based on the value of their jobs. The job grade consists of G5 to G8 (staff), G9 to G10 (supervisor/executive/ specialist), L to K (junior management), J to G (middle management) and F to D (senior management). The competency evaluation system is based on five core competencies such as *making customers more successful, shaping direction, driving high performance, developing others* and *developing self.* The evaluation system distinguishes between what to do and what not to do, provides action guides for each action item and reflects the evaluated competencies on performance appraisal. The competency evaluation is conducted separately from the job grade and managers decide who gets a promotion.

Employee pay is based on their job grades only and is not related to their positions. There is a pay range for each job grade and the company has management by objective and a competency-based performance appraisal system.

DHL Korea also has excellent labor relations. With the support of a labor-management council and a regular communication channel between the CEO and employees, there have been no labor disputes. DHL has made many achievements such as pay increases and improvement of various benefits to better the needs of employees. The company is also well known for its relatively egalitarian culture and active, open communication among all members. With the high commitment and motivation of employees, DHL Korea won the Best Employer of Commitment to Engagement Award in 2013.

## Source

Bae, J. S. 2018. *Human resource theories: Values, people and regulations.* Seoul: Hongmoonsa.

# Bibliography

## Key references

Froese, F. J., Sekiguchi, T., & Maharjan, P. 2017. Human resource management in Japan and Korea: Challenges and opportunities. In F. L. Cooke & S. Kim (Eds.), *Asian HRM handbook*: 275–294. New York: Routledge.

Horak, S., & Yang, I. 2019. Whither seniority? Career progression and performance orientation in South Korea. *The International Journal of Human Resource Management*, https://doi. org/10.1080/09585192.2017.136259.

Tung, R. L., Paik, Y., & Bae, J. 2013. Korean human resource management in the global context. *The International Journal of Human Resource Management*, 24(5): 905–921.

## Online sources

Korea Labor Institute. 2019. www.kli.re.kr Accessed 18 March 2019.

## References

Ahn, J. T. 2008. A comparative study on the human resource management of big enterprise in Korea and Japan under the High Performance System. *Korean Corporation Management Review*, 15(2): 195–212.

Amsden, A. 1987. *Asia's next giant: South Korea and late industrialization*. New York: Oxford University Press.

Bader, K., Froese, F. J., & Kraeh, A. 2018. Clash of cultures? German expatriates' work-life boundary adjustment in South Korea. *European Management Review*, 15: 357–374.

Bae, J. S. 2018. *Human resource theories: Values, people and regulations*. Seoul: Hongmoonsa.

Bae, J., Chen, S., & Rowley, C. 2011. From a paternalistic model towards what? HRM trends in Korea and Taiwan. *Personnel Review*, 40: 700–722.

Froese, F. J. 2013. Work values of the new generation of business leaders in Shanghai, Tokyo and Seoul. *Asia Pacific Journal of Management*, 30: 297–315.

Froese, F. J., Kim, K., & Eng, A. 2016. Language, cultural intelligence, and inpatriate turnover intentions: Leveraging values in multinational corporations through inpatriates. *Management International Review*, 56: 283–301.

Froese, F. J., & Kishi, Y. 2013. Organizational attractiveness of foreign firms in Asia: Soft power matters. *Asian Business & Management*, 12: 281–297.

Froese, F. J., Pak, Y. S., & Chong, L. C. 2008. Managing the human side of cross-border acquisitions in South Korea. *Journal of World Business*, 43(1): 97–108.

Froese, F. J., Sekiguchi, T., & Maharjan, P. 2017. Human resource management in Japan and Korea: Challenges and opportunities. In F. L. Cooke & S. Kim (Eds.), *Asian HRM handbook*: 275–294. New York: Routledge.

Hemmert, M. 2017. *The evolution of Tiger management: Korean companies in global competition*. New York: Routledge.

Hildisch, K., Froese, F. J., & Pak, Y. S. 2015. Employee responses to a cross-border acquisition: The role of social support from different hierarchical levels. *Asian Business and Management*, 14, 327–347.

Horak, S. 2017. The informal dimension of human resource management in Korea: Yongo, recruiting practices and career progression. *The International Journal of Human Resource Management*, 28(10): 1409–1432.

Horak, S., & Yang, I. 2019. Whither seniority? Career progression and performance orientation in South Korea. *The International Journal of Human Resource Management*, https://doi.org/10.1080/09585192.2017.136259.

Jöns, I., Froese, F. J., & Pak, Y. S. 2007. Cultural changes during the integration process of acquisitions – A comparative study between German and German-Korean acquisitions. *International Journal of Intercultural Relations*, 31: 591–604.

Jun, I. W., & Rowley, C. 2014. Change and continuity in management systems and corporate performance: Human resource management, corporate culture, risk management and corporate strategy in South Korea. *Business History*, 56(3): 485–508.

Kim, D., & Bae, J. 2004. *Employment relations and HRM in South Korea*. London: Ashgate Publishing.

Kim, D. B., & Oh, G. T. 2018. The trend of HR practices in Korean companies. *Korea Labor Institute Monthly Labor Review*, 2018(06): 47–64.

Kim, K. S. 2008. Nonstandard employment in Korea and its impact on human resource management. *Korean Journal of Economics and Management*, 26(3): 183–205.

Kim, N., Kim, S., & Park, K. 2017. Aging workforce and human resource management: Making sense of research on aging and work in Korea. *Korean Journal of Management*, 25(4): 45–96.

Kim, Y. J., Kim, S. K., & Kim, K. S. 2015. *New human resource management*. Seoul: Topbooks.

Kraeh, A., Froese, F. J., & Park, H. 2015. Foreign Professionals in South Korea. In A. P. D'Costa (Ed.), *After-development Dynamics: South Korea's contemporary engagement with Asia*, 185–200. Oxford University Press.

Lee, B. C., Lee, K., & Jeon, Y. 2012. Human resource management in the Era of Korean unification: Present and the future. *Korea Business Review*, 16(2): 229–261.

Li, J. M., & Kim, S. K. 2014. Improving cross-cultural training programs in Korea. *Korean Journal of Economics and Management*, 32(1): 27–49.

Li, J. M., Liu, Y., & Chung, D. S. 2016. The effects of social capital on cultural adaptation and job satisfaction among Korean-Chinese workers in Korea. *Journal of Human Resource Management Research*, 23(1): 1–18.

OECD. 2017. *Population with tertiary education*. https://data.oecd.org/eduatt/population-with-tertiary-education.htm. Accessed 18 March 2019.

Park, W. S. 2004. *Are foreign establishments really different from local establishments in managing human resources? An evidence from KLI establishment survey*. www.google.com/url?url=www.kli.re.kr/wps/downloadCnfrncSjIemFile.do%3FiemNo%3D381&rct=j&frm=1&q=&esrc=s&sa=U&ved=0ahUKEwiS57vL3OzeAhVET7wKHb0DBHcQFggTMAA&usg=AOvVaw2_d08h57iY8aoiRQ1T_ScE. Accessed 24 November 2018.

Park, W. W. 2001. Human resource management in South Korea. In P. S. Budhwar & Y. A. Debrah (Eds.), *Human resource management in developing countries*: 34–55. London, New York: Routledge.

Tung, R. L., Paik, Y., & Bae, J. 2013. Korean human resource management in the global context. *The International Journal of Human Resource Management*, 24(5): 905–921.

Universum. 2018. *Universum Korea employer ranking*. https://universumglobal.com/rankings/south-korea/. Accessed 18 March 2019.

Worldbank. 2018. *Human capital project*. www.worldbank.org/en/publication/human-capital. Accessed 18 March 2019.

# 11

# EXPATRIATES IN KOREA

## Live to work or work to live?

*Samuel Davies and Fabian Jintae Froese*

## Introduction

The rapid economic growth of Korea, along with an increasingly mobile workforce, have made Korea an attractive destination for employees from across the globe. In Korea, international talent is vital to fill skills gaps and transfer knowledge across borders (Froese, 2012). Thus, Korea has become a dynamic player in the global war for talent, competing with its regional economies such as Japan (Froese & Peltokorpi, 2011) and China (Han & Froese, 2010) to attract global talent. Attracted by these prospects, the number of foreigners in Korea has increased dramatically. From as low as 65,000 foreigners in 1992, more than 1.4 million foreigners lived in Korea in 2016 (Korea National Statistical Office, 2017). The vast majority are of Chinese nationality (about 800,000) and live in the greater Seoul area. Although approximately 900,000 foreigners are employed, the vast majority occupy low- to medium-skilled jobs, for example, construction workers and service employees, and only about 100,000 foreigners occupy professional or managerial positions (Korea National Statistical Office, 2017). In this chapter, we focus on highly skilled employed foreigners who do not intend to live in Korea permanently, so-called expatriates.

Expatriation research distinguishes between two different types of expatriates. First, there are organizational expatriates (OEs) – those who are sent by their organizations, to a subsidiary in Korea, or vice versa, from a Korean subsidiary abroad, to the Korean HQ, known as inpatriates (Froese et al., 2016; Sarabi et al., 2017). OEs, as highly qualified professionals, among a variety of reasons, are sent to, for example, transfer knowledge (Chang et al., 2012), coordinate and control between HQ and subsidiary, and for career development purpose (Biemann & Andresen, 2010; Sarabi et al., 2017; Sarabi et al., 2019). OEs often do not make the decision to move abroad for their assignment but are sent by their employer and usually receive support from their organization's headquarters during their assignment (Peltokorpi & Froese, 2009).

The second type, self-initiated expatriates (SIEs) (Froese, 2012), are those who decide to move abroad of their own volition, often to experience a new environment and culture, without additional support and expatriate benefits (Peltokorpi & Froese, 2009). SIEs find employment at different types of organizations, both local and foreign, to fill skills and knowledge gaps. The investment banking, IT, engineering, R&D and education sectors are industries where SIEs find employment, as their skills and knowledge can be transferred across national boundaries. (Froese, 2012).

Whichever type, expatriates in Korea are presented with several challenges, reflected by Korea's unique culture. This chapter discusses the unique aspects of Korean culture and the resulting challenge of adjustment, how expatriates can prepare for the move, factors that present challenges and benefits for expatriates, and finally presents a case study of a self-initiated expatriate who worked for a software company in Korea.

## Korean culture – Confucianism causing confusion

Korean culture is vastly different from Western European culture and presents itself in several interesting ways (see also Chapter 5). First, Korea is a relatively homogenous society, and although more expatriates and foreigners are living and working there, especially over the last 20 years, it is still a vastly majority ethnic Korean society. Korean society operates around its central cultural component of Confucianism and, of all Asian countries, is arguably the most Confucian in its day-to-day cultural practices (Kraeh et al., 2015; Park et al., 1996; Yum, 1988). In the 15th century, Confucius influenced society to be structured along lines of individuals of important status, for example, parents, teachers, siblings, and so on, and their salient characteristics, for example, age, gender, and the relative status between people resulting from these relative characteristics, for example, how a young person should address their elder, a student their teacher, an employee their supervisor and so on (Kraeh et al., 2015; Yum, 1988). There is a deep recognition within Confucianism of authority and social harmony. This hierarchical verticality runs so deeply that it is even integrated within Korean grammar, where verbs are altered according to the relative status of another (Kang, 2003). Korea is therefore, to this day, a hierarchical, culturally authoritarian society and is further a collectivist society, stressing the importance of the group, above the importance of the individual (Kraeh et al., 2015). Korea is furthermore characterized by high in-group preference, which describes preferring members of one's own group to another (Kraeh et al., 2015). These Confucian characteristics precipitated macro-characteristics of Korean culture, of formality, hierarchy, authoritarianism, and in-group collectivism, along with its rapidly developed economy. Korean culture's macro characteristics have partly or wholly resulted in intriguing cultural micro-characteristics.

The work- and non-work environment can be very stressful for expatriates. Korean working hours are the third highest in the OECD (OECD, 2018). However, reform in 2018 legislated this to a 52-hour working week maximum (The Guardian, 2018), and OECD statistics show working hours have been steadily decreasing over time, with 2,512 annual hours worked in 2000, compared to 2,069 annual hours worked in 2016 (OECD, 2018). This number is still very high compared to Germany, with slightly more than 1,300 hours per year. Employees, including expatriate employees, might be expected to show their loyalty, and commitment, by maintaining long hours and, further, undertaking extra work in times of crisis for the company. This willingness to go above and beyond for the company, is rooted in the notion of *Jeong*, which is essentially a feeling of bonding and warmth for one's peers, which is rooted in Confucianism, and which arguably leads to Korean employers wishing to fulfill their social commitments to their superiors and colleagues (Kraeh et al., 2015). Relatedly, another issue faced by expatriates, is the Korean after work, dinner/drinking culture of *hoesik*. This tradition means that employees are expected to attend late-night drinking sessions, usually once a month, or sometimes, once a week (Kraeh et al., 2015). Furthermore, Korea has a *bbali-bbali* culture, which means to do things as quickly, and often as last minute as possible. *Bbali-bbali* causes problems for some expatriates, who expect to plan, rather than hurriedly perform tasks at the last minute (Kraeh et al., 2015). You will see examples of some of these, and other aspects of macro- and micro-level cultural issues, within the case study later in this chapter.

The maelstrom of unusual cultural components of Korea, often rooted in Confucianism, and often alien to the cultural norms of the West, means that expatriates, especially Western expatriates, face significant challenges in adapting to both work and life within Korea (Bader et al., 2018; Kraeh et al., 2015; Park et al., 1996). This adaption has been conceptualized by scholars as *cross-cultural adjustment* and is critical when working and living in Korea.

## Cross-cultural adjustment – riding the roller coaster

One of the primary concerns of an expatriate while in Korea is the task to become adjusted to the work and life of Korea. Cross-cultural adjustment (henceforth – adjustment) is broadly the process of adjusting to a foreign culture's working and living environment. Adjustment is comprised of three facets: general adjustment (comfort with things outside of work, for example, food, housing, culture, entertainment), interaction adjustment (comfort with interactions with host-country nationals in and out of work), and work adjustment (comfort with work-related factors, e.g., jobs or tasks at work; Black et al., 1991). Adjustment is crucial for individuals and organizations, as good adjustment positively affects important outcomes, such as job satisfaction, organizational commitment, job performance, and employee turnover (Bhaskar-Shrinivas et al., 2005).

Upon arrival in Korea, expatriates are likely to suffer stress from the salient cultural differences previously discussed (Kraeh et al., 2015). Because of these cultural

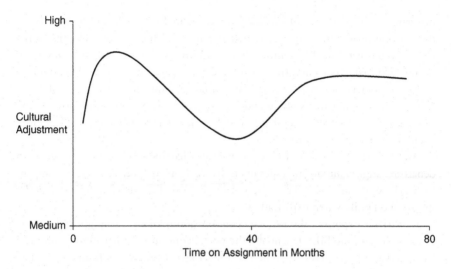

**FIGURE 11.1**    Expatriate adjustment U-curve

*Source:* Bhaskar-Shrinivas et al. (2005).

stressors, strain results and adjustment are contextual measures of the levels of that stress. Over time, as expatriates adjust to the Korean environment, they will experience less strain (Bhaskar-Shrinivas et al., 2005). Bhaskar-Shrinivas et al. (2005) found that the adjustment process takes several years, and follows a U-shaped curve beginning with, first, the honeymoon stage, which lasts about one year, and then, much like a rollercoaster, dips down and back up to finally result in an adjusted state.

Adjustment is a rather emotional journey, and before and during this journey various important factors affect an expatriate's adjustment (Bhaskar-Shrinivas et al., 2005). Some of these factors are especially relevant to the experience of expatriates within Korea. We next outline the factors that are especially relevant to expatriates in Korea, beginning with the pre-departure stage.

## Before moving to Korea – motivation and preparation

Expatriates have different motivations for why they go to Korea. Willingness to expatriate is a crucial part of expatriates' motivations (Froese, 2012), and the first major hurdle to making the decision to work in Korea. Cosmopolitanism, essentially an "openness to diverse cultural experiences" (Froese et al., 2013: 3249) and foreign exposure, for example, foreign contacts, foreign language proficiency, and positively predicted expatriation willingness to expatriate (Froese et al., 2013). These factors are beneficial for expatriates in Korea (Froese, 2010). In another study, Froese (2012) interviewed 30 foreign professors in Korea to explore the reasons why they relocated to Korea. First, in line with findings by Froese et al. (2013) on expatriate willingness, international experience was a dominant theme in terms of SIEs' motivation to live and work in Korea. The study found two themes of international experience that affected SIEs motivations. The first was a general interest in the Asia region, and the second, a general interest in any form of international experience. Indeed, some expatriates in this study had previously had some experience within Korea; for instance, James from the US had come to Korea as an exchange student and had studied Korean. Others reported living experience in other Asian countries, such as Japan (Froese et al., 2013), before deciding to expatriate to Korea.

Another motivational factor was expatriates having a Korean spouse prior to departure. Eight out of 30 respondents had a Korean spouse before moving to Korea (Froese et al., 2013). This chapter later discusses the crucial importance of the spouse and family when expatriating.

Expatriates expressed the Korean economy/job market as a significant motivational factor among SIEs. Essentially, the poor economies of their home countries had acted as a push factor to come to Korea. Expatriate scholars from the US had problems in the US in obtaining tenure track positions, due to high job competition. Korea provided an opportunity for these scholars to obtain tenure track status, albeit outside their home nation. Indeed, as one SIE said regarding his move to Korea: "Why not?" (Froese et al., 2013: 1102). Similarly, host-country characteristics (measured as economic level and language) have been shown to be a crucial factor when assessing potential expatriate's willingness (Kim & Froese, 2012). For instance, Froese et al. (2016) found that the majority of expatriates in Korea hail from less developed, mostly Asian nations.

Once motivation has been established, and the decision to expatriate to Korea has been made, certain pre-departure factors might aid later adjustment. First, if an expatriate has previously been abroad, this is an advantage for adjustment as the expatriate knows some of what to expect, having experienced the adjustment process in another country (Bhaskar-Shrinivas et al., 2005). Prior experience in Korea and/or Asia seems advantageous. It might also matter if expatriates plan to stay for a relatively short or a relatively long time in Korea. Those who only stay for a short period, for example, less than six months, described only a few problems, while those who stay longer complained more often about the challenges in daily life in Korea (Froese et al., 2013). The reason behind this might be different adjustment phases, implying that short-stayers remain as guests who enjoy the visit, while long-stayers must immerse into the different sociocultural environment, for example, visiting doctors and negotiating with property owners.

Pre-departure cross-cultural training prepares expatriates to know what to expect abroad and might aid adjustment. (Caligiuri et al., 2001). Expatriates can learn about the sociocultural background and business etiquette, which can be helpful, particularly at the beginning. In addition, learning the host country language can be even more effective than their pre-departure cross-cultural training (Puck et al., 2008). We next discuss the vital importance of Korean language ability.

## Language and host-country nationals – communication breakdown?

Host-country language ability represents one's ability to speak, read, and listen to the host country language, as well as the ability to understand the local dialect, and non-verbal communications common to that location (Selmer & Lauring, 2015). Host-country language ability was found to positively affect interaction adjustment across several studies (Bhaskar-Shrinivas et al., 2005). Furthermore, Korean language ability specifically was further found to affect both interaction *and* work adjustment, indicating it might be even more necessary in Korea (Froese et al., 2012). Indeed, the Korean language is particularly difficult for English speakers to learn, and vice versa, due to one of the highest linguistic distances between the respective languages (Chiswick et al., 2005). A recent study found that host country language ability had benefits for adjustment in countries with particularly difficult languages for English speakers to learn (Selmer & Lauring, 2015). This is further support for the suggestion that expatriates considering a move to Korea should make a special effort to learn the language. Froese (2012) found that 15 out of 30 expatriate respondents in Korea expressed that their poor Korean language skills negatively affected their general adjustment. This importance of Korean language might be partially due to divergent communication styles between expatriates and Koreans (Kraeh et al., 2015; Park et al., 1996). Froese et al. (2012) found that convergent communication styles and even the amount you talk to your Korean colleagues increased adjustment. Park et al. (1996), describe some of these fundamental differences in communication style between Koreans and Westerners. For instance, Koreans have a high tolerance for ambiguous communication, whereas Westerners might prefer clarity and specificity in the workplace. Furthermore, Korean employees use silence in the workplace for various reasons, among them to conceal a limited command of a foreign language, to avoid conflict, and to save face (essentially maintaining one's social reputation), which might cause significant frustration for expatriate colleagues. Relatedly, how much support is received from co-workers is also a further indicator of good adjustment across several studies (Bhaskar-Shrinivas et al., 2005), so it seems important when expatriated to use language skills to have as good a relationship with Korean colleagues as possible.

In summary, it helps to have even a little Korean-language ability before moving abroad and learning it while on the work stint to use it to overcome communication and cultural barriers and to use it to engage with your co-workers, who can help you become adjusted. Due to similarities in language, we recommend all Chinese and Japanese expatriates to become fully proficient in the Korean language to work more effectively in Korea. Talented Korean and Chinese expatriates could become proficient in Korean within one year. Given the large difference of languages, it would be unrealistic to expect Western expatriates to acquire fluent Korean-language skills. Nevertheless, we recommend Western expatriates to learn Korean before and during their stay. Even if they speak only little Korean, that would help them get better adjusted and accepted in Korean work- and non-work environments. For instance, Korea employees would appreciate if the foreign CEO uses (at the beginning) Korean language when he/she gives an official speech.

However, using language skills is one thing, but communicating *effectively* with culturally different co-workers, and empathizing with the way they do things, is another. Cultural intelligence can play a vital role in improving this, and how you interact with your colleagues in the workplace.

## Cultural intelligence – be mindful

Cultural intelligence is broadly the ability to observe culturally different others, model their differing behaviors, and adapt one's own thinking and behavior to suit the cultural context (Stoermer et al., 2017; Thomas et al., 2008). Cultural intelligence has aspects of meta-cognition – that is, being mindful of one's own behavior, and communications in a cross-cultural situation, and adapting this behavior/communication style to suit. This could be a particularly useful skill within Korea, given the multiple cultural elements already discussed. To take an example, Korean colleagues might remain silent, even if they disagree with your instructions or opinions (Park et al., 1996). Culturally intelligent expatriates should be more likely to pick up the lack of response as disagreement and adapt or change their instructions in the face of this disagreement, maintaining social harmony. Cultural intelligence is also important for integration into the organization. Stoermer et al. (2017) found that cultural intelligence increased expatriates' embeddedness (i.e., their level of enmeshment in the organization) and boosted their ability to share knowledge with their cross-cultural colleagues. The good news is that Stoermer et al. (2018) note that cultural intelligence is malleable and can be improved.

Organizations can provide training, coaching, and mentoring to increase expatriates' cultural intelligence. Furthermore, organizations wishing to hire expatriates for Korea might want to consider motivation, Korean language abilities, and cultural intelligence in their recruiting and selection processes.

## Exclusion and inclusion

Racially based social exclusion at work is defined as the "exclusion of the target [individual] from work-related or social interactions as a result of his or her race or ethnicity" (Schneider et al., 2000: 3). Stoermer et al. (2017) note that racially based social exclusion is the opposite of receptivity to outsiders. Predictably, in Korea, arguably due to its homogeneity and in-group collectivist cultural characteristics, social exclusion at work has been shown to be present and to negatively affect expatriates' job satisfaction. The good news is that the authors found that when cultural intelligence was greater than the perceived amount of social exclusion, job satisfaction was positively affected (Stoermer et al., 2017). This indicates that you can affect the success of your job path in Korea, by working on your (malleable) cultural intelligence.

There has been further evidence of racial discrimination causing problems for expatriates. Stoermer et al. (2017) found that employees' race affects their self-perceived racial harassment and that this perceived racial harassment can have negative knock-on effects for their job satisfaction. But not only race can be a target for discrimination. A study by Bader et al. (2018) found that female expatriates can be particularly vulnerable to perceptions of gender-based discrimination, when compared with male expatriates, and that this discrimination can lead to lowered expatriate job satisfaction. As Korea is a masculine society (Hofstede et al., 2010), this might present itself as a problem for female expatriates and should thus be considered. So, while individual differences are crucial, they might not always bring disadvantages, and indeed, some characteristics can be leveraged.

Froese (2010) discussed acculturation experiences as a self-initiated expatriate and foreign professor working in Korea. Among various factors, a notable issue was the authors' demographic characteristics. Even being half ethnically Korean the author notes, "No matter how assiduously I attempted to conform to Korean culture, several critical incidents made me aware that it was impossible for me to assimilate entirely" (Froese, 2010: 341). However, the author also notes the advantages of being part Korean, such as greater trust from Korean colleagues and assumed expertise of Korea by other expatriates.

More on the upside, the author notes that Korea is becoming increasingly more global, and thus more accepting of foreigners (Froese, 2010). In line with the nature of Confucianism and its emphasis on the status of individuals (Kraeh et al., 2015; Yum, 1988) the author notes that job position matters, and Koreans recognize the status inherent in certain jobs, for example, university professor. Thus, as senior managers in Korea, expatriates will have a relatively easy life compared to low-ranked expatriates who must adjust to senior Korean supervisors.

There is also hope in the form of support from the organization in Korea via an inclusion climate. An inclusion climate measures the level at which employees perceive their organization values diversity and the degree to which their organization includes minorities and women in the workplace (Mor Barak et al., 1998; Nishii, 2013). From a sample of expatriates residing in Korea, Davies et al. (2019) found that a perceived inclusion climate has positive implications for expatriate's workplace adjustment, by conserving and fostering their personal resources.

## Work and life

The vast majority of expatriates live in Seoul, with many of them congregated in certain districts. For instance, many Germans live in Hannam-dong near the Deutsche Schule (German school), while many French live in Bangbae-dong near the Lycée Francaise (French school). The schools serve as a magnet for expatriates with and without children. In consequence, several shops cater to the needs of expatriates, for example, German-style bread in Hannam-dong, and more Western-style apartments are available. Seoul has become an increasingly affluent metropolis with various food, social, and cultural offerings. However, the offering is mainly catered to Koreans and not all Western expatriates are satisfied with it (Bader et al., 2018; Froese, 2012).

The understanding of what work and life mean often varies between expatriates and their Korean colleagues. Work plays a central role in the lives of Korean employees. Koreans "live to work", while Europeans "work to live" (Bader et al., 2018). Moreover, while Europeans like to separate work and life, Koreans tend to integrate work and life (Bader et al., 2018). Based on the four-dimensional framework of Kreiner et al. (2009). Bader et al. (2018) investigated what work-life challenges German expatriates experienced and how they coped with it. First, in terms of *temporal influences*, the long working hours, time pressure, and short-notice working culture present major challenges for German expatriates. Unlike Germany, where flexible time arrangements are commonplace, the employer/supervisor dictate the time in Korea. Second, expatriates are also confronted with *behavioral influences*. Since Koreans usually do not clearly separate work and life, employees, including expatriates, are expected to participate in various off-work activities, for example, after-work meetings and social gatherings. This limits the time expatriates can spend with their family, friends, or on their own. Third, *physical influences* are visible in the structure and usage of space. While some expatriates live in company-sponsored housing, often in proximity with their colleagues, many live in expatriate districts. This limits the perceived freedom as they could at any time bump into their colleagues, customers, or suppliers. One problem is also the distance to family and friends back home. Fourth, *mental influences*, that is, a different understanding of work and life, also complicate the situation of expatriates in Korea. Rigid gender expectations and strict authorities limit self-development, particularly of younger and female expatriates. The strength of these influences varies substantially across the type of organization, for example, foreign versus Korean organization, and supervisor, for example, foreign versus Korean. Expatriates working at foreign companies often find an environment that mixes some elements of the foreign and Korean work culture, for example, shorter working hours and fewer off-work activities than traditional Korean companies do.

Expatriates have different options to deal with these differences. Bader et al. (2018) distinguish between four different strategies. First, in an *ethnocentric style*, expatriates simply maintain their work–life balance as before. This is usually only possible if expatriates work at foreign institutions and occupy senior positions. Otherwise, expatriates might be penalized by their Korean colleagues. Second, in the *disconnected style*, expatriates are under constant pressure to adjust to the Korean work lifestyle but do not appreciate it. This is a problematic situation for expatriates. They either adopt one of the following styles, re-negotiate, or leave the situation. Third, the *localized style* applies to expatriates who have adopted the Korean work lifestyle. While being aware of differences, these expatriates appreciate the Korean style and/or believe that this would be beneficial for personal/business success in Korea. Most of these expatriates were highly career oriented. Traditional Korean organizations wishing to hire expatriates might want to recruit such expatriates. Fourth, expatriates applying a *flexible style* find a mix between foreign and Korean work–life boundaries. They adopt some Korean practices while maintaining some features that are important to them. Foreign organizations can support them. For instance, because Germans enjoy holidays, their employing organizations could send them for extended "business trips" over the summer or Christmas.

## Cost of living and compensation

As described in Chapter 2, Korea has risen from a poor developing country to a rich industrialized economy. The GDP per capita is comparable with southern European countries. Likewise, the cost of living has increased substantially. While locals and foreign students can live on a relatively small budget, the cost for expatriates are very high. According to various rankings (e.g., Mercer, 2018), the cost of living for expatriates is usually among the 10 highest in the world, in a similar league with, for example, Hong Kong or London. The main drivers of the cost are housing and foreign products. While local cuisine at a local restaurant can be very cheap, Western food ingredients and cuisine can be very expensive. For instance, while 50 grams of Parma ham costs about 2 euro in Italy, it costs about 8 euro in Seoul. The property prices in Seoul have soared in recent years. For instance, Hyundai bought a piece of land in downtown Seoul in 2014 for USD10 billion to build a new headquarters. Moreover, Korea has a different housing rent system where the tenant is expected to pay a large amount up front ( *Jeonse* or key money), for example, USD300,000. Cost for rent in desirable locations such as the expatriate districts and Gangnam, a posh southern district, is extremely expensive. The monthly rental cost for a CEO of a large foreign company usually exceeds USD10,000, while most corporate expatriates receive rent allowances higher than USD5,000. SIEs who do not receive such corporate benefits need to find smaller places and/or in more local districts. This leads to our next topic: compensation.

In line with increased economic development, the salary level has risen in Korea. Korea is a financially attractive destination both for self-initiated and corporate expatriates. Foreigners from certain countries and under certain conditions can receive two years' tax-free income. Even after that period, the tax rate is lower than in most European countries. Foreigners can choose between a flat rate of 20.9% or the regular progressive rates ranging from 6.6% to 44%. Thus, the maximum tax rate for foreigners would be 20.9%. Apart from that, organizations find numerous creative ways to reduce the tax rates for its employees.

Depending on their contracts, expatriates enjoy different types of benefits. Corporate expatriates usually enjoy generous expatriate benefits. Most multinational enterprises have adopted a balance sheet approach of expatriate compensation (Bonache & Zarraga-Oberty, 2017; Briscoe et al., 2012), that is, offering an equivalent salary compared to a referent group. To ease relocation and satisfy expatriates, multinational organizations usually offer attractive expatriate benefits (Bonache & Zarraga-Oberty, 2017). Table 11.1 provides an exemplary composition of an expatriate's compensation package. The logic behind the benefits is that expatriates should be able to maintain a similar lifestyle as in their home country.

**TABLE 11.1** Typical expenses of a corporate expense from Munich to Seoul

| Item | Euro |
|---|---|
| **Direct compensation cost** | |
| Base salary | **80,000** |
| Foreign service premium | 25,000 |
| Goods and services differential | 50,000 |
| Housing | 96,000 |
| **Company paid cost** | |
| Education (for 2 children) | 30,000 |
| Transfer moving costs | 30,000 |
| Working spouse allowance | 50,000 |
| Annual home leave expenses | 20,000 |
| Add'l insurance, pension & evacuation coverage | 30,000 |
| **Total** | **411,000** |

Typical expatriate benefit packages include allowances for housing, education, and a foreign service premium. As a result, expatriate compensation and benefit packages are usually three to five times the amount of the pay back home, often making the expatriate the most expensive employee on the payroll of the foreign subsidiary. Most expatriates can save some money during their international assignment. Given the plurality of expatriate assignments, increasing global mobility, skill upgrade of Korean managers, and the increasing attractiveness of Korea, multinational organizations may consider ways to reduce expatriate benefits, for example, cut foreign service premium (Bonache & Zarraga-Oberty, 2017).

In contrast, SIEs usually do not receive any expatriate benefits. They receive comparable salaries with other Korean employees. Thus, SIEs usually must adjust their living style to local conditions. Some Korean-based organizations that are interested in hiring SIEs offer some expatriate benefits, for example, limited housing allowance or tuition support for accompanying children. The net salary in Korea is comparable to other industrialized nations in America and Europe. This makes Korea an attractive destination for foreign professionals from other less developed Asian countries, those from industrialized countries who have difficulties obtaining employment at home, and those who have a special interest in Korea.

## The family – help or hindrance?

The family and the partner, in particular, have an important influence on the success of the expatriate (Bhaskar-Shrinivas et al., 2005). Many have probably experienced that their partner can make or break their day. Takeuchi et al. (2002), found similarly, that the adjustment of an expatriate's partner can affect the adjustment of the expatriate. This effect is theorized to happen through crossover – an affect state (e.g., strain) that transfers from one individual to another. This crossover effect means that a poorly adjusted spouse can result in a poorly adjusted expatriate and is one of the major reported reasons for the ultimate decision to leave the job and/ or country. (Bhaskar-Shrinivas et al., 2005; Takeuchi et al., 2002). As a highly in-group-oriented country, Korea can be difficult for the spouse, as an outsider, to adapt to, and cultural factors might make it difficult to form close friendships with Koreans. Even if spouses were highly qualified and employed back home, it is very difficult for foreign spouses to find jobs in Seoul, partially due to language and visa issues. Instead of paying spouse allowances, it would be better if organizations helped spouses find employment.

In a study subtitled "Burden or Support?" expatriates with Korean partners, and to a lesser extent, third-country partners showed increased adjustment over expatriates with non-Korean partners (Davies et al., 2015), indicating that non-Korean, and especially home-country partners, may have a harder time getting used to life in Korea, affecting the expatriate through a crossover effect. Furthermore, Froese (2012) found that having a Korean spouse in Korea was advantageous for adjustment. So, it's important for an expatriate in Korea to also make sure their partner is happy, and not only for the purposes of expatriation.

Children of corporate expatriates usually attend international kindergarten and schools. Tuition is substantial and ranges between USD10,000 and USD30,000, depending on the age of children and the school. The student population at these international schools is international, including both Korean and students from all over the world. Given the transient nature of the expatriate communities, schools are used to integrate children and most children easily adapt to the new school and community. These schools also serve as the social contact point for expatriates and their families. Due to the high cost, some SIEs send their children to local schools. While children must adapt to the strict Korean school system with long hours, an advantage would be that they learn the Korean language.

## Conclusion

In this chapter, we discussed first (and possibly foremost), the importance of recognizing vital higher order aspects of Confucian and Korean culture. We recommend individuals to take note of the resultant lower order cultural aspects detailed within this chapter (e.g., *bbali-bbali, jeong, hoesik*, etc.) that are likely to be encountered (Kraeh et al., 2015) and to be mindful of their existence and standing within Korean culture (also see Chapter 4). We further brought attention to the importance of cross-cultural adjustment while working as an expatriate, to avoid negative consequences and increase positive outcomes (Bhaskar-Shrinivas et al., 2005), and recommend paying close attention to the challenges of adjustment while finding a path to it. Indeed, it may be wise to prepare before leaving for Korea in order to obtain the most optimal outcomes for adjustment and further integration into the workplace and society. The importance of language in Korea cannot be overstated (Froese et al., 2012) and has a vital impact on adjustment (Bhaskar-Shrinivas et al., 2005). and applying any language skills mindfully, and with respect to the cultural differences of Koreans, is vital. While exclusion can be a problem in Korea

(Stoermer et al., 2017), applying cultural intelligence aside other skills can help find a way to negotiate problematic experiences.

It is crucial for expatriates to make sure that work/life boundaries are not too blurry in Korea, given different preferences in approach to work–life balance for Koreans versus Westerners (Bader et al., 2018), and we recommend, per the discussion in this chapter, that not just career but also leisure and family life are given satisfactory, separate attention. Expatriates in Korea may find that certain foods are expensive, or certain leisure activities are unavailable, but nevertheless, there will be plenty to do, and one can have a great lifestyle while working and living in Korea, a vibrant, modern economy.

Korea can be a land of significant opportunity for a wide range of potential Expatriates. Those wishing to adapt to such a challenging cultural environment should take heed of the recommendations within this chapter, and note the experiences described within the case study to form an approach best suited to their own set of circumstances, and one that allows them to fully reap the rewards of expatriating to South Korea and, more important, succeeding there.

## Case study: "Thomas", an expatriate in Seoul

Thomas, a male college graduate in his late 20s from Canada, found a job in Seoul in a game software company, as an English localization expert. As an SIE, he does not receive any expatriate benefits or preferential treatment. Thomas experiences many of the upsides and significant challenges of working in Korea as an expatriate. The strict hierarchy confused him:

> The Korean workplace is far more hierarchical than workplaces in Canada, which are far more egalitarian, and this is something that could be felt in every facet of working in a Korean company. What was particularly difficult for me was how often my perspective as a foreigner, which was often important in the decision-making process within our team and the department as we were concerned with a product's viability in Western countries, was disregarded due to my place at the bottom of the hierarchy [. . .].

At the beginning, he found it difficult to integrate into the team. He wondered why he was the only foreigner in his team. He noticed that the situation greatly improved when he started to learn the Korean language.

> After I made an honest effort to learn the Korean language, I found that my situation improved quite a bit in a number of ways, as did my

view of the country. I learned that certain types of exchanges I previously thought were unpleasant actually weren't, and that some perceptions I had were incorrect due to me not knowing the language or understanding the culture (the two are intertwined) [. . .].

Thomas found family life in Korea a significant challenge, and Korea presented blurry work/life boundaries. Company priorities were frequently placed above that of the individual's own private and family life. This tension was difficult to handle for Thomas, and his refusal to accept work spillover into his private life, ultimately led to a promotion refusal:

> The most challenging aspect of this was the unspoken (and occasionally spoken) rule requiring all employees to remain at their desks well past 6pm [. . .] with many employees remaining at their desks until 11pm at night. This was coupled with an expectation to work on weekends as well. When I was refused a promotion at the end of my second year, my desire to leave work "on time" (30–45 minutes late each day) was the reason given.

Despite these cultural differences, Thomas had a positively enriching experience in Korea, discovering a change in his outlook, learning the Korean language, and engaging more deeply with the Korean culture and people, that ultimately seems to have led to his personal growth:

> I found upon learning the language, getting to know the culture on a deeper level and marrying into a Korean family that I got to experience more warmth and kindness from Korean people than I did as an isolated expat filling a specific role in Korean work environments.

Finally, Thomas notes an increased flexibility in both his career and personal life due to his stint in Korea:

> More generally, being an expat and having lived abroad made it easier for me to cope with difficulties in the transition from country to country. I think I can handle "restarting" my career, going back to school, moving to a new city/country more easily than someone who hasn't lived abroad

After five years in Korea, Thomas continued his career in the US. The time in Korea was an important step for him both from a professional and personal perspective.

### Source

Based on an interview with an expatriate but slightly modified. Thomas is an alias to protect the interviewee's anonymity.

## Bibliography

### Key references

Bader, K., Froese, F. J., & Kraeh, A. 2018. Clash of cultures? German expatriates' work-life boundary adjustment in South Korea. *European Management Review*, 15: 357–374.

Froese, F. J. 2010. Acculturation experiences in South Korea and Japan. *Culture & Psychology*, 16(3): 333–348.

Froese, F. J. 2012. Motivation and adjustment of self-initiated expatriates: The case of expatriate academics in South Korea. *The International Journal of Human Resource Management*, 23(6): 1095–1112.

Kraeh, A., Froese, F. J., & Park, H. 2015. Foreign professionals in South Korea. In A. P. D'Costa (Ed.), *After-development Dynamics: South Korea's contemporary engagement with Asia*: 185–200. Oxford University Press.

### Online sources

Information for Expats Living, Moving, Visiting, Working in Korea. n.d. *Korea4expats*. www.korea4expats.com/ Accessed 14 March 2019.

InterNations. n.d. www.internations.org/ Accessed 14 March 2019.

The World on Arirang. n.d. www.arirang.com/Index.asp?sys_lang=Eng Accessed 14 March 2019.

## References

Andresen, M., & Bergdolt, F. 2016. A systematic literature review on the definitions of global mindset and cultural intelligence – Merging two different research streams. *The International Journal of Human Resource Management*: 1–26.

Bader, K., Froese, F. J., & Kraeh, A. 2018. Clash of cultures? German expatriates' work-life boundary adjustment in South Korea. *European Management Review*, 15: 357–374.

Bader, B., Stoermer, S., Bader, A. K., & Schuster, T. 2018. Institutional discrimination of women and workplace harassment of female expatriates: Evidence from 25 host countries. *Journal of Global Mobility*, 6(1): 40–58.

Bhaskar-Shrinivas, P., Harrison, D. A., Shaffer, M. A., & Luk, D. M. 2005. Input-based and time-based models of international adjustment: Meta-analytic evidence and theoretical extensions. *Academy of Management Journal*, 48(2): 257–281.

Biemann, T., & Andresen, M. 2010. Self-initiated foreign expatriates versus assigned expatriates: Two distinct types of international careers? *Journal of Managerial Psychology*, 25(4): 430–448.

Black, J. S., Mendenhall, M., & Oddou, G. 1991. Toward a comprehensive model of international adjustment: An integration of multiple theoretical perspectives. *Academy of Management Review*, 16(2): 291–317.

Bonache, J., & Zarraga-Oberty, C. 2017. The traditional approach to compensating global mobility: Criticisms and alternatives. *International Journal of Human Resource Management*, 28: 149–169.

Briscoe, D., Schuler, R., & Tarique, I. 2012. *International human resource management: Policies and practices for multinational enterprises*. New York: Routledge.

Caligiuri, P., Phillips, J., Lazarova, M., Tarique, I., & Burgi, P. 2001. The theory of met expectations applied to expatriate adjustment: The role of cross-cultural training. *International Journal of Human Resource Management*, 12(3): 357–372.

Caplan, R. D. 1987. Person-environment fit theory and organizations: Commensurate dimensions, time perspectives, and mechanisms. *Journal of Vocational Behavior*, 31(3): 248–267.

Chang, Y. Y., Gong, Y., & Peng, M. W. 2012. Expatriate knowledge transfer, subsidiary absorptive capacity, and subsidiary performance. *Academy of Management Journal*, 55(4): 927–948.

Chriswick, B. R., Lee, Y. L., & Miller, P. E. 2005. Family matters: The role of the family in immigrants' destination language acquisition. *Journal of Population Economics*, 18: 631–647.

Davies, S. E., Stoermer, S., & Froese, F. J. 2019. When the going gets tough: The influence of expatriate resilience and perceived organizational inclusion climate on work adjustment and turnover intentions. *The International Journal of Human Resource Management*, 1–25.

Davies, S., Kraeh, A., & Froese, F. 2015. Burden or support? The influence of partner nationality on expatriate cross-cultural adjustment. *Journal of Global Mobility: The Home of Expatriate Management Research*, 3(2).

Froese, F. J. 2010. Acculturation experiences in South Korea and Japan. *Culture & Psychology*, 16(3): 333–348.

Froese, F. J. 2012. Motivation and adjustment of self-initiated expatriates: The case of expatriate academics in South Korea. *The International Journal of Human Resource Management*, 23(6): 1095–1112.

Froese, F. J., Jommersbach, S., & Klautzsch, E. 2013. Cosmopolitan career choices: A cross-cultural study of job candidates' expatriation willingness. *The International Journal of Human Resource Management*, 24(17): 3247–3261.

Froese, F. J., Kim, K., & Eng, A. 2016. Language, cultural intelligence, and inpatriate turnover intentions: Leveraging values in multinational corporations through inpatriates. *Management International Review*, 56: 283–301.

Froese, F. J., & Peltokorpi, V. 2011. Recruiting channels of foreign subsidiaries in Japan. *Zeitschrift Für Betriebswirtschaft*, 81(3): 101–116.

Froese, F. J., Peltokorpi, V., & Ko, K. A. 2012. The influence of intercultural communication on cross-cultural adjustment and work attitudes: Foreign workers in South Korea. *International Journal of Intercultural Relations*, 36(3): 331–342.

The Guardian. 2018. *South Korea cuts "inhumanely long" 68-hour working week*. www.theguardian.com/world/2018/mar/01/south-korea-cuts-inhumanely-long-68-hour-working-week. Accessed 29 May 2018.

Han, Z., & Froese, F. J. 2010. Recruiting and retaining R&D professionals in China. *International Journal of Technology Management*, 51(2): 387–408.

Hofstede, G., Hofstede, G. J., & Minkov, M. 2010. *Cultures and organizations: Software of the mind*. Revised and expanded. New York: McGraw-Hill.

Inkson, K., Arthur, M. B., Pringle, J., & Barry, S. 1998. Expatriate assignment versus overseas experience: Contrasting models of international human resource development. *Journal of World Business*, 32: 351–368.

Kang, M. A. 2003. Negotiating conflict within the constraints of social hierarchies in Korean American discourse. *Journal of Sociolinguistics*, 7(3): 299–320.

Kim, J., & Froese, F. J. 2012. Expatriation willingness in Asia: The importance of host-country characteristics and employees' role commitments. *The International Journal of Human Resource Management*, 23(16): 3414–3433.

Korea. n.d. *OECD Observer*. http://oecdobserver.org/news/categoryfront.php/id/85/Korea. html. Accessed 27 May 2018.

Korea National Statistics Office. 2017. http://kostat.go.kr. Accessed 27 May 2018.

Kraeh, A., Froese, F. J., & Park, H. 2015. Foreign professionals in South Korea. In A. P. D'Costa (Ed.), *After-development dynamics: South Korea's contemporary engagement with Asia*: 185–200. Oxford University Press.

Kreiner, G. E., Hollensbe, E. C., & Sheep, M. L. 2009. Balancing borders and bridges: Negotiating the work-home interface via boundary work tactics. *Academy of Management Journal*, 52: 704–730.

Mercer. 2018. *Mercer's annual cost of living survey finds Asian, European, and African cities most expensive locations for employees*. www.mercer.com/newsroom/cost-of-living-2018.html. Accessed 21 February 2019.

Mor Barak, M. E., Cherin, D. A., & Berkman, S. 1998. Organizational and personal dimensions in diversity climate: Ethnic and gender differences in employee perceptions. *The Journal of Applied Behavioral Science*, 34(1): 82–104.

Nishii, L. H. 2013. The benefits of climate for inclusion for gender-diverse groups. *Academy of Management Journal*, 56(6): 1754–1774.

OECD iLibrary. 2018. *Hours worked*. www.oecd-ilibrary.org/employment/hours-worked/indicator/english_47be1c78-en. Accessed 21 February 2019.

Park, H., Dai Hwang, S., & Harrison, J. K. 1996. Sources and consequences of communication problems in foreign subsidiaries: The case of United States firms in South Korea. *International Business Review*, 5(1): 79–98.

Peltokorpi, V., & Froese, F. J. 2009. Organizational expatriates and self-initiated expatriates: Who adjusts better to work and life in Japan? *International Journal of Human Resource Management*, 20(5): 1095–1111.

Peltokorpi, V., & Froese, F. J. 2014. Expatriate personality and cultural fit: The moderating role of host country context on job satisfaction. *International Business Review*, 23(1): 293–302.

Puck, J. F., Kittler, M. G., & Wright, C. 2008. Does it really work? Re-assessing the impact of pre-departure cross-cultural training on expatriate adjustment. *The International Journal of Human Resource Management*, 19(12): 2182–2197.

Sarabi, A., Froese, F. J., & Hamori, M. 2017. Is international assignment experience a ticket to the top of a foreign subsidiary? The moderating effect of subsidiary context. *Journal of World Business*, 52: 680–690.

Sarabi, A., Hamori, M., & Froese, F. J. 2019. Managing global talent flows. In D. Collings, H. Scullion & P. Caligiuri (Eds.), *Global talent management*: 59–74, London: Routledge.

Schneider, K. T., Hitlan, R. T., & Radhakrishnan, P. 2000. An examination of the nature and correlates of ethnic harassment experiences in multiple contexts. *Journal of Applied Psychology*, 85(1): 3.

Selmer, J., & Lauring, J. 2015. Host country language ability and expatriate adjustment: The moderating effect of language difficulty. *The International Journal of Human Resource Management*, 26(3): 401–420.

Stoermer, S., Bader, A. K., & Froese, F. J. 2016. Culture matters: The influence of national culture on inclusion climate. *Cross Cultural & Strategic Management*, 23(2): 287–305.

Stoermer, S., Davies, S., & Froese, F. J. 2017. Expatriates' cultural intelligence, embeddedness and knowledge sharing: A multilevel analysis. *Academy of Management Proceedings*, 2017(1): 16294.

Stoermer, S., Haslberger, A., Froese, F. J., & Kraeh, A. L. 2018. Person – Environment fit and expatriate job satisfaction. *Thunderbird International Business Review*, 60(6): 851–860.

Stoermer, S., Hitotsuyanagi-Hansel, A., & Froese, F. J. 2017. Racial harassment and job satisfaction in South Africa: The moderating effects of career orientations and managerial rank. *The International Journal of Human Resource Management*: 1–20.

Takeuchi, R. 2010. A critical review of expatriate adjustment research through a multiple stakeholder view: Progress, emerging trends, and prospects. *Journal of Management*, 36(4): 1040–1064.

Takeuchi, R., Yun, S., & Tesluk, P. E. 2002. An examination of crossover and spillover effects of spousal and expatriate cross-cultural adjustment on expatriate outcomes. *Journal of Applied Psychology*, 87(4): 655.

Thomas, D. C., Elron, E., Stahl, G., Ekelund, B. Z., Ravlin, E. C., Cerdin, J. L., et al. 2008. Cultural Intelligence Domain and Assessment. *International Journal of Cross Cultural Management*, 8: 123–143.

Yum, J. O. 1988. The impact of Confucianism on interpersonal relationships and communication patterns in East Asia. *Communications Monographs*, 55(4): 374–388.

# 12

# ESTABLISHING A START-UP BUSINESS IN KOREA AS A FOREIGN ENTREPRENEUR

*Stephan Gerschewski*

## Introduction

With the rise in economic wealth and political clout, and as a result of globalization drivers (see Chapters 2 and 3), a growing number of foreign companies have invested in the Korean market with a sharp increase in foreign-invested companies from 3,000 in 1997 to 17,100 in 2016 (KOTRA, 2017; Hemmert, 2017). As a result, the number of foreigners living and working in Korea has grown considerably over the past 30 years. For example, the number of foreigners in Korea has doubled from 1 million people in 2007 to 2.18 million people in 2016, which accounts for about 4% of the entire Korean population. It is expected that the number of foreigners in Korea is likely to exceed 3 million people by 2021 (Ock, 2016). The majority of foreigners consists primarily of expatriates working in subsidiaries of MNEs and in educational institutions, such as universities and private institutes (*hagwons*; see Chapter 11). In addition, partly due to the ease of doing business in Korea (World Bank, 2018), an increasing number of foreigners attempt to establish their own start-up businesses, ranging from small consultancies to independent craft stores and high-tech companies.

In 2013, the then Korean president Ms. Park Geun-hye introduced the so-called Creative Economy with one of the main aims of considerably boosting the start-up industry in Korea and shifting the balance of 'economic power' from the 'chaebols' (i.e., large conglomerates, such as Samsung) to SMEs. As a result of the 'Creative Economy' initiative, the Korean government has implemented and established several high-profile projects, including the K-Startup Grand Challenge, in order to foster and promote Korea as an Asian regional tech hub and to develop the 'Korean Silicon Valley' (K-Startup Grand Challenge, 2018). The Korean government has invested more than US$2 billion in the start-up industry per year since

2013, and it made a further pledge to establish a US$9 billion venture fund with public and private finances. Thus, Korea provides the highest government backing per capita for start-ups in the world (Guttmann, 2018). As a result of this generous government investment, Google, Spark Labs and other renowned companies have ventured into the Korean market over the past three years with the start-up scene in Korea expanding rapidly, resulting in a growing number of accelerators, such as 500 Startups' Korea fund (Guttmann, 2018).

The purpose of this chapter is to provide an overview on how foreign entrepreneurs can start a business in Korea, including the rules and regulations in the Korean market, and general advice on doing business in Korea. The chapter first outlines and analyses the key features of the Korean economy, including its key industry sectors and main export industries, and then conducts an analysis of the SME sector in Korea and its challenges and barriers, in order to provide a comprehensive and detailed overview for foreign entrepreneurs interested in starting a business in the dynamic market of Korea.

## The Korean economy

According to a recent McKinsey (2013) study, Korea has become a world leader in several technology industries, including DRAM memory chips, LCD displays, automobiles, and mobile phones. As described in Chapter 9, this provides an excellent opportunity for foreign companies and individuals to learn.

Korea has transformed from one of the poorest countries in in the 1950s to one of the wealthiest and most technologically advanced countries in the world in the 2000s. This is reflected in the shift of industries in Korea from light industry and labour-intensive sectors in the 1960s to heavy and chemical industries in the 1970s, until a strong shift towards technology and ICT-intensive industries in the 1980s and 1990s. From the 2000s onwards, the key sectors of the Korean economy lie in knowledge-intensive industries with innovation as being one of the main drivers of competitiveness.

Figure 12.1 illustrates an overview of the development of the different industry sectors in Korea from the 1960s to the 2000s.

|  | 1960s | 1970s | 1980 | 1990s | 2000s |
|---|---|---|---|---|---|
| Industry for Promotion | Light Industry | Heavy and Chemical Industry | Technology-intensive Industry | New Industry, including ICT | Knowledge-intensive Industry |
| Factors of Competitiveness | Simple Labour | Skilled Labour | Capital | Technology | Innovation |

**FIGURE 12.1**   Industry sectors in Korea from the 1960s to 2000s

*Source:* Adapted from Hwang (2007).

**TABLE 12.1** The development of Korea's export items from 1970 to 2009

|  | 1970 | 1980 | 1990 | 1995 | 2000 | 2005 | 2009 |
|---|---|---|---|---|---|---|---|
| 1st | Textiles (40.8%) | Textiles (28.8%) | Clothing (11.7%) | Semiconductor (14.1%) | Semiconductor (15.1%) | Semi-conductor (10.5%) | Ship (12.4%) |
| 2nd | Plywood (11%) | Electronics (11.4%) | Semiconductor (7.0%) | Automobile (6.7%) | Computer (8.5%) | Automobile (10.4%) | Semiconductor (8.5%) |
| 3rd | Wig (10.8%) | Iron & Steel (9.0%) | Footwear (6.6%) | Ship (4.5%) | Automobile (7.7%) | Mobile Phone (9.7%) | Mobile Phone (8.5%) |
| 4th | Iron Ore (5.9%) | Footwear (5.2%) | Media Equipment (5.6%) | Artificial Fiber (4.3%) | Petroleum Products (5.3%) | Ship (6.2%) | Display (7.0%) |
| 5th | Electronics (3.5%) | Ship (3.5%) | Ship (4.4%) | Media Equipment (3.9%) | Ship (4.9%) | Petroleum Products (5.4%) | Automobile (7.0%) |
| TOTAL | 72.0% | 57.9% | 35.2% | 33.6% | 41.4% | 42.2% | 43.5% |

*Source:* KOTRA (2016).

The transformation of the Korean economy is manifested in the development of its top five export products. While textiles and plywood were the main export items for Korea in the 1970s and 1980s, semiconductors, mobile phones, LCD screens, automobiles, and ships were the biggest export products in the 2000s. Table 12.1 provides an overview of the main export items from 1970 to 2009.

The strengths of the IT sector and knowledge-intensive industries in Korea open up many potential opportunities for foreign entrepreneurs to start their own businesses. With the establishment of the OASIS start-up visa in 2013 (see later in this chapter), foreigners have easier access to start their businesses in the IT and technology sectors, representing attractive career and growth paths in these emerging industries in Korea.

One of the main challenges of the Korean economy is the relatively uneven proportion and balance of the various industry sectors. Korea has generally too many low-value-added local services, such as restaurant and personal services, and relatively few high-value services, including health care, financial services, and IT services (McKinsey Global Institute, 2013).

As a result, foreign entrepreneurs are well advised to focus more on high-value-added industries and sectors, such as IT, financial services and architectural/engineering services, as these sectors are rather underdeveloped in terms of employment share in Korea, but offer relatively high added value, thus providing potentially highly profitable business opportunities.

The majority of self-employed Koreans generally operate low-value-added local services, such as restaurant, retail, land transport, and personal services. A notable proportion of 30% of the total Korean workforce is self-employed. This compares to only 11% of self-employed people in Germany in 2009. In addition, more than 80% of the self-employed workforce in Korea work in local services (McKinsey Global Institute, 2013).

The high concentration of Korean people who are self-employed in low-value-added local services, such as retail and restaurants, suggests a potential market entry strategy into new and different industries (i.e., 'blue oceans') for foreign entrepreneurs, in order to stay competitive and grow their businesses rather than being eaten by the existing big 'sharks' in 'red oceans' (Kim & Mauborgne, 2005). Attractive industries for starting a business are generally related to technology and high-value-added service industries, such as professional services, consulting, and IT services, which tend to resemble 'blue oceans' rather than 'red oceans' (Kim & Mauborgne, 2005).

## SMEs in Korea

### Numbers and trends of SMEs in Korea

According to the Ministry of SMEs and Startups (2019), an SME in Korea is commonly defined as

- A corporation whose total assets are less than 500 billion won
- A business entity that has less than 300 full-time workers
- A business entity with less than 8 billion won of equity capital

In 2014, there were approximately 3.5 million SMEs in Korea which accounts for 99.9% of all firms in Korea. Taken together, SMEs employ almost 16 million people, corresponding to 88% of all employees in Korea. Table 12.2 provides an overview of the number of SMEs and the respective number of employees in Korea between 2010 and 2014 (Ministry of SMEs and Startups, 2018).

SMEs account for approximately 88% of domestic jobs in Korea, and they tend to be dominated by very small enterprises with only 0.07% of SMEs growing to become large enterprises. The average salary of SMEs is about 62% of large-company rates (McKinsey Global Institute, 2013).

## Productivity of SMEs

The productivity of manufacturing SMEs in Korea is only 27% of that of large firms (McKinsey Global Institute, 2013). In contrast, the productivity of manufacturing SMEs in Germany is more than double compared to Korea, with 62% of the productivity levels of large companies. The productivity of SMEs versus large manufacturing companies in Korea has continuously decreased since the 1990s (McKinsey Global Institute, 2013).

According to the latest 'Doing Business' report by the World Bank, Korea is scoring very highly, being ranked fourth out of 190 countries (World Bank, 2018). There has been a marked improvement in the 'Doing Business' rankings for Korea moving from 24th in 2013 to the top five in 2018. This can be partly attributed to the digitalization of the Korean economy (e.g. e-government) and the technologically advanced infrastructure (e.g., communications, high-speed internet, physical infrastructure, and logistics). Table 12.3 shows the top 10 countries according to the 'Ease of Doing Business' ranking by the World Bank (2018).

**TABLE 12.2** Number of SMEs in Korea

|  |  | 2010 | 2011 | 2012 | 2014 |
|---|---|---|---|---|---|
| Number of Company | Total | 3,125,457 | 3,234,687 | 3,354,320 | 3,545,473 |
|  | SMEs | 3,122,332 | 3,231,634 | 3,351,404 | 3,542,350 |
|  | (Ratio, %) | (99.9) | (99.9) | (99.9) | (99.9) |
|  | Large Firms | 3,125 | 3,053 | 2,916 | 3,123 |
|  | (Ratio, %) | (0.1) | (0.1) | (0.1) | (0.1) |
| Number of Employees | Total | 14,135,234 | 14,534,230 | 14,891,162 | 15,962,745 |
|  | SMEs | 12,262,535 | 12,626,746 | 13,059,372 | 14,027,636 |
|  | (Ratio, %) | (86.8) | (86.9) | (87.7) | (87.9) |
|  | Large Firms | 1,872,699 | 1,907,484 | 1,831,790 | 1,935,109 |
|  | (Ratio, %) | (13.2) | (13.1) | (12.3) | (12.1) |

*Source:* Ministry of SMEs and Start-ups (2019).

**TABLE 12.3** Ease of doing business

| Rank | Economy | Score |
|------|---------|-------|
| 1 | New Zealand | 86.55 |
| 2 | Singapore | 84.57 |
| 3 | Denmark | 84.06 |
| 4 | Korea | 83.92 |
| 5 | Hong Kong SAR, China | 83.44 |
| 6 | United States | 82.54 |
| 7 | United Kingdom | 82.22 |
| 8 | Norway | 82.16 |
| 9 | Georgia | 82.04 |
| 10 | Sweden | 81.27 |

*Source:* World Bank (2018).

The high ranking of Korea in terms of 'ease of doing business' seems very attractive to foreign entrepreneurs who are likely not fluent in the Korean language. Thus, the favourable institutional environment in Korea for doing business is generally conducive to the foreign entrepreneurs' overall success, which ties in well with institutional theory (e.g., North, 1990; Peng et al., 2008).

## Ways for foreigners to do business in Korea

### Establishing a business as a foreigner

There are several options for foreigners to establish separate, legal entities, including local corporations, private businesses, branches, and liaison offices, in order to do business in Korea. These legal forms are governed by the Foreign Investment Promotion Act and the Foreign Exchange Transactions Act, respectively. Figure 12.2 provides an overview of how foreigners can do business in Korea.

### Local corporation

Provisions of the Foreign Investment Promotion Act and the Commercial Act apply to investments made through local corporations established by a foreigner or a foreign company, and the established corporation shall be treated equally as domestic corporations. However, the investment amount should be at least KRW100 million (KOTRA, 2016).

### Private business

Where a foreigner operates his/her private business in Korea with an investment amount of more than KRW100 million, the investment is recognized as FDI. Private businesses are treated equally as local corporations in their business activities.

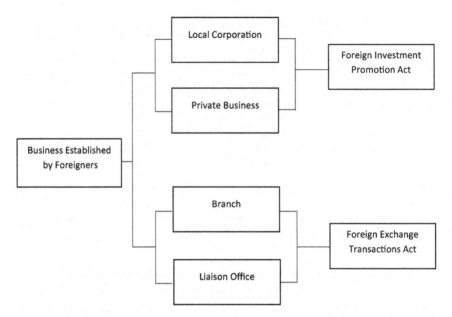

**FIGURE 12.2**   How foreigners can do business in Korea
*Source:* Adapted from KOTRA (2016).

The opening and temporary and permanent closure of a private business are less complex compared to a local corporation, and their corporate social responsibilities are generally not as heavy as local corporations. However, private businesses experience limitations in financing and securing manpower since they have a lower credit rating, and, therefore, private businesses are usually small-sized operations.

### Branch

A foreign company that intends to carry out business activities in Korea should appoint a representative for its local branch, undergo the branch establishment procedure stipulated by the Foreign Exchange Transactions Act, and complete court registration. A branch is recognized as a permanent establishment under the tax laws, and the same tax rate applied to domestic companies shall apply to the profits generated by a branch (KOTRA, 2016).

### Liaison office

While a branch undertakes sales activities in Korea to generate profit, a liaison office only carries out non-sales functions, such as business contacts and market research, among others, on behalf of the head company. Unlike branches, liaison offices do not need court registration and are given a unique business code number, which is equivalent to business registration at a jurisdictional tax office in Korea (KOTRA, 2016).

## Visa types for foreigners to do business in Korea

Before considering starting up a business in Korea as a foreigner, it is crucial to analyze and research the market in Korea, in order to determine the appropriate, legal type of business. Depending on the respective visa status, foreign entrepreneurs may have better conditions to start a business in Korea immediately. Another factor that impacts on the amount of investment required to start a business is whether the foreigner graduated from a Korean school or not.

The detailed visa regulations are as follows (Seoul Global Center, 2015):

> Foreigners with an F-2 (Long-Term Resident), F-4 (Overseas Korean), F-5 (Permanent Foreign Resident), and F-6 (Foreign Spouse) visa, can do business in the same way as native Koreans. In addition, they can freely choose the legal type and form of company, such as corporation, or sole proprietorship, and operate it accordingly. Upon deciding on sole proprietorship, the foreigners need to choose between the simplified taxation system or general taxation system.

Foreigners with visas not listed above have two different pathways to start a business in Korea:

1   FDI: At least KRW100 million is needed as an investment amount for a corporation and KRW300 million for sole proprietorship (KRW100 million are required for foreigners with a Korean master's or higher degree)
2   Start-Up Visa (OASIS): Persons with an application for a patent or equivalent accomplishment recognized by the Korean Ministry of Justice can obtain an OASIS visa through a start-up, which is explained in detail in the next section.

## Technology-based start-up for foreigners

An increasingly popular and common way of starting a business as a foreigner relates to the technology-based start-up visa OASIS (Overall Assistance for Startup Immigration System), which is a relatively new visa type implemented by the Korean government in October 2013 (OASIS, 2018). The OASIS start-up visa does not include a minimum capital requirement, and is, thus, particularly suited for foreigners, who do not have the generally required KRW100 million capital for starting a business. There are certain prerequisites that must be met in order to be eligible for the OASIS visa (Seoul Global Center, 2015).

First, the technology must be recognized for the start-up visa. More specifically, the recognition of technology developed must meet certain conditions, such as the possession of a patent, application for a patent, or any other equivalent conditions.

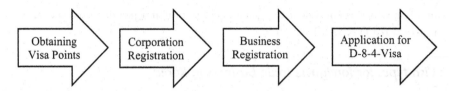

**FIGURE 12.3**   Establishing a business using the start-up visa system in Korea

*Source:* Seoul Global Center (2015).

The OASIS start-up visa is based on a point system, which consists of required and elective items. A key to obtaining a start-up visa is gaining enough points in the required items (Ramirez, 2015a).

Separate programs, which are offered by the Seoul Business Agency (Seoul Global Center), are recognized as OASIS-4 (foreigner start-up university), OASIS-5 (business coaching), OASIS-6 (start-up idea audition), and OASIS-7 (incubation). The Korea Invention Promotion Association, Korea Immigration Service Foundation, and Korea Institute of Startup & Entrepreneurship Development also operate separate, but relevant programs. The yearly OASIS schedule can be viewed at www.ipcampus.kr/oasis-visa.

After the required points are obtained for the visa, foreigners can establish a business by following the process outlined in Figure 12.3 (Seoul Global Center, 2015).

In conclusion, obtaining a start-up visa requires sufficient advanced preparation time. Each programme tends to be operated independently and obtaining enough points from required items for OASIS takes a considerable amount of time. Obtaining a work visa can help prepare for subsequently getting a start-up visa at a later stage.

## Start-up operations in Korea

### Incubators for foreign start-ups

In 2016, the Korean government introduced its first incubator programme for foreign start-ups. Named the K-Startup Grand Challenge, the programme is organized by the Ministry of SMEs and Startups, National IT Promotion Agency (NIPA), Korea Innovation Center (KIC), Korea IT Cooperation Center, Korea-India Software Cooperation Center, and accelerators, including CNTTech, Global Entrepreneurs Foundation, Kingsley Ventures, and Shift among others. The start-ups are located in Pangyo Techno Valley, which is an innovation park located south of Seoul and focuses on information, biotech, cultural and fusion technology. It is considered as Korea's best ICT-based R&D innovation cluster with a total of US$4.2 billion invested by the Korean government. It was completed in 2015 and covers an area of about 454,964 square miles with support facilities such as the global R&D Center, Public Support Center, and the Industry-Academy R&D Center. The Pangyo

Techno Valley is an environment where SMEs and start-ups can mutually exchange information with high-technology research institutes and large, global companies. This complex aims to merge different industrial sectors, mostly within the information and communications technology, to create new business opportunities and foster the growth of start-ups. Korea's top 60 start-ups and K-Global 300 start-ups are all located in the Pangyo Startup Campus.

After the initial incubator programme, K-Startup Grand Challenge was established in 2015, other incubators have followed suit in a relatively short amount of time. For example, the Seoul Global Startup Center (Seoul GSC) opened in Yongsan in 2016 and selects 40 foreign companies for each programme to participate in six-month accelerator programmes with a number of benefits: 24/7 office space with makerspace for hardware developers, a voucher for expenses and services worth KRW10 million, business development workshops, peer-mentoring, in-house expert liaisons, and a two-week all-expenses-paid trip to China or Vietnam to learn about and network in the market. The Seoul GSC is not only open to tech start-ups, but it also invites start-ups with innovative and sustainable business ideas and models.

With the rise in start-ups, the importance of office space has come to the forefront of entrepreneurs. Co-working spaces are a recent trend in the global economy, with about 17,225 co-working spaces worldwide in 2018. This is projected to rise to 30,432 co-working spaces in 2022 with 5.1 million co-working people. The biggest proportion of co-working space is located in Asia/Pacific and India with about 4,000 co-working spaces and a proportion of approximately 30% of the total number of co-working spaces in the world (GCUC, 2018).

Korea has an increasing number of co-working spaces, and these are used not only by start-ups but also by traditional companies. The reasons for the popularity of co-working spaces mainly relate to the high costs of real estate property in Seoul and the rising cost of 'traditional' office space. Co-working spaces generally offer affordable, and low-cost office spaces in prime locations, such as Gangnam in the South of Seoul. In addition, a key benefit of co-working spaces usually relates to the closely knit communities and networks with other entrepreneurs and start-ups that facilitate mutual learning and sharing of experiences among entrepreneurs. Some of the most popular co-working spaces in Seoul include Google Campus Seoul, WeWork, Heyground, and Idea Factory. The role of co-working space and creating networks and business relationships should be emphasized in light of the highly collectivistic culture of Korea (Hofstede, 1991) and the critical role of networks and *inmaek* (ties to people) when doing business in Korea. Foreigners may face the 'liability of outsidership' (Johanson & Vahlne, 2009) in Korea due to their country of origin and may, thus, face disadvantages while doing business in Korea without strong, local business networks and relationships. By interacting and connecting with local Koreans as well as foreigners in co-working spaces, a valuable benefit is to learn the so-called rules of the game in Korean institutions for conducting business successfully (North, 1990; Peng et al., 2008).

## Tax information for foreign entrepreneurs in Korea

The Korean Hometax website (www.hometax.go.kr) provides comprehensive information on taxation in Korea, while the taxation processing is handled by the National Tax Service in Korea. The National Tax Service website also offers professional materials, such as tax information and tax consultation cases for foreigners online. These documents, which are available in Korean and English, are useful for both Koreans and foreigners. In addition, tax invoices and proof of tax payment can be issued, and taxes can be reported and paid online through the Hometax website.

The most basic taxes to know when operating business are valued-added tax, composite income tax, and corporate tax. Value-added tax is levied to the value added in the process of carrying on business. It is levied to entire goods (services). Customers who purchase goods and services are responsible for the value-added tax. However, customers do not pay the tax directly; they only pay for the price of goods that already include value-added tax. Sellers of goods and services report their revenue and sales to the appropriate tax office and pay the tax on behalf of customers.

## Registration for four major social insurances when hiring workers in Korea

A business employing one or more full-time employees must obtain the four major social insurances programs and pay for them regularly based on determined rates. The four major social insurances programs include (1) National Health Insurance (for diseases and injuries), (2) National Pension (for death and ageing), (3) Employment Insurance (for unemployment), and (4) Industrial Accident Compensation Insurance (for accidents occurring during work). The insurance rates are income-dependent (Seoul Global Center, 2015).

## Conditions for hiring foreign workers in Korea

A business must meet the following conditions to hire foreigners in Korea (Seoul Global Center, 2015).

*   *Number of Korean employees*
    To hire foreign employees, the company is required to hire at least five Korean workers. This is the standard to protect the employment of Koreans, and this condition must be met by all companies operating in Korea (i.e., foreign and domestic firms). If the number of Korean workers is less than five, the invitation of foreign workers is limited, in principle. However, different business types may require different hiring conditions to be met.
*   *Previous year's revenue*
    Depending on jobs, different work visas can be issued for foreigners. For example, there are visas such as E-3 (researcher), E-4 (technical instructor), E-5

(professional consultant), E-6 (entertainer), and E-7 (specially designated profession). The E-7 visa has 85 occupational guidelines, for which proper qualifications and additional documents may be required.

- *Relationship between workers to be hired and job obligations*
  Persons with a degree obtained in Korea can be hired even though their study major may not correspond to their actual job obligations. However, persons without a degree obtained in Koreas have to prove that there is relevance between their degree as well as career and obligations of the job for which they are to be hired.

## Conclusion

Korea has become an increasingly attractive market for Foreign Direct Investment (FDI), and the Korean economy has grown rapidly over the past years, becoming the 11th-largest economy in the world. In addition, the number of foreigners working in Korea has increased considerably since the 1990s. While the majority of foreigners work as expatriates in subsidiaries of MNEs and as academic staff at universities and private language institutions (*hagwons*), foreign entrepreneurs increasingly attempt to establish their own start businesses in Korea (Hemmert, 2012).

Several factors influence how foreigners can start a business in Korea. First, the visa status of foreigners is very important. Foreigners with an F-series visa, such as F-5 (Permanent Residence) or F-6 (Foreign Spouse visa), can do business in Korea like native Koreans. For foreigners without these visas, there are relatively high investment thresholds of KRW100 million to start a corporation or KRW300 million for sole proprietorship. One notable exception is the start-up visa (OASIS), which does not require a minimum capital amount, but it depends on obtaining a patent/other intellectual property and successfully completing a selection of various mentoring and business courses offered by different Korean government agencies, such as the Seoul Global Center.

Second, when operating a business in Korea as a foreigner, several areas need to be considered carefully, including taxation, registration of social insurances, and employment restrictions for foreign employees.

The Korean government seems to attempt to encourage, promote, and invest in the start-up sector by providing several business incubators for foreign start-ups, such as K-Startup Grand Challenge. Government-funded agencies, including the Seoul Global Center and the Seoul Global Startup Center, provide valuable complimentary resources for foreign entrepreneurs, including free co-working space, start-up lectures, networking opportunities, and legal advice. These developments, along with the rise of the 'side hustle economy' and a simultaneous increase in co-working office spaces, suggest that the number of foreign entrepreneurs establishing start-up businesses in Korea is likely to keep growing in the future.

## Case study:   moonROK – the door to K-Pop news in English

MoonROK is the world's premier source of K-Pop news and entertainment. Founded in 2014 by US citizen Hannah Waitt, moonROK addresses a large gap in the existing K-Pop market: an English-language news site. Prior to 2014, despite millions of K-Pop fans worldwide, this critical news resource was still missing for people who were unable to speak and understand the Korean language. In addition, the purpose of moonROK is to provide a legitimate, trustworthy news source, which publishes accurate, fast, and unbiased K-Pop news.

MoonROK has partnered with multiple prominent Korean entertainment media outlets that have agreed to share their stories with moonROK. Instead of fans having to sit around and wait for someone to translate Korean news for them, moonROK can publish the news at the same time as their partners, but in English. This way the fans can read the news as it is happening, not an hour after it has already happened. One of the intriguing things about K-Pop is that the community that surrounds it is one of the most unique, diverse, and passionate groups of people in the world. People of all ages, races, sexes, religions, and nationalities are united by their love of culture and music perhaps entirely different from anything in their home country. This explains the company name 'moonROK'. In Korean, the word 문 is pronounced *moon*, and it means 'door'. South Korea's official country name is the 'Republic of Korea', commonly abbreviated R.O.K. In other words, moonROK is the 'door to Korea'.

The 'founding story' of moonROK seems to be quite intriguing as it was founded in Seoul in 2014 by a foreign female entrepreneur, Hannah Waitt, from the US. Hannah Waitt participated in the K-Startup Grand Challenge in 2016, and she achieved third prize with her start-up business moonROK. According to Hannah Waitt,

> We were able to raise our company funds through investors we met during the competition, and were able to produce various media contents for free at the production and studio facilities provided by the K-Startup Grand Challenge. Participating in the Grand Challenge 2016 was the best thing we did for our company, and being in Korea has been nothing but awesome for our company so far.

The programme partnered with Korean businesses, including Samsung, Hyundai, Kakao, KT Corporation, and SK Group, who would lend their expertise of the local Korean and global markets to the start-ups. Those running the programme on the ground took a genuine interest in making sure the start-ups succeeded in Korea; said Hannah Waitt, "I got the feeling that yes, this is a government project . . . but never felt that it hindered our ability to accomplish anything". The programme also helped them network with some big Korean companies that they would likely not have met otherwise, such as leaders in automobiles, transportation, music, and entertainment as well as local investors, not to mention the other participating start-ups from around the world.

Today, moonROK has shifted its headquarters to the US, and it is growing continuously by satisfying the news needs of the English-speaking K-Pop community around the world. Hannah Waitt, who hopes to connect with investors who already understand the K-Pop phenomenon's magnitude, noted that Korea is a trend-conscious society not only in fashion and pop culture but also in tech – so even if Korea is not known as a startup or entrepreneurial hub, it's a great market to test out a product or service: "Korea's startup investment is a relatively new thing for the country, which is dominated by conglomerates, so that makes it a little scary environment in which to start a business that are hard to compete with," she said. "But if Korea continues to invest in cultivating small businesses here and the startup ecosystem, then it will slowly but surely develop into more of a startup hub in Asia".

## Sources

K Startup Grand Challenge. 2017. *Interviews with KGSC 2016 Top 20 teams: Hannah Waitt, CEO of moonROK.*

www.kstartupgc.org/board/board_view.do?bd_idx=4&searchVal=&searchMonth=&searchCate=&searchDate=&listSize=10&searchKind2=&searchArea=&searchKey=&searchYear=&bmt_idx=2&searchState=&page=1&searchKind=&searchOrder=1&searchDel=N. Accessed 5 January 2019.

Official Company Website of moonROK. www.moonrok.com. Accessed 10 January 2019.

Ramirez, E. 2017. Why entrepreneurs come to South Korea, and why they don't. *Forbes.* Accessed 25 May 2017. www.forbes.com/sites/elaineramirez/2017/05/25/why-entrepreneurs-come-to-south-korea-and-why-they-dont/#4f4b2ab97dbf. Accessed 15 February 2019.

Reyes, L. (2017). *K Startup Grand Challenge helps startups become globally competitive, uses Korean market as gateway to Asia.* Accessed 25

May 2017. https://e27.co/k-startup-grand-challenge-helps-start-ups-globally-competitive-korean-market-entryway-20170525/. Accessed 1 March 2019.

## Bibliography

KOTRA. 2016. *Guide to establishing a business in Korea.* Seoul: KOTRA.
McKinsey Global Institute. 2013. *Beyond Korean style: Shaping a new growth formula.* Seoul: McKinsey & Company.
Seoul Global Center. 2015. *Consulting casebook for foreign start-ups.* Seoul: Seoul Business Agency/Seoul Global Center.

## Online sources

K-Startup Grand Challenge. 2018. *Pangyo techno valley.* www.k-startupgc.org/about/pangyo.do.
National Tax Service Korea. 2018. www.hometax.go.kr.
OASIS. 2018. *OASIS start-up visa.* http://ipcampus.kr/oasis-visa/eng/about/visa.jsp.
World Bank. 2018. *Republic of Korea.* www.worldbank.org/en/country/korea/overview.

## References

GCUC (Global Coworking Conference Unconference). 2018. *Global co-working forecast.* https://gcuc.co/2018-global-coworking-forecast-30432-spaces-5-1-million-members-2022/. Accessed 14 September 2018.
Guttmann, A. 2018. *South Korea triples its financial commitment to startups.* www.forbes.com/sites/amyguttman/2018/02/28/south-korea-triples-its-financial-commitment-to-startups/#6574200855fc. Accessed 18 October 2018.
Hemmert, M. 2012. *Tiger management: Korean companies on world markets.* Abingdon: Routledge.
Hemmert, M. 2017. *The evolution of Tiger management: Korean companies in global competition.* Abingdon: Routledge.
Hofstede, G. 1991. *Cultures and organizations: Software of the mind.* Maidenhead: Mc-Graw-Hill.
Hwang, Y. 2007. *Role and performance of S&T policy for transformative demand of economic development.* Paper presented at the Special Symposium of 40th Anniversary of S&T Administration and 3rd Anniversary of Vice Prime Minister of S&T Administration. Seoul, 29 October 2007.
Johanson, J., & Vahlne, J. E. 2009. The Uppsala internationalization process model revisited: From liability of foreignness to liability of outsidership. *Journal of International Business Studies*, 40(9): 1411–1443.
Kim, W., & Mauborgne, R. (2005). *Blue ocean strategy: How to create uncontested market space and make the competition irrelevant.* Boston, MA: Harvard Business School Press.
KOTRA. 2016. *Guide to establishing a business in Korea.* Seoul: KOTRA.
KOTRA. 2017. *Doing business in Korea.* Seoul: KOTRA.
K-Startup Grand Challenge. 2018. *Pangyo Techno Valley.* www.k-startupgc.org/about/pangyo.do Accessed 30 September 2018.

Lindic, J., Bavdaz, M., & Kovacic, H. 2012. Higher growth through the blue ocean strategy: Implications for economic policy. *Research Policy*, 41(5): 928–938.

McKinsey Global Institute. 2013. *Beyond Korean style: Shaping a new growth formula*. Seoul.

Ministry of SMEs and Start-ups. 2019. *Status of Korean SMEs*. www.mss.go.kr/site/eng/02/10202000000002016111504.jsp on 2 October 2018. Accessed 10 March 2019.

North, D. C. 1990. *Institutions, institutional change, and economic performance*. Cambridge: Cambridge University Press.

OASIS. 2018. *OASIS start-up visa*. http://ipcampus.kr/oasis-visa/eng/about/visa.jsp. Accessed 25 October 2018.

Ock, H. J. 2016. *Number of foreigners exceeds 2 million*. www.koreaherald.com/view.php?ud=20160727000493 Accessed 8 April 2018.

OECD Observer. 2017. *The OECD and Korea: Celebrating a milestone*. http://oecdobserver.org/news/fullstory.php/aid/5645/The_OECD_and_Korea:_Celebrating_a_milestone.html. Accessed 21 September 2018.

Peng, M., Wang, D.Y. L., & Jiang, Y. 2008. An institution-based view of international business strategy: A focus on emerging economies. *Journal of International Business Studies*, *39*(5): 920–936.

Ramirez, E. 2015a. *Support for foreign startups reveals redundancies*. www.koreaherald.com/view.php?ud=20150618001028. Accessed 19 October 2018.

Ramirez, E. 2015b. *Labor laws hurt startups*. www.koreaherald.com/view.php?ud=20150604000895. Accessed 18 August 2018.

Seoul Global Center. 2015. *Consulting casebook for foreign start-ups*. Seoul: Seoul Business Agency/Seoul Global Center.

United Nations. 2018. *Republic of Korea – Country profile*. www.un.org/esa/earthsummit/rkore-cp.htm. Accessed 9 August 2018.

World Bank. 2018. *Doing business 2018 – Reforming to create jobs*. Washington, DC.

# INDEX